John G. Hodgins

The Legislation and History of Separate Schools in Upper Canada

From 1841, Until the Close of the Rev. Doctor Ryerson's Administration

John G. Hodgins

The Legislation and History of Separate Schools in Upper Canada
From 1841, Until the Close of the Rev. Doctor Ryerson's Administration

ISBN/EAN: 9783337189006

Printed in Europe, USA, Canada, Australia, Japan

Cover: Foto ©ninafisch / pixelio.de

More available books at **www.hansebooks.com**

THE LEGISLATION AND HISTORY OF SEPARATE SCHOOLS IN UPPER CANADA:

FROM 1841, UNTIL THE CLOSE OF THE REVEREND DOCTOR RYERSON'S ADMINISTRATION OF THE EDUCATION DEPARTMENT OF ONTARIO IN 1876:

INCLUDING VARIOUS PRIVATE PAPERS AND DOCUMENTS ON THE SUBJECT.

BY

J. GEORGE HODGINS, M.A., LL.D., F.R.G.S.,

BARRISTER-AT-LAW,

LIBRARIAN OF THE EDUCATION DEPARTMENT FOR ONTARIO, AND EDITOR OF THE "DOCUMENTARY HISTORY OF EDUCATION IN UPPER CANADA, 1791-1876."

The School Law of Upper Canada recognizes Individual Rights; deals with each Individual for himself, and does not ignore, or proscribe, him from the Public Schools, and all the privileges connected with them, except at his own request.—(*Rev. Dr. Ryerson to the Hon. John A. Macdonald, 2nd of April, 1855. Page 89.*)

It must be acknowledged that a combined Secular, with Separate Religious Instruction, is the only safe, just, and defensible system of National Education.—(*Rev. Dr. Ryerson to the Governor-General, Sir Edmund Head, January, 1858. Page 121.*)

TORONTO:
PRINTED BY WILLIAM BRIGGS, WESLEY BUILDINGS.
1897.

Entered according to Act of the Parliament of Canada, in the year one thousand eight hundred and ninety-seven, by JOHN GEORGE HODGINS, at the Department of Agriculture.

PREFATORY REMARKS.

IN the outline of "THE STORY OF MY LIFE," prepared by the Rev. Dr. Ryerson, during his later years, he briefly summed up what he had been able to accomplish, as Head of the Education Department for Upper Canada, during his incumbency from 1844 to 1876. He then added these words:—

"I leave to Dr. J. George Hodgins, my devoted Friend of over forty years, and my able Colleague for over thirty of these years, the duty of filling up the details of our united labours in founding a System of Education for my native Province, which is spoken of in terms of strong commendation, not only within, but by people outside of, the Dominion."

Feeling that an almost filial duty was thus devolved upon me, I prepared a Prospectus, in 1884, of such a Volume as I then projected, including a sketch of the "Legislation and History of Separate Schools in Upper Canada," which I now publish, intending, at some future time, to carry out further the wishes of my revered Friend. In that Prospectus I said:—

Not only did Dr. Ryerson entrust me with the whole of his private correspondence with Public Men and Ministers of State on educational matters, but I have also had a voluminous correspondence, from time to time, with him myself, when he was absent, on several important subjects connected with our School System. These, with various private memoranda and other information, will be available for the Volume.

I then thought, (as I expressed it,) that such a personal record would likely be of more interest to the next generation than it would be to the then present one,—especially as so many storms and personal conflicts had marked the era of Dr. Ryerson's administration,—creating, at the time, much undue prejudice, which might still linger in the memories of men, and exert an undue influence on the minds of many. Time, and a calm review of what has been accomplished, notwithstanding the adverse circumstances, and the opposing influences, under which our School System was founded, would, I then felt, alone dissipate that prejudice, and do full justice to Dr. Ryerson, and to those who stood by him, in his efforts to place our National System of Schools upon a broad, safe, and comprehensive basis.

Having been intimately and confidentially connected with Dr. Ryerson for thirty-two years, in the great work of his later life, (*i.e.*, from his appointment, in 1844, to 1876,) the projected work would necessarily largely partake of a personal character,—so far as he and I and others were concerned.

This, on the whole, will be found to greatly add to its interest and value. Besides, I alone am in a position to verify some facts which were mentioned in private conversation, or in his correspondence with me, and which are known only to myself.

It was twelve years since the Prospectus, to which I have referred, was written. Time warns me that if the work, projected in 1884, is to be published, it is now time to prepare it. I have, therefore, determined to issue the first instalment of it, in the shape of the "LEGISLATION AND HISTORY OF SEPARATE SCHOOLS IN UPPER CANADA," from 1841 to the close of Dr. Ryerson's administration, in 1876.

A second Volume, containing a more general review of our Educational System, from 1844 until its later development, will be prepared, (D.V.,) and will be issued in due time. Such a publication will include a large number of private and confidential Letters and Papers of my own, together with those which were entrusted to me by Dr. Ryerson,—in fact, a Volume containing what may be called the private, or "inner," history of the Education Department for Ontario, including many facts and incidents of my long personal connection of fifty-two years.

with it and with those "in authority" in the Department, and in the Executive Government of the Province, during that time.

I have been the more convinced as to the desirability of publishing the present somewhat condensed, yet sufficiently detailed, history of the Roman Catholic Separate Schools in Upper Canada, as a contribution to our Educational History and Literature, from the fact that men, in whose practical wisdom and judgment I have confidence, have encouraged me to do so.

I have received the following Letter on the subject from my esteemed friend, Dr. W. T. Harris, the United States Commissioner of Education, at Washington, which I may very appropriately insert in this place. He says:—

I am much interested in your proposed Work on the Separate Schools of Upper Canada. The problem, of which it will treat, is one of great importance; and Ontario has found a solution of it that can never fail to interest Public men and Educators.

Certainly, no other Person has equal facilities with yourself for elucidating every condition bearing upon the expediency of Separate Schools.

The references called forth by your valuable "Documentary History of Education in Upper Canada," are such as to awaken interest in the new work; and, it seems to me a wise measure to have them both distributed in printed form.

Among the champions of Roman Catholic Separate Schools in Upper Canada, whom Dr. Ryerson encountered, none was more pronounced, or even bitter, in his language than the Editor of the *Canadian Freeman* newspaper of Toronto.

On his retirement from the editorial chair, in 1873, he bade Dr. Ryerson good-bye, in language which, on the whole, was generous and kind. In his valedictory he gives so graphic a sketch of Dr. Ryerson's somewhat stormy life, and yet also of him as a man of purpose, of nerve, and of unswerving fidelity to the cause which he had espoused, that I cannot forbear quoting it. The Editor said:—

Before relinquishing the editorial pen, we should like to say a few words on a gentleman whom we have for years steadfastly opposed, and whose opinions on many, but especially educational, matters, we have strenuously combated, and, nevertheless, have in a certain sense admired, and would, were he aught but the Chief Superintendent of Education, hold in the highest esteem. . . .

The Reverend Egerton Ryerson holds what the civilization of this age terms "liberal" views: he advocates the advancement of the masses, or educating every one, no matter what his position in society may be. The best part of an eventful life has been devoted by him to carry out his peculiar opinions on this subject. He is essentially a man of one idea, and he is a very determined, resolute, and personally courageous person. It is individuals of his stamp who have made their mark in the world. As to politics, he has really none; but in free thought, in educating the masses, he does believe. From the various Educational Systems of constitutional England, despotic Prussia, republican America, Holland, Ireland, and Scotland, with the assistance of his own powerful intellect, he has perfected a plan, according to non-Catholic ideas, an improvement on all of them, maintaining their best, rejecting their worst, features. He has been assailed by various Denominations and classes of our citizens, by dissatisfied freeholders, by childless ratepayers, by Representatives of Churches, by Grit and Conservative newspapers, by politicians, and by administrations holding the most opposite views, and yet he has managed to stand his ground, and not only this, but to enforce his educational opinions on the great majority of the people of this Province. At one time he is reported by a Tory Governor as "a dangerous man," and a certain Toronto journal has pursued him with fierce malignity for years, and all kinds of politicians have at different periods attacked him in the bitterest way, and yet Egerton Ryerson has triumphed, and is at this day, in spite of all opposition, the great and successful vindicator of free, universal education. This is the man whom Governments do not care to interfere with, and who cannot be crushed; who, in spite of his seventy years, is still as fresh and as vigorous as ever, and as ready, in defence of his ideas, to smite his enemies "hip and thigh," either through a public journal, or in a pamphlet of 365 pages. During our entire career we have opposed the Doctor; but we are fully aware how difficult it is to make headway against a man of his ability, holding but one idea, and resolved to win. We have often wished that a Ryerson would present himself as a representative of our Catholic masses, to fight as determinedly for us as he has for his Protestant fellow-countrymen,—a man who would endeavour, under all circumstances, to procure what his Eminence Cardinal Cullen and the Irish Hierarchy are now labouring to attain,—a Catholic, purely Catholic, education for Catholic people. . . .

In retiring from the management, [of the *Canadian Freeman*,] we would wish to offer the right hand of fellowship to all we have encountered, . . .

and to part on amicable terms with all from whom we have differed. Foremost among these is the Chief Superintendent of Education, and we have, therefore, devoted this, our last article, to him. We have written column upon column against him, for the past fifteen years. We have tried with all our might to put him down, and yet he is a man for whose talents, resolution, and dogged perseverance we have the highest respect, and for whose courtesy and gentlemanly bearing towards our co-religionists we offer our acknowledgments, and for whom the Protestant people of this Province will, at some not very distant period, do, what a learned American historian stated the North-West would do for Marquette,—"build his monument."*

A word as to the attitude of the Church of England on this question. It always held, (as a Church established in Upper Canada by the Constitutional Act of 1791,) that, if the Church of Rome were legally entitled to establish Separate Schools, in which the dogmas of that Church were to be taught, and to receive a portion of the public funds for their support, much more should that branch of the Church of the Empire in Canada receive a like share of the public revenue, and for a like purpose. Beyond that, the Church of England was not disposed to go, nor to enter into any of the local controversies on the subject.

Traditionally the Church of England in Canada always held the doctrine, which was so clearly stated by Dr. Ryerson, in his Confidential Report to the Governor-General, in 1858, (page 121,) and in which he maintained :—

That a combined secular, with separate religious instruction, is the only safe, just, and defensible system of National Education.

No one was more sensible of the efforts made by Dr. Ryerson to carry into effect this combined system of Education, than was the venerable Dr. Strachan, the first Anglican Bishop of Toronto. In his Charge to the Clergy, in 1856, he said :—

So far as Dr. Ryerson is concerned, I am one of those who appreciate

* It would, no doubt, gratify the former Editor of the *Canadian Freeman*, (James G. Moylan, Esq., now of Ottawa,) to know, that a few years after Dr. Ryerson's death, in 1882, a handsome Monument was erected, in 1889, to his memory, in front of the Building in which he spent the last years of his official life.

very highly his exertions, his unwearied assiduity, and his administrative capacity. I am also most willing to admit that he has carried out the meagre provisions of the several School enactments, that have any leaning to Religion, as far as seems consistent with a just interpretation of the law.

No less cordial were the words used by Bishop Bethune, in his Letter to Dr. Ryerson, of the 3rd of July, 1872, in which he said :—

I have to thank you for your Letter of the 1st instant, . . . and to express my gratification that I had the opportunity, [in the Synod,]* to bear my humble testimony to your zealous and righteous efforts to promote the sound education of the youth of the Province.

I believe that, in the endeavour to give this a moral and religious direction, you have done all that, in the circumstances of the country, it was in your power to accomplish.

None have been more true and faithful in their maintenance of the Public School System in Upper Canada, than have been Members of the Church of England. This was promptly and very heartily acknowledged by Dr. Ryerson, in his Letter of the 31st of December, 1858, to the Hon. George Brown, when he said :—

To the honour of the Church of England, and to the honour of Canada, and especially to the honour of the Gentlemen themselves, the Episcopalians stood forward as a phalanx against the seductions presented to them by the Taché Bill, as introduced in 1855. . . . I feel it no less my duty, than my pleasure, to express my own gratitude, and, I believe, that of Upper Canada generally, to Messrs. J. W. Gamble, W. B. Robinson, John Langton, George Crawford and D. B. Stevenson, for the earnest and noble stand which they took on that occasion, as the champions of the unmutilated Common School System of Upper Canada.

It was often a matter of surprise to me, during the long years of conflict on the Roman Catholic Separate School Ques-

---

* In his Address to the Anglican Synod of 1872, Bishop Bethune said :—
"I have confidence in the good intentions and righteous efforts of that venerable gentleman, (Dr. Ryerson,) to do what he can for the amelioration of the evils which the absence of systematic religious teaching of the young must induce ; so that we may have a hope that, from his tried zeal and unquestionable ability, a way may be devised by which such essential instruction shall be imparted, and the terrible evils we deplore to some extent corrected."

tion, that so many of our public men shrank from a full, fair, and patriotic discussion of it as a matter of public concern,—apart from politics and denominational influences,—involving, as that discussion would, the further question of appropriating public funds for the support of Denominational Schools.*

And, after all, such a general and united expression of public opinion would have practically narrowed the question down to a simple determination, (1,) to maintain the integrity of our Public School System against all who would seek to undermine it; and, in case Separate Schools were allowed, (2,) to recognize and uphold the individual right of parents,—without compulsion or interference,—to choose for themselves the School to which they should send their children.†

Even after the passage of the Clergy Reserve Secularization Act of 1854, in which it was declared that "all semblance of the Union of Church and State" was abolished, very many of the men who had aided to crystallize this declaration in an Act of Parliament, seemed unable to resist the pressure put upon them to give the opposite doctrine a practical application, in their maintenance and partial endowment, by public grants and by Municipal assessments, of purely Denominational

---

* In his confidential Letter to Dr. Ryerson, in March, 1857, (page 117,) the Hon. John Elmsley urged Dr. Ryerson to press for an "enquiry" into "the whole of the Separate School question," by a Committee of the House of Assembly, where a "combat," as he expressed it, "of dispassioned argument," and a "battle of cool investigation," would take place. How he could expect either of these results from a purely political body does not appear. All such discussions, or enquiries, to be effective or satisfactory, must be conducted by a totally different class of men, far removed from either political or denominational influences.

† This right is expressly reserved to Roman Catholic Parents by Cardinal Satolli, in his Letter to the Roman Catholic Archbishops assembled in New York, in November, 1892. He said :—
We strictly forbid anyone, whether Bishop, or Priest, and this is the express prohibition of the Sovereign Pontiff, through the Sacred Congregation, either by Act, or by Threat, to exclude from the Sacraments, as unworthy, Parents who choose to send their children to the Public Schools. As regards the children themselves, this enactment applies with still greater force.—(*Conc: Plen: Balt: Number 198, page 104, Conf. Tit. VI., Cap. I., II.. Tit. VII.*)

Schools, the latter mode of aiding such Schools, Dr. Ryerson characterized, in his Letter to the Provincial Secretary, in 1866, as "one of the worst and most degrading features of Church and State connection, so formally renounced by our Legislature." And, in general, these men either misrepresented Dr. Ryerson's attitude on the question, or, when they did not, they left him to wage the war for unequivocal "equal rights" and "no denominational preferences" alone.

It is singular that the promoters of Separate Schools, in their desire for Legislation in the interest of these Schools, often unwittingly placed weapons in Dr. Ryerson's hands against themselves. They frequently assumed that to be law which was only so in their imagination: and that to be fact, which was, in reality, pure fiction. They generally, in framing "projects of law," provided, in their guileless zeal, for far more than they desired, and embraced in their Bill a far wider range of assumed "rights" than they had intended. This unpractical mode of dealing with practical matters led, no doubt, to the merciless dissection of the "project of Bill," drawn up by the three Bishops of Upper Canada, in 1854-5, by Dr. Ryerson, which is given on pages 87–92. His remarks, on page 91, although severe, are, nevertheless, borne out by the fact that a careless use of terms was employed, which were already too comprehensive in their application, but which were, nevertheless, used by the framers of the Bill. Thus, the careless and ignorant use of legal terms, in drawing up a will, has often led to vexatious and protracted litigation.

I would ask attention to the two Chapters in this Book near its close,—the XXX. and the concluding Chapter.

In Chapter XXX., the Question is asked,—"Was the Roman Catholic Separate School Act of 1863 a Finality?"

So far as the facts therein narrated go, the answer is in the

PREFATORY REMARKS.

affirmative. The Chapter is, however, specially interesting as a psychological study. In it are curious examples of mental reservation,—in which silent assent meant negative acquiescence, and personal concurrence a dumb show,—passive and unreal. Such examples of mental unconsciousness of simple, plain facts is somewhat akin to mental colour-blindness, and furnish striking illustrations of the subtleties of this somewhat new, yet interesting, science of psychology.

The concluding Chapter will, I trust, appeal to all thoughtful men and lovers of their Country.

I have added, as Appendices to this Volume, two important Documents. The first is a most carefully prepared " Analysis and Comparison of the Roman Catholic Separate School Acts of 1855 and 1863," by Dr. Ryerson. The second is the " Decisions and Statements of Cardinal Satolli,—in regard to the Canons of the Plenary Council of Baltimore,"—addressed, in the form of a Letter, to the eleven Roman Catholic Archbishops of the United States, at their Meeting held in New York, on the 13th–17th of November, 1892."

J. GEORGE HODGINS.

TORONTO, March 17th, 1897.

CONTENTS.

CHAPTER	PAGE
I. Preliminary Remarks	9
II. The Educational State of Upper and Lower Canada	11
III. Educational Proceedings of the Canadian Legislature of 1841	14
IV. Petitions, praying that the Bible be used as a Class Book in the Schools	19
V. Effect of these Petitions—Adoption of the Principle of Separate Schools in Upper Canada	22
VI. Separate School Legislation as affecting Upper Canada	25
VII. Proceedings in regard to the Schools—Bishops Strachan, Power and Charbonnel—Bishop Macdonell	27
Bishop de Charbonnel and his Changed Attitude in 1857	35
VIII. The Controversy with Bishop de Charbonnel in 1852	37
IX. The Separate School Legislation of 1846–1850	44
1. Episode of the Disallowed Common School Bill of 1849	46
2. Original Draft of the 19th Section of the Common School Bill of 1850, and as passed	50
3. The First Toronto Separate School Case, in 1851	53
4. Unrest and Uncertainty—Mr. W. L. Mackenzie in 1851	55
5. The Separate School Question, from 1841 to 1851	56
X. Incidents of the Separate School Contest, from 1852 to 1855	59
XI. Claim for Additional Grants to Separate Schools—Pressure on the Government in 1852	61
1. The Belleville Separate School Case, 1852	63
XII. Second Appeal to the Government—Renewed Demands of Bishop de Charbonnel	71
1. Second Toronto Case—Separate School Difficulties in Two Wards	71
2. Third Separate School Difficulty in the City of Toronto	73
3. Renewed Agitation by Bishop de Charbonnel—The Taché Act Foreshadowed	75
4. Documents Submitted by the Roman Catholic Bishops of Upper Canada to the Government, in 1854	81
(1) Comparative Table of Separate School Legislation in Upper and Lower Canada	82
(2) Preliminary Statement of the Three Roman Catholic Bishops of Upper Canada	85
(3) Draft of an Act Bttter to Define Certain Rights to Parties therein-mentioned	85

CONTENTS.

CHAPTER	PAGE
XIII. The Taché Roman Catholic Separate School Bill of 1855	92
1. The Taché Separate School Act, as Amended	95
2. Passage of the Taché Separate School Bill, 1855	99
3. Sir John Macdonald and the Taché Separate School Act, (Pope's Memoirs)	100
XIV. Private and Confidential Correspondence relating to the Passage of the Taché Act of 1855	102
1. Hon. John A. Macdonald to Dr. Ryerson	102
2. Telegram from Dr. Ryerson to J. George Hodgins	102
3. Bishop Phelan to Hon. John A. Macdonald	102
4. Hon. John A. Macdonald to Dr. Ryerson	104
5. Hon. John A. Macdonald to Dr. Ryerson	105
6. J. George Hodgins to Dr. Ryerson, (in England)	106
7. J. George Hodgins to Dr. Ryerson, (in England)	106
8. J. George Hodgins to Dr. Ryerson, (in England)	107
XV. Effect of the Charbonnel Separate School Controversy upon Lower Canadians—Nova Scotia	107
XVI. Renewed Controversy—The Bowes' Separate School Bill, 1856	110
1. Letter from J. George Hodgins to Dr. Ryerson	110
2. Letter from J. George Hodgins to Dr. Ryerson	111
3. Dr. Ryerson on the Bowes' Separate School Bill	111
XVII. The Bruyère-Pinsoneault-Dallas Controversy	113
1. Bishop de Charbonnel Selected Roman Catholic Library Books	114
2. Cardinal Wiseman Consulted in London on Library Books, in 1851	114
3. Pamphlet Summaries of the Separate School Discussions, 1856-1858	115
XVIII. Renewed Efforts to Promote Separate School Legislation, 1857-1860	117
XIX. Confidential Report to the Governor-General on the Separate School Question, in 1848	118
1. Letter from Dr. Ryerson to J. George Hodgins	121
2. Letter from Hon. John A. Macdonald to Dr. Ryerson	123
XX. Special Report on Roman Catholic Separate Schools, in 1858	123
XXI. Abortive Separate School Legislation, in 1858-1861	125
Analysis of the Scott Separate School Bills of 1860, '61	126
XXII. Failure of Separate School Legislation, in 1862	127
Draft of Bill by Dr. Ryerson, in 1862, with Memorandum	128
The Bishop Lynch Appointment Episode, in 1862	130
Dr. Ryerson's Letter to *The Leader*, 29th April, 1862	130
R. W. Scott's Attack on Dr. Ryerson in the House	132
Private Letter of Bishop Horan, of Kingston	133

CONTENTS.

Chapter		Page
XXVI.	Dr. Ryerson on the Passing of the Act of 1863	160
XXVII.	Incidents of the Passing of the Act of 1863	164
XXVIII.	Separate School Act of 1863—Mr. Scott's Statement	166
	Reply of Sir Oliver Mowat, re B. N. A. Act, 1867	167
XXIX.	Hon. John A. Macdonald on the Separate School Act of 1863	168
	Hon. A. Mackenzie on the Separate School Act of 1863	170
	Hon. George Brown on Separate Schools	171
XXX.	Was the Separate School Act of 1863 a Finality?	172
	Compact with the Representatives of the Roman Catholic Church in 1862 and 1863	174
	Hon. G. Brown and Hon. T. D. McGee on the Separate School Settlement of 1863	177
	Disclaimer of the Vicars-General that they were Parties to the Settlement of 1863	179
	Dr. Ryerson reiterates his Statement that these Vicars-General were Parties to the Settlement	180
	Further Testimony as to the Finality of the Separate School Settlement of 1863	182
	Fruitless Appeal to Mr. R. W. Scott for Information on the subject	183
XXXI.	British North America Act relating to Education	184
	Legal Opinion of Messrs. Richards, Crooks and Blake on that Act	185
XXXII.	Inspection of Roman Catholic Separate Schools	187
XXXIII.	French and German Separate Schools	189
	Why Perpetuate Nationalities in Elementary Schools?	192
XXXIV.	Dr. Ryerson's Final Utterances on Separate School Agitation	193
	The Separate School Bill of 1866	195
	Letter to the Provincial Secretary on this Bill	196
XXXV.	End of Dr. Ryerson's Difficulties in Separate School matters	199
Concluding Chapter.	Expediences of Separate Education considered by Dr. Ryerson and Archbishop Ireland	200

APPENDICES.

1. The Roman Catholic Separate School Acts of 1855 and 1863 Analyzed and Compared, by Dr. Ryerson 206
2. Letter of Cardinal Satolli to the American Roman Catholic Bishops, in November, 1892, on the Canons of the Plenary Council of Baltimore 214

Consecutive Index of Subjects 220
Principal Personal References 221

CONTENTS.

CHAPTER		PAGE
XXIII.	Private and Confidential Letters in 1862	134
	1. Telegram from Dr. Ryerson to Hon. John A. Macdonald	135
	2. Letter from Hon. John A. Macdonald to Dr. Ryerson	135
	3. Telegram from Dr. Ryerson to Hon. John A. Macdonald	135
	4. Note from Dr. Ryerson to J. George Hodgins	135
	5. Telegram from Dr. Ryerson to Mr. William Ryerson	135
	6. Telegram from Dr. Ryerson to Mr. A. Morris	135
	7. Letter from Hon. John A. Macdonald to Dr. Ryerson	136
	8. Letter from Mr. William Ryerson to Dr. Ryerson	136
	9. Letter from Dr. Ryerson to J. George Hodgins	137
	10. Letter from Dr. Ryerson to J. George Hodgins	137
	11. Letter from Dr. Ryerson to Mr. A. Morris	138
	12. Letter from Dr. Ryerson to J. George Hodgins	139
	13. Letter from J. George Hodgins to Dr. Ryerson	139
	14. Letter from J. George Hodgins to Dr. Ryerson	140
	15. Letter from Dr. Ryerson to J. George Hodgins	140
	Detailed Proceedings in regard to the Bill of 1862	140
XXIV.	Separate Schools in the Anglican Synod, 1862	145
	School Bill relating to Neglected Children	148
	Dr. Ryerson's Explanation in regard to this Bill	150
XXV.	Passage of the Separate School Bill of 1863	152
	1. Letter from Hon. J. S. Macdonald to Dr. Ryerson	153
	2. Letter from Dr. Ryerson to J. George Hodgins	153
	3. Letter from J. George Hodgins to Dr. Ryerson	153
	4. Letter from Dr. Ryerson to J. George Hodgins	154
	5. Letter from Dr. Ryerson to J. George Hodgins	154
	6. Letter from J. George Hodgins to Dr. Ryerson	154
	7. Letter from Dr. Ryerson to J. George Hodgins	155
	8. Letter from Dr. Ryerson to J. George Hodgins	155
	9. Letter from J. George Hodgins to Dr. Ryerson	155
	10. Letter from Dr. Ryerson to J. George Hodgins	156
	11. Letter from Dr. Ryerson to J. George Hodgins	156
	12. Letter from J. George Hodgins to Dr. Ryerson	156
	13. Letter from Dr. Ryerson to J. George Hodgins	157
	14. Telegram from Dr. Ryerson to J. George Hodgins	158
	15. Letter from Dr. Ryerson to J. George Hodgins	158
	16. Letter from J. George Hodgins to Dr. Ryerson	159
	17. Letter from Dr. Ryerson to J. George Hodgins	159
	18. Letter from Dr. Ryerson to J. George Hodgins	159
	19. Letter from J. George Hodgins to Dr. Ryerson	159
	20. Letter from J. George Hodgins to Dr. Ryerson	159
	21. Letter from Rev. M. Stafford to Dr. Ryerson	160

LEGISLATION AND HISTORY OF SEPARATE SCHOOLS IN UPPER CANADA.

CHAPTER I.

THE HISTORY OF SEPARATE SCHOOLS IN UPPER CANADA.

PRELIMINARY REMARKS.

MOST of the prominent actors on the stage of provincial politics, or public affairs, of fifty-six years ago, when Separate Schools were first established in Upper Canada, have passed away. And yet the impress of their hands, in framing the legislative measures of those days, is felt and recognized in the outlines and main features of the school, municipal and fiscal laws of to-day. Up to that time, most of the statutes which were passed were, it is true, either temporary in their object, or more or less crude in their character. They have long since been repealed or have been greatly modified in their purpose and scope, especially those relating to Education. A brief reference, however, to the school laws and policy of these times may prove interesting.

Up to 1841, only three enactments had passed the Legislature of Upper Canada, providing for the establishment of Primary Schools, viz., those of 1816, 1820 and 1824. Grants were made by the Legislature from time to time, but no specific enactments for the regulation, or management, of the Primary Schools were made by it, except those mentioned.

What the state of education was, in Upper Canada previous to the school legislation of 1841, may be stated in a few words.

In a petition of the United Presbytery of Upper Canada, presented to the House of Assembly in 1830, the signers say:—

> It is with deep regret that your Petitioners, (in their ministerial capacity, connected with a very large portion of His Majesty's subjects in this Province,) are compelled to say that the state of education is, in general, in a deplorable condition.

In 1831, a Resolution was introduced into the House of Assembly which further stated:—

> That there is in this Province a very general want of education; that the insufficiency of the Common School Fund to support competent, respectable and well-educated Teachers, has degraded Common School teaching from a regular business to a mere matter of convenience to transient persons, or common idlers, who often stay but for one season, and leave the Schools vacant until they accommodate some other like person, whereby the minds of the youth of this Province are left without due cultivation, or, what is worse, frequently with vulgar, low-bred, vicious and intemperate examples before them in the persons of their monitors, (*i.e.*, Teachers).

In 1837, the Legislative Council refused to concur in a Common School Bill, passed by the House of Assembly, and gave as a reason for not doing so, that:—

> It could not pass the Bill, because it proposes to levy an assessment at the discretion of the Justices of the Peace, to the extent of 1½d. [3 cents] in the £ [$4], to support Common Schools; and as Acts have lately passed imposing rates on the inhabitants of several of the Districts, for the purpose of defraying the expense of building Gaols and Court-houses, and for the construction of macadamised roads, the Council fear that the proposed assessment for Common School Education might be found burthensome.

Thus, because Gaols, Court-houses and Roads were considered more necessary and important than Schools, the last Act for the promotion of Education ever passed by the Upper Canada House of Assembly was rejected by the Legislative Council! Such was the untoward state of affairs when the Legislative Union of Upper and Lower Canada took place in 1840.

CHAPTER II.

EDUCATIONAL STATE OF UPPER AND LOWER CANADA, 1841.

DURING the first Session of the Parliament of United Canada, in 1841, a vigorous effort was made to induce the Government and Legislature of the day to provide, in the Common School Act, for the use of the Bible as a class, or text, book in the Schools of the Province.

The Governor-General, Lord Sydenham, who so strongly recommended to the Legislature that "due provision be made for the Education of the People,"—which he declared to be "one of the first duties of the State," had evidently misgivings as to the unanimity of the Legislature on the subject. He, therefore, counselled the Members of both Houses, in his opening speech, that:—

> If it should be found impossible so to reconcile conflicting opinions so as to obtain a measure which may meet with the approbation of all, . . . steps may, at least, be taken by which an advance to a more perfect system may be made.

Nor were the apprehensions of the Governor-General on this subject of dealing with the subject of popular education groundless. It was well known that, in the newly-elected House of Assembly, there were two active opposing educational forces. The one was desirous of giving, as they expressed it, a decidedly Christian and scriptural character to the proposed educational legislation. With this object in view, they addressed vigorously expressed petitions to both Houses of the Legislature—to the number of forty—praying that the Bible, in its entirety, should be definitely prescribed as a class, or text, book in the Common Schools, about to be established, and liberally endowed, in the United Provinces of Canada. One section of this objecting force, representing the Church of England, petitioned the

Legislature that children of that Church should be educated by it, with the aid of Public Grants and School Assessments. The other section of this opposing force contented itself with objecting to the principle of the proposed Common School Bill, and desiring that the Bill "should not become law until the opinion of the Roman Catholic, and that of other Religious Denominations, be known."

This twofold question, thus raised in the first Legislature of United Canada, was felt at the time to present an almost unsurmountable difficulty in dealing with School legislation. Its being raised there, when the establishment of a general and comprehensive system of elementary education was determined upon by the Government, need not have been a matter of surprise. It was inevitable, considering the past educational history of each of the Provinces, now united under one Government and Legislature. The Hon. Mr. Day, Solicitor-General, in introducing his Common School Bill, stated that were it not for—

> A few institutions, supported by private benevolence, and maintained by the exertions of a class of men to whom he, (Mr. Day,) could not pay too high a tribute of praise—he alluded to the Roman Catholic clergy—no means for public instruction existed (in Lower Canada).

In other words, the only education which existed in Lower Canada was provided by the Roman Catholic clergy. It was natural, therefore, that the petition of the Roman Catholic Bishops to the Legislature should desire that no educational measure should pass "until the opinion of the Roman Catholic and other Religious Denominations be known."

In the case of Upper Canada, it was generally known at the time, that the Bible was in use in the Schools of the Province, generally, chiefly with a view to verses from it being learned off, or memorized, by the pupils attending the Schools.

From the very first, public sentiment in Upper Canada was strongly in favour of public education being "based on Christian principles," as it was expressed, more or less distinctly, in the successive Charters of King's, Victoria and Queen's Colleges. This was the special plea of those who, more than fifty years ago, advocated the secularization of the Clergy Reserves to purely educational purposes. Some even favoured the diversion of this "Church Property" to educational purposes, on the ground that the education, which it would promote, would be so entirely "based upon Christian principles," that the so-called "secularization" would be the means—by reason of the wide diffusion of the Clergy Reserve moneys—"of promoting the Christian education of the whole people."

The first Legislative enactment on behalf of Common Schools, in Upper Canada was passed in 1816, nine years after Grammar Schools were established. There was no direct provision in that Act for giving religious instruction in the schools; the practice then being for pupils to learn verses from the Bible as already intimated. But, the Trustees were directed to "examine into the moral character and capacity of any person willing to become a Teacher"; but this had reference only to moral conduct, and not to his religious opinion.

Experience, however, showed that something in the shape of religious instruction was desirable, and that it should be "disseminated among the people." In 1824, therefore, a Common School Act was passed, the preamble of which stated that,—

It would greatly advance the happiness of society to disseminate moral and religious instruction among the people.

The Act, therefore, declared that :—

For the benefit of all classes of His Majesty's subjects, and for the encouragement of Sunday Schools, and for affording the means of moral and religious instruction in the more indigent and remote settlements in the several Districts of this Province, there shall be annually paid the sum of One Hundred and Fifty pounds (£150), to be laid out and expended for the purchasing of books and tracts, designed to afford moral and religious instruction, to be distributed among the several Boards of Education throughout the Province. . . .

CHAPTER III.

EDUCATIONAL PROCEEDINGS OF THE CANADIAN LEGISLATURE OF 1841.

In 1840, the Provinces of Upper and Lower Canada were, by Act of the Imperial Parliament, (3rd and 4th Victoria, Chapter 35,) united under one Government and Legislature. On the 20th of July, 1841, the Hon. Solicitor-General Day introduced a Bill into the House of Assembly, "to make provision for the Establishment and Maintenance of Common Schools throughout the Province." This School Bill of 1841 was introduced into a mixed Legislative Body, composed of Members from both sections of the Province, elected to act together for the first time, in a matter on which the Representatives from each section held very diverse views, and, in the main, very ill-defined ones on "religious education." The result may easily be imagined. A dead-lock ensued; and this dead-lock was only ended by the Government entirely abrogating its functions, as defined by itself at the beginning of the Session, and submitting its own measure—carefully prepared, as Mr. Day, its framer, had explained—to a mixed general Committee of the House, not chosen geographically, or fairly, in proportion to the Members representing each section of the Province, but at haphazard, and by giving Lower Canada about two-thirds of the Members of the Committee, and Upper Canada a little over one-third. The number on the Committee, therefore, stood as follows: Lower Canada, fifteen, and Upper Canada, eight; or twenty-three in all.

The result of such a proceeding may have been easily anticipated by the more thoughtful men in the Legislature; but, if so, it could scarcely then have been provided for by them. No Committee under strong pressure from without, as this one was, could have given that judicious and careful consideration to the subject, which was necessary in dealing with so difficult and delicate a matter as this was. The time was too short; and the immediate object to be gained was too general and undefined to enable the Committee to lay down, at once, a safe and practical rule by which Separate Schools could be established. As it was, it recommended to the House that any number of persons, of either faith, by merely dissenting "from the regulations, arrangements and proceedings of the Common School Commissioners," could establish a Separate School! The practical need of such a School, on conscientious grounds, was not to be the motive, or grounds, of action on the part of dissentients, but simply that if they objected to the official School Regulations, they could express their dissent, and then be free to establish a rival school, and claim funds to support it,—not according to the number of children in attendance at that school, but according to the number of the residents who had expressed their dissent from the official School Regulations, or from the "arrangements" and "proceedings" of the Township School Commissioners.

It is a matter of fact, that up to 1841, no Religious Body, or other persons, mooted, much less advocated, the question of the necessity, or desirability, of Separate Schools, as part of a general system of education. Their establishment was, as I have shown, due to peculiar circumstances, and as the result of a dead-lock in the Legislature, and of an effort, in consequence thereof, at compromise and conciliation, under strong pressure from various opposing influences. These influences, as pointed out, were brought to bear on the Government, and compelled it to abrogate its functions; and these influences were also brought to bear, with ill effects, on the mixed Legislature of the newly united Provinces of Upper and Lower Canada, and its Special School Committee.

It was this introduction, in 1841, of the principle of Separate Schools which gave rise to that prolonged and bitter controversy, and which produced that unhappy discord which prevailed during the earlier period of Dr. Ryerson's administration,—especially from 1850 to 1863.

A far more troublesome and difficult question to deal with was the apathy on the part of some, and the persistent opposition, on the part of others, to a National System of Education, projected, as it was, on the comprehensive lines laid down by Dr. Ryerson, in his elaborate and illustrative preliminary Report of 1845-46.

These two passive, and yet opposing, forces were sure to give way in time, which they did; but the purely denominational, or sectarian, questions, as they were characterized, remained, to be a source of irritation for many years. And this feeling was greatly increased by the persistent efforts made by the opponents of Separate Schools to hold Dr. Ryerson personally responsible for the very introduction, and afterwards, for the extension, of the principle of Separate Schools in Upper Canada; whereas his desire was to deal with this difficult and delicate question rather as an incident, or adjunct, to a provincial system of education, (and that solely with reference to the conscientious convictions of individuals,) and not as affecting a religious community, as a unit, or as a Church. He thus sought to settle the question on sound principles and, as he believed, on a safe and prudential basis.

In reply to a Letter, which I addressed to the late Sir Francis Hincks, (who was a Member of the first Parliament of United Canada,) asking him why it was that the Government referred the School Bill to a general Committee of the House of Assembly, he wrote as follows, under date of Montreal, 15th August, 1884:—

> The School Bill was, as you state, introduced into the Legislature by the Hon. C. D. Day, Solicitor-General, (late Hon. Mr. Justice Day,) without any clause in it relating to Separate Schools. Petitions were presented to the House, praying that the Bible should be made a class-book in the Schools; and I imagine that the Government, to get rid of the responsibility of dealing with a very difficult question, proposed and carried a reference of the Bill and the petitions to a Select Committee of all parties in the House. That Committee was about twenty-one (23) in number. . . I think that Dissentient Schools in Lower Canada, [and Separate Schools in

Upper Canada,] were provided for in the same way; although, of course, the Separate Schools would have been generally Roman Catholic in Upper Canada and Protestant in Lower Canada. The Bill was passed, as reported from the Select Committee, on which all parties were represented.*

F. HINCKS.

MONTREAL, 15th of August, 1884.

The appointment of this Select, or Mixed General, Committee to deal, at its pleasure, with a Government measure, was clearly a violation of the principle advocated by the Government Members of the House in the early part of the Session. For instance, a motion was made by the Hon. George Moffatt on the 8th of June, 1841, to appoint a number of Standing Committees, among them one on "Education and Schools." This, the Attorney-General and Solicitor-General, resisted, on the ground that it was the duty of the Government—

To originate all important measures of public utility.

And these gentlemen asked, how the Government could—

Obtain the confidence of the House if those measures were to be taken out of their hands, and brought before the House in the shape and detail essentially different from that in which the Government desired to bring them forward?

Mr. William H. Merritt explained what had been the former practice in the Upper Canada House of Assembly, and stated that in that House—

They had been in the habit of appointing Committees on all subjects, . . . But now they had a different system; and they had reason to expect that satisfaction would hereafter be given, because . . . the Members of His Excellency's Administration assert that we have now "Responsible Government."

---

* The only reference to this matter which Sir Francis Hincks gives in the "Reminiscences of [his] Public Life" is the following:—"The Bill for establishing Common Schools, and for granting a liberal sum annually for their maintenance, was introduced by Mr. Solicitor Day, whose recent death, after a most honourable public career, has been very greatly deplored by his fellow-citizens, and was carried without opposition. It is worthy of notice that, after the introduction of the School Bill, a number of Petitions were presented, praying that the Bible should be adopted as a School Book. This led to the reference of the Bill to a large Select Committee, which recommended the introduction of the Separate School clause, which was not in the Bill as originally introduced." (*Pages 68 and 69.*)

Nevertheless, the Government Common School Bill of 1841 was referred, with the consent of the Government, to a mixed General Committee of the House, and by it was reported to the House essentially different, in "shape and detail," and in important particulars, from that in which the Government had introduced it. It was in this way that the Separate School principle was incorporated in the Bill, when it came out of the hands of this mixed and irresponsible Committee of the House of Assembly.

The Members of the Government in 1841 were: The Honourable Messieurs Robert Baldwin Sullivan, John Henry Dunn, Dominick Daly, Samuel Bealey Harrison, Charles Richard Ogden, William Henry Draper, Robert Baldwin and Charles Dewey Day.

The select General Committee of the House, to which Mr. Day's Common School Bill was referred, consisted of twenty-three members—eight only from Upper Canada, and fifteen from Lower Canada. The Upper Canada members were: Messieurs Samuel B. Harrison, John S. Cartwright, Malcolm Cameron, William H. Merritt, Thomas Parke, David Thorburn, Francis Hincks and John Prince—8.

The members from Lower Canada were: Messieurs Charles D. Day, John Neilson, John Simpson, George Moffatt, Frederick A. Quesnel, John W. Dunscombe, Thomas C. Aylwin, Robert Christie, Augustus N. Morin, Marcus Child, Etienne Parent, Colin Robertson, Benjamin Holmes, Stephen S. Foster, Amable Berthelot and Denis B. Viger—15.

Having asked Sir Francis Hincks if there had been, in 1841, any understanding among Lower Canada Members of the House of Assembly that, by the treaty of Capitulation of Quebec, Lower Canada Roman Catholics could demand Schools of their own faith, as a right, he replied as follows:—

I can assure you that no such question was raised as that of the right to Separate Schools, on the ground of the stipulations of the old Treaty of Capitulation.

I was entirely opposed myself to the Bible being made a class-book in the Schools. F. H.

CHAPTER IV.

PETITIONS PRAYING THAT THE BIBLE BE USED AS A CLASS-BOOK IN THE SCHOOLS.

Dr. Ryerson, as is well known, had thus nothing to do with the introduction of the principle of Separate Schools into our School System. That was done, as I have shown, in 1841, three years before his appointment to office. It was owing principally, as pointed out, to the well-intentioned, but misdirected, zeal of those who sought to influence the newly elected and mixed Legislature of the time, to make the Bible a class-book, in the Common Schools. The Hon. William Morris advocated this view; and, in his remarks in the Legislative Council, on the Common School Bill of 1841, he said:—

> With respect to the difficulty which is presented to our view by the Petitions which daily come before the House, from Roman Catholic and Protestant Bodies, I would just observe, that if the use, by Protestants, of the Holy Scriptures in their Schools, is so objectionable to our fellow-subjects of that other faith, the children of both religious persuasions must be educated apart; for Protestants never can yield to that point, and, therefore, if it is insisted upon that the Scriptures shall not be a class-book in Schools, we must part in peace, and conduct the education of the respective Bodies according to our sense of what is right.

The Hon Peter B. DeBlacquiere, on the other hand, contended that—

> To attempt the introduction of the Holy Scriptures, as received by Protestants, as a class-book in the Common Schools, when Roman Catholics were to be educated in the same School, was worse than useless; it was oppressive; it was dangerous; and it must arrest all progress in education. . . .

The petitions presented to both Houses of the Legislature, praying that the Bible be prescribed as a class-book in the Schools, were from different Religious Bodies, and were more or less diverse in their character. They were all, however, equally embarrassing to the Government of the day. As from their effect upon the School legislation of the time, they may be considered of historical interest.* Of those which were printed by the Legislature, I give a specimen, as follows:—

1. A petition from the Clergymen and Members of the Church of England at St. Armand West, Lower Canada, stated that:—

The Petitioners, while they are anxious to promote throughout the Province the diffusion of general knowledge, are, in their own minds convinced that knowledge, to be productive of any real benefit, or substantial good, to the people, must be guided by the unerring wisdom of God, as revealed in His Word. . . .

That humbly, also, but conscientiously believing that the Bible, as given by God, must be received as a whole, and cannot, without rashness, or detriment, either be added to or diminished from, . . . your Petitioners consider that they would ill discharge their duties as Christians, and, consequently, as believers in the whole Book of Revelation, if they did not deprecate in any contemplated establishment of Schools, every attempt to introduce into them extracts only from the Holy Scriptures, whereby the Word of God would be abridged and mutilated, and the imperfect selections of uninspired men be substituted for the inspired Word of the Almighty, expressly revealed for man's benefit and guidance ;†

---

* In one of Dr. Ryerson's Letters, he says:—"The principal opposition which, in 1846, and for several years afterwards, I encountered was that I did not make the Bible compulsory in the Schools, but simply recognized the right of Protestants to use it in the School, (not as an ordinary reading book, as it was not given to teach us how to read, but to teach us the way to Heaven,) as a book of religious instruction, without the right, or the power, of compelling any one to use it."—"*Story of My Life*," *page 429.*

† This strong language is not borne out, or confirmed, by experience. The Hon. P. B. DeBlacquiere, in his remarks on the Common School Bill of 1841, in the Legislative Council, stated that "judicious selections, suited to the age and capacities of those to be instructed" was a practical want in the Schools. This practical want was supplied by the Education Department for Ontario in 1888, and also in Chicago, "under the supervision of the Chicago Woman's Educational Union, in 1896. The latter is a Book of 150 selections from the Bible, entitled: "Readings from the Bible, selected for Schools, and to be read in Unison." It is also suggested that the selections be "memorized." The publication of this Book was the result of a largely signed petition to the Chicago Board of Education, asking that a "Reading Book, consisting of selections from the Sacred Scriptures, such as in use in the Schools of Toronto, Canada, or similar selections, (with the approval of both the Roman Catholic and Protestant Churches,) be put into use in the Public Schools of Chicago." The "Scripture Readings" issued by the Education Department of Ontario, and to which reference is made above, embraces 292 Selections, or Lessons, and extends to 434 8vo pages. The Chicago Selections number 150, and extend to 190 12mo pages. In addition to the Table of Contents, as in the Ontario Selections, the Chicago Book contains a Topical Index, and an Index of Texts.

Wherefore Petitioners humbly pray that not only may the Bible . . . be recognized as the class-book, to be universally taught in all Public Schools and Seminaries throughout the Province, in which Protestants shall receive their education, but that it may be put into the hands of all such scholars, in its full and unabridged state, and that no part of it may be withheld from them.

These strong sentiments, expressed by Members of the Church of England in Lower Canada, were re-echoed by their brethren in Upper Canada, through the medium of *The Church* newspaper, which had been established in 1837 by the Rev. Dr. A. N. Bethune, afterwards, (in 1867,) second Bishop of Toronto. *The Church*, of July 24th, 1841, said:—

In the Provincial Parliament, an attempt will be made to introduce a new and comprehensive System of Education. In anticipation of this, Members of various Christian Denominations have presented petitions to the Legislature, praying that provision may be made for the use of the Holy Scriptures in all Schools receiving any Public Grant. In such a petition as this, we consider it the duty of every man to join, and thus record, (to borrow the forcible language of the *Quebec Mercury*,) "their abhorrence of the principle that would recommend the putting of garbled extracts from the Sacred Volume in the hands of the rising generation."

The whole subject will, we fear, be found environed with many difficulties, and we have a shrewd suspicion that something like the Irish System of Education will be thrust upon our acceptance. We confess that we cannot, at present, see any likelihood of a speedy and satisfactory settlement of this question; for its discussion must necessarily bring to the surface every element of political and religious discord. At all events, however, there is one point of Protestant unanimity—and that is, to insist on the free and unmutilated use of the Authorized Version of the Holy Scriptures in every School supported by the State.

2. A petition was also presented to the Legislature on the 18th of August, 1841, from the Right Reverend Remegius Gaulin, Roman Catholic Bishop of Kingston, and from the Reverends A. Manseau and H. Hudon, Administrators of the Diocese of Montreal, stating objections to the principle of the School Bill of 1841, and desiring—

That it may not become law, until the opinion of the Catholic and other Religious Denominations be known.

3. A petition was presented on the same day from the Right

Reverend the Bishop and Clergy of the Church of England in Toronto, praying—

That the education of the children of their own Church may be entrusted to their own pastors; and that an annual grant from the asssessments may be awarded for their instruction.

4. In a petition presented to the Legislature from the Right Reverend the Roman Catholic Bishop of Quebec, and the Bishop of Sidyme, his Coadjutor, on the 23rd of August, 1841, it was stated that they entertained a hope that:—

When the House will adopt a law for the encouragement of Education in this Province, they will watch carefully that it shall contain no enactment which can prejudice the interests of Her Majesty's Catholic subjects; also, that it will be based on the principles of justice.

5. The petition presented to the House of Assembly by the Reverend James George, "Moderator of the Presbyterian Church of Canada, on behalf of said Church," prayed that an enactment be made prescribing the use of the Bible in all the Schools of the Province.

CHAPTER V.

EFFECT OF THESE PETITIONS—ADOPTION OF THE PRINCIPLE OF SEPARATE SCHOOLS IN UPPER CANADA.

OF the forty-two petitions presented to the House of Assembly in regard to the Honourable Solicitor-General Day's Common School Bill, thirty-nine prayed for the use of the Bible in the Schools. All of these, as well as the Government Bill itself, were referred to the Special and Select Committee already named. The result was that, in the attempt to deal with, and to provide for, the diverse circumstances of Upper and Lower Canada alike, a far more ill-digested and unwise scheme for Separate and Dissentient Schools was framed by the Committee than was evidently intended, or desired, by the Upper Canada Members of the House, or by the Petitioners from that part of the Province. This is apparent from the fact that, after a year's trial, the Act was wholly repealed; and that, in the special School Act for Upper Canada, framed by the Hon. Francis Hincks, none of the Separate School provisions of the Common School Act of 1841 were retained. The conditions on which Separate Schools could be established were greatly restricted, and the principle, or basis, on which they were aided was narrowed down from the indefinite, yet collective, one of the total number of dissentient inhabitants interested, to that of the actual one of the attendance of individual pupils at the School concerned. Nevertheless, the Government, having adopted the unusual course of submitting one of its Cabinet measures to the revision of a mixed Select Committee, had no option but to concur in what that Committee proposed as a solution of the difficulty. With this now memorable addition to the Government Education Bill of 1841, made solely by the Select Committee, it received the Royal assent on the 18th of September of that year.

The principal provisions, relating to Separate Schools, introduced into Mr. Solicitor-General Day's Common School Bill of 1841 by the Select Committee, to which it was referred by the Government, were as follows :—

XI. Be it enacted, That whenever any number of the Inhabitants of any Township, or Parish, professing a Religious Faith different from that of the majority of the Inhabitants of such Township, or Parish, shall dissent from the Regulations, Arrangements, or Proceedings of the Common School Commissioners, [elected in each Township,] with reference to any Common School in such Township, or Parish, it shall be lawful for the Inhabitants, so dissenting, collectively to signify such dissent in writing to the Clerk of the District Council, with the name, or names, of one or more persons elected by them, as their Trustee, or Trustees, for the purposes of this Act; and the said District Clerk shall forthwith furnish a certified copy thereof to the District Treasurer; and it shall be lawful for such Dissenting Inhabitants, by and through such Trustee, or Trustees, who, for that purpose, shall hold and exercise all the rights, powers and authorities, and be subject to the obligations and liabilities hereinbefore assigned to, and imposed upon the Common School Commissioners, to establish and maintain one or more Common Schools, in the manner and subject to the Visitation, Conditions, Rules and Obligations in this Act provided, with reference to other Common Schools, and to receive from the District Treasurer their due proportion, according to their number, of the moneys appropriated by Law and raised by assessment for the support of Common Schools, in the School District, or Districts, in which the said Inhabitants reside, in the same manner as if the Common Schools, so to be established and maintained under such Trustee, or Trustees, where established and maintained under the said Common School Commissioners, such moneys to be paid by the District Treasurer, upon the Warrant of the said Trustee, or Trustees.

XVI. Be it enacted, That it shall be lawful for the Governor of this Province to appoint, from time to time, in each of the Cities and Towns Corporate therein, not less than six, nor more than fourteen persons, (one-half of whom shall, in all cases, be Roman Catholics, and the other ha'f Protestants,) to be a Board of Examiners for each City, or Town, Corporate; of which said Board the Mayor shall be Chairman, but shall have no vote other than a casting vote; and the said Board shall be divided into two Departments, one of which shall consist of Roman Catholics, and shall exercise the duties hereinafter assigned to the Board of Examiners in and over the Common Schools attended by Roman Catholic Children only, and shall, in such case, appoint their Chairman; and the other Department shall consist of Protestants, who shall exercise their said duties in and over the Common Schools attended by the Protestant Children only, and shall, in such cases, appoint their Chairman;—and, in all cases, in which the said Common Schools are attended by Roman Catholic Children and Protestant Children together, the said duties shall be exercised in and over the same by the whole Board of Examiners; and the duties of the said Board, and of the said Departments hereof, in the several cases above mentioned, in and for the said Cities and Towns Corporate, respectively, shall be to examine the persons recommended as Teachers by the corporation, and reject them, if unqualified, on the ground of character or ability; and to regulate for each School separately the course of study to be followed in such School, and the books to be used therein, and to establish general rules for the conduct of the Schools, and communicate them in writing to the respective Teachers. . . .

The same Act provided that no person should be appointed a Teacher, unless he were a British subject, and had been duly examined. An exception to this provision was made in Section four of the Act, in favour of "persons known as *les Freres de la Doctrine Chretienne.*"

CHAPTER VI.

SEPARATE SCHOOL LEGISLATION AFFECTING UPPER CANADA ALONE, 1843.

It was soon found that the general Education Law, framed in 1841 for the whole Province, was not acceptable to Upper Canada, or suitable to its needs, or condition. Nothing, however, was done in regard to education during the Legislative Session of 1842. But, in the next Session, the Hon. Francis Hincks, having, since 1841, become a Member of the Government as Inspector General, introduced a Common School Bill into the Legislature of 1843.* In that Bill, no part of the Separate School legislation of 1841 was included—it being considered at the time objectionable in principle, and unjust and unwise in its financial detail. The strongest objection which was felt at the time to the law of 1841, so far as it related to Separate Schools, was to the element of discord in neighbourhoods which it authorized and sanctioned, by the general permission which it gave to those, who might express dissent to the official Regulations prescribed for the government of the Common Schools, to withdraw their children from the School, and set up a rival one in the same place. The law also provided that if even the Regulations were unobjectionable, dissent might be expressed to the "arrangements" or even to the "proceedings" of the School Commissioners, and then the right would arise to the dissentients; and they would, under the law, be justified in setting up a rival School, with the same right as the local School to share in the School moneys, "according to their number," (*i.e.*, of dissentients.)

---

* The School Law of 1841 was also found to be unsuited to Lower Canada; and, in the same Session of 1843, the Hon. A. N. Morin introduced a School Bill for Lower Canada into the House of Assembly.

Such an unstatesmanlike mode of dealing with a difficult social question was seriously felt on all sides; and the Law of 1841 was, in 1843, wholly repealed. The Hon. Francis Hincks, a Member of the Government, undertook the task of providing, in that year, (1843,) a School Law for Upper Canada alone, in place of the General School Act of 1841. In his Bill, he omitted the whole of the provisions for Separate Schools, which were contained in the School Act of 1841, and introduced the following provisions for such Schools in its place:—

LV. And be it enacted, That in all cases wherein the Teacher of any Common School shall happen to be a Roman Catholic, the Protestant inhabitants shall be entitled to have a School with a Teacher of their own Religious Persuasion, upon the application of ten or more resident freeholders, or householders, of any School District, or within the limits assigned to any Town, or City, School; and, in like manner, when the Teacher of any such School shall happen to be a Protestant, the Roman Catholic inhabitants shall have a Separate School, with a Teacher of their own Religious Persuasion, upon a like application.

LVI. And be it enacted, That such applications shall be made in writing, signed with the names of each resident freeholder, or householder, and addressed and delivered to the Township, Town, or City, Superintendent, [with names of Trustees], and upon the compliance of such Trustee, and of the Township, Town or City Superintendent, with the requirements of this Act, such School shall be entitled to receive its share of the public appropriation, according to the number of children of the religious persuasion who shall attend such Separate School, which share shall be settled and adjudged by the Township, Town or City Superintendent, subject to an appeal to the County Superintendent; and such Separate School shall be subject to the visitations, conditions, rules and obligations provided in this Act, with reference to other Common Schools, or to other Town, or City, Schools established under this Act.

It will be noted that these provisions of the Upper Canada School Bill of 1843 are much less general than those in the Act of 1841. They dealt with a practical case, and gave no room for capricious action, founded on mere difference of opinion in regard to the "regulations, arrangements, or proceedings, of the School Commissioners." The Act of 1843 provided that the course of study and text-books agreed upon by the Trustees were subject to the approval of the Local Superintendent.

Provision was first made in this Act for the protection of

those children, whose parents or guardians objected to have them " read or study in, or from, any religious book, or join in any exercise of devotion or religion."

Hon. Francis Hincks, in a Speech which he delivered in 1843, thus explained the reason why the Common School Act of 1841 was superseded by an Act introduced by himself in 1843, and, in the case of this Province, confined to Upper Canada alone. He said:—

No one is more sensible than I am of the defects of the late School Law, (of 1841,) so great, indeed, were they, that it has been found impossible to work it. That . . . School Law was not framed by any Ministry, responsible, or otherwise; it was hastily put together in a Select Committee of the House of Assembly, consisting of [twenty-three] Members; without that deliberation and care which such a measure ought to have and received.

CHAPTER VII.

PROCEEDINGS IN REGARD TO THE SCHOOLS—OF BISHOPS STRACHAN, POWER AND CHARBONNEL—BISHOP MACDONELL.

I. BISHOP STRACHAN.

BISHOP STRACHAN strongly opposed the Separate School provisions in the Hincks' School Act of 1843, which applied to Upper Canada alone. He wished to have Church of England Schools, "pure and simple." In his Charge to his Clergy in 1844, the Bishop said:—

When the School Act was under discussion in the Legislature, in 1841, I petitioned that the Church should be allowed her share of the public money in proportion to her numbers.* With this reasonable request, there was a disposition to comply, as appears from the eleventh section; but the Act was found contradictory and impracticable, and no benefit

---

* This was the provision in the discarded Act of 1841, which the Bishop wished to be restored in the Act of 1843. The same request was invariably preferred, and that very frequently afterwards by promoters of Separate Schools, but was as invariably refused by Dr. Ryerson.

could be derived from it during its continuance. I petitioned again, while the new Act [of 1843] was under consideration, praying that the sum appropriated by the Legislature for the use of Common Schools might be divided among the recognized Denominations of Christians, in proportion to their respective numbers,* or in proportion to the funds raised by each, or from the combination of both. . . . No notice was taken of this application. . . . The former law of 1841 was dropped, and a new statute was enacted (in 1843), in which, throughout its seventy-one clauses, there is no reference to Christianity.—(*Bishop Strachan's Charge to his Clergy, January, 1844, page 39.*)

It is proper to remark here that this proposition of Bishop Strachan to have Separate School moneys divided among the Denominations "in proportion to their respective numbers" was a principle which, during his administration, Dr. Ryerson strenuously opposed. He held that to do so would be practically to endow churches, as such,—professedly for school purposes,—but, nevertheless, a recognition of the right of these Churches, in their corporate capacity, to a share of the public funds, for the promotion of Sectarian Education. Reference to this matter is made in a subsequent part of this Book.

For several years after the passage of the Acts of 1841 and 1843, no demand was made by the Representatives of the Roman Catholic Church for any extension of the principle of Separate Schools, as it had been agreed upon and settled by all parties in the House of Assembly in these years. The Church of England, however, persistently made a claim, year after year, for a share of the School moneys for Parochial Schools; but the claim was never recognized, nor acted upon, by the Government, or Legislature.

II. BISHOP POWER.†

During the life-time of the Right Reverend Dr. Michael Power, first Roman Catholic Bishop of Toronto, he acted in a

---

* Dr. Ryerson was invariably opposed to this proposal, as it involved the principle of Church Endowment. See Note on the preceding page.

† The Right Reverend Michael Power, D.D., was a native of Nova Scotia. He was elected Bishop of Toronto on the 17th of December, 1841; was consecrated on the 8th of May, 1842; died from fever, caught while ministering to the fever-stricken Irish emigrants in Toronto, on the 1st of October, 1847.

friendly way with Dr. Ryerson on the Provincial Board of Education, (afterwards the Council of Public Instruction,) of which he was Chairman until his death. This I knew as a matter of fact, for I was at every Meeting of that Board up to the time of the greatly lamented death of Bishop Power, on the 1st of October, 1847.

Years afterwards, this friendliness of action on the part of Bishop Power was questioned by the Hon. John Elmsley, of Toronto, by Vicar-General Bruyere, of Toronto, and by Bishop Pinsoneault, of London. In a Letter from the latter to the Vicar-General, published in *The Leader* newspaper of the 20th of February, 1857, the Bishop said :—

Need I say it is notorious that both these zealous Prelates, (Bishops Macdonell and Power,) laboured most faithfully and strenuously—in their own times—to establish thorough Catholic Schools, whenever and wherever circumstances permitted them.

Dr. Ryerson dissented from this strong statement of Bishop Pinsoneault, and, in *The Leader* of the 27th of February, 1857, said :—

In reply to this statement (of the Bishop), I remark :

1st. There is not a vestige of proof to sustain it in any circular or letter, or writing, put forth by either of the excellent Prelates mentioned.

2nd. That, although the provisions of the law for Separate Schools have existed since the commencement of the present system in 1841, and although Bishop Macdonell chiefly resided in Kingston, and Bishop Power in Toronto, but two Separate Roman Catholic Schools were established under the law, in either Kingston, or Toronto, until after the death of these Bishops.

3. That Bishop Power not only acted with the Board of Education, (a mixed Board,) and presided at its Meetings until the week before his death, but his name stands first of the six Members who individually signed the first Circular to the Municipalities of Upper Canada, on the establishment of the Normal School,* (a mixed School,) as the great instrument of giving effect to our system of Common Schools.

4. The late Bishop Macdonell died before I had any connection with

---

* The opening and closing paragraphs of this Circular are as follows :
" We to whom the duty has been assigned, (to select and recommend proper books and libraries, and to establish a Normal School for the better education of School Teachers in Upper Canada,) have undertaken it with a deep conviction of its importance and difficulty, and with an earnest desire to perform it in a

our School System; but I knew the sentiments of Bishop Power from frequent intercourse and consultation with him on School matters, and I know that he and Bishop Charbonnel—on his first coming to Toronto—professed not to desire Separate Schools beyond what they, (Roman Catholics,) termed 'protection from insult;' that is, in such cases only where Roman Catholic children could not attend the Common Schools without being insulted and being imposed upon on account of their religion. The necessity of a Separate School they lamented as a misfortune, instead of advocating it as a principle. In this feeling I entirely sympathized.

In reply to a Letter of mine, dated the 1st of October, 1847—in which I informed Dr. Ryerson, then absent from Toronto, of the death of Bishop Power,—in a Letter, dated the 3rd of October, he said:—

The death of Bishop Power astonished and deeply affected me. He was a very valuable Member of the Provincial Board, and an exceedingly agreeable man. I hope the Board has a suitable Resolution in reference to him. (Such a Resolution was passed by the Board.)

In a Letter addressed, in 1855, to the Hon. John A. Macdonald, Dr. Ryerson thus referred to Bishop Power:—

Bishop Power, virtually a Canadian, being born in Nova Scotia, had a patriotic desire to elevate the Roman Catholic population of the Country, and believed that it would be best effected by their children being educated with the children of other creeds, wherever party feeling did not oppose insurmountable obstacles to it.—(*Correspondence between the Chief Superintendent and other persons on the subject of Separate Schools, 1853-1855, page 50.*)

---

manner that will promote, to the greatest possible extent, the best interests of the Country.

. . . .

The Board of Education earnestly hope that this subject (the Normal School) will receive the favourable consideration of the several District Councils; and to their early as well as patriotic and benevolent attention we earnestly recommend it. It is the purpose of the Board to educate young men *for* Canada, as well as *in* it, etc.

J. GEORGE HODGINS,
Recording Clerk.

† MICHAEL, BISHOP OF TORONTO,
Chairman.
EGERTON RYERSON.
H. J. GRASETT.
S. B. HARRISON.
JOSEPH C. MORRISON.
HUGH SCOBIE.
J. S. HOWARD.

Education Office, Toronto, August 4th, 1846.

In his address at the opening of the Normal School for Upper Canada, in November, 1847, Dr. Ryerson thus referred to the then recent decease of Bishop Power, and to the harmony which had characterized the Meetings of the Provincial Board of Education, up to that time:—

> One event, indeed, has occurred, over which the Members of the Board have reason to mourn—the decease of the Right Reverend Prelate, who, by his colleagues, had been unanimously chosen Chairman of the Board, and whose conduct, as Chairman and Member of the Board, was marked by a punctuality, a courtesy, a fairness, a zeal and intelligence which entitle his memory to the affectionate remembrance of his colleagues and the grateful esteem of every member of the community. . . . I cannot reflect upon the full and frequent conversations which I have had with him on subjects of public instruction, and with the scrupulous regard which he ever manifested for the views and rights and wishes of Protestants, without feelings of the deepest respect for his character and memory.

Further, in referring to the preparation of the Regulations in regard to Religious Instruction in the Schools, Dr. Ryerson said, in his Annual Report:—

> It affords me pleasure to record the fact . . . that before adopting the section in the printed *Forms and Regulations* on the "Constitution and Government of the Schools in Respect to Religious instruction," I submitted it to the late Roman Catholic Bishop Power, Chairman of our Board, who, after examining it, said that he would not object to it, as Roman Catholics were fully protected in their rights and views, and as he did not wish to interfere with Protestants in the fullest exercise of their rights and views.

In addition, I may say that Dr. Ryerson, in a private Letter to Hon, Attorney-General Draper, dated December 17th, 1846, thus explained his proceedings in regard to the preparation of the clause in the Regulations relating to Religious Instruction in the Schools. He said:—

> I submitted the clause first to Reverend Mr. Grasett, as a Member of the Board. He quite approved of it, as he felt exceedingly anxious that there should be such an explicit recognition of Christianity in our School system. . . . I showed it also to Bishop Strachan. After he had read the Section, he said he believed I had done all that could be done on that subject, and that . . . he would write a Circular to his Clergy, recommending them to act as School Visitors, and to do all in their power to promote the efficiency and usefulness of the Common Schools.

The Hon. W. H. Draper, in a private note, to Dr. Ryerson, in reply, dated the 1st January, 1847, said :—

I am more gratified than I can express that you have so successfully met the difficulty about the Religious Instruction of children in Common Schools. You, (to whom I expressed myself about three years ago on the subject of the importance of not dividing religion from secular instruction,) will readily understand the pleasure I feel that, in Common Schools at least, the principle and proposed application of it, for mixed Schools, has been approved by the Bishop of my own Church, and by the Roman Catholic Prelate.

W. H. DRAPER.

MONTREAL, 1st of January, 1847.

The first and last paragraphs of these Regulations on Religious Instruction in the Schools were as follows :—

As Christianity is the basis of our whole system of elementary education, that principle should pervade it throughout. Where it cannot be carried out in mixed Schools to the satisfaction of both Roman Catholics and Protestants, the law provides for the establishment of Separate Schools. And the Common School Act, securing individual liberty, as well as recognizing Christianity, provides :—

"That in any Model or Common School, established under this Act, no child shall be required to read or study in or from any religious book, or to join in any exercises of devotion or religion which shall be objected to by his parents or guardians."

With this limitation, the peculiar religious exercises of each School must be a matter of understanding between the Teacher and his employers. This must be the case in regard both to Separate and Mixed Schools.

(2. *Quotation from the Regulations of the Irish National Board.*)

3. The foregoing quotations (which might be greatly extended) from the Irish Commissioners' Reports are made because their system may be considered as the basis of the Upper Canadian system—their books having been adopted and their methods of instruction being about to be introduced in the Provincial Normal School. That system is Christian, but not sectarian ; secures individual right and denominational privileges, and is founded on revealed truth. The *General Lesson,** hung up in every School of the Irish National Board, and carefully inculcated upon the pupils, is recommended for universal adoption in Upper Canada.—(*Special Report on the Measures which have been adopted for the establishment of a Normal School, and for carrying into effect generally the Common School Act, 9 Vict. ch. xx. By the Chief Superintendent of Schools ; Montreal, 1847, pages 60, 61.*)

---

* This *General Lesson* is practically the substance of the *Golden Rule.*

III. BISHOP MACDONELL.*

As to Bishop Macdonell, his proceedings in regard to Schools are detailed pretty fully in the examination of the Reverend Dr. O'Grady, Parish Priest at York, by the W. L. Mackenzie's *Grievance Committee*, in 1835, and also in the evidence of other Witnesses. This evidence goes to show that the British Government authorized a grant to be made to Bishop Macdonell for Mission and Educational purposes, of One Thousand pounds (£1,000) sterling a year. Four Teachers were brought out by him from Scotland, viz.: Messrs. Hammond, Murdoch McDonald and McPherson. Colonel Alexander Chisholm, M.P.P. for Glengarry, in his evidence before the Grievance Committee, stated

---

* The Right Reverend Bishop Macdonell was born in July, 1762, near Loch Ness, Inverness-shire, Scotland. He was educated at the Scottish Colleges, first at Paris and afterwards at Valladolid, where he was ordained in 1787. In 1794, Mr. Macdonell conceived the idea of forming some Scotch Roman Catholic operatives, out of work, into a Regiment. This was done with the King's sanction, and he became Chaplain to the Glengarry Fencible Regiment, first in Guernsey, and then in Ireland. In 1802, the Regiment was disbanded; and in March of that year, Mr. Macdonell obtained the Sign Manual for a grant of land for every Officer and soldier of the Regiment whom he could introduce into Upper Canada. On his own arrival, he was appointed to the Mission of St. Raphael, Glengarry. On the 12th of January, 1819, he was nominated Bishop of Rhæsina, and Vicar Apostolic of Upper Canada, and was consecrated as such in Quebec on the 31st of December, 1820. On the 27th of January, 1826, he was appointed Bishop of Regiopolis, or Kingston. On his return from England, he resided in York, at the corner of Nelson (Jarvis) and Duchess Streets. In 1836, he removed to Kingston. In 1839, he went to England. On a visit to Ireland, he took cold from exposure of rain, and also in Scotland, where he died on the 14th of January, 1840. His remains were, in 1861, removed to Kingston, and buried there. Mr. D. A. O'Sullivan, Q.C., LL.D., in his "Essays on the (Roman Catholic) Church in Canada," speaking of Bishop Macdonell, says:—"He was a martial figure in the history of (that) Church in this country, and had many difficulties to encounter. He had been Chaplain in Ireland during the trouble of '98; . . . he was missionary in Canada during the War of 1812, and Bishop of Kingston during the Rebellion of 1837. . . . He was named a Legislative Councillor in 1834 (*see page 27 of this volume*), shortly after the creation of his See, and was in receipt of a considerable pension from the (British) Government of the day (*pages 131, 132*). Archbishop Cleary, in a letter to the Toronto *Catholic Register*, of October 7th, 1894, says that Bishop Macdonell "raised two regiments of Scotch Fencibles from amongst his own people, and led them forward and cheered them on by his presence and bravery in several battles with the enemy in Eastern Ontario. This," the Archbishop says, "profoundly touched the hearts of the statesmen in the Foreign Office in London, and in the Governor-General's Citadel in Quebec; so much so, that in token of high appreciation, he received from the King a pension for life, which was afterwards doubled, and then quadrupled, and made hereditary in perpetuity to his successors in office after he had become Bishop of Kingston."

that three of these Teachers taught Roman Catholic Schools in Glengarry, and one a Common School. The Bishop himself, in a letter to the Reverend Dr. O'Grady, dated December 1st, 1830, stated that:

> After receiving the Prince Regent's thanks for my own conduct in defence of the Province during the late war, (1812,) the Colonial Minister, Earl Bathurst, increased my own salary, and sent orders to the Executive Government of Upper Canada to pay so much—in the aggregate One Thousand pounds (£1,000)—annually to a certain number of Clergymen and Teachers, that I was to recommend.

A Letter from Sir John Colborne, about the same time, informed the Bishop that one-fourth of this grant was to be expended in paying the salaries of Teachers.

BISHOPS MACDONELL AND POWER.

As to Bishop Macdonell's proceedings in educational matters, the late lamented Reverend M. Stafford, Parish Priest at Lindsay, in a private Letter to me, written in May, 1885, said:—

> There are Letters in manuscript by Bishop Macdonell—first Roman Catholic Bishop in Upper Canada—which you will find very interesting. . . . He imported Teachers from Scotland, . . . and wrote strongly to the Government against allowing Teachers from the United States into this country, and advocated the training of native Canadians for Teachers. . . .

In this matter of training Teachers for Canada, and in Canada, Bishops Macdonell and Power were quite agreed. See the Circular on the subject to District Councils, in a note on page 22, *ante*. The exclusion of Teachers from the United States, as suggested by Bishop Macdonell, was provided for in the Common School Acts of 1841 and 1843.

I have referred to these matters relating to Bishops Macdonell and Power the more fully, from the fact that, in the Separate School discussions of later years, it was frequently asserted that these Representatives of the Roman Catholic Church in Upper Canada had, during this period, and always, demanded Separate Schools as a right. This was not so; for, as a matter of fact, the desire for "protection from insult," and the claim for individual right of conscience in the Schools, were the only pleas put forth by them from 1841 to 1851, and then, only in special cases requiring such protection, or intervention. This will be apparent, not only from the proceedings of Bishops Macdonell and Power, but also from the moderate language of the only two petitions from Bishops sent in to the House of Assembly in 1841, and quoted on pages 13 and 14. The single petition sent from Representatives of the Roman Catholic Church, addressed to the House of Assembly, in 1850, only asked that such a measure be granted as to enable Roman Catholics to establish Separate Schools in Upper Canada, but without specifying details.

BISHOP CHARBONNEL AND HIS CHANGED ATTITUDE IN 1852.*

Such, as a matter of history, was the attitude of the acknowledged Representatives of the Roman Catholic Church in Upper Canada towards the Public Schools down to 1851-52. Even Bishop Charbonnel, who, in addition to his hierarchical rank, was a French nobleman, (Count de Charbonnel,) gave abundant evidence that, if left free to exercise his own judgment, he would have continued to act in harmony with Dr. Ryerson, as a Member of the Council of Public Instruction. Of this, as an Officer of the Council, I felt assured, from my knowledge of the Bishop, and from the nature of my intercourse with him. He was an accomplished gentleman, and was always most agree-

---

* The following sketch of Bishop Charbonnel is taken from the *Mail* newspaper of the 26th of March, 1891:—"The Right Reverend Armand Francis Marie Charbonnel was born in 1802, in Monistrol, Department of Haute-Loire, France. His uncle was the celebrated Cardinal Charbonnel, of Puy. His mother was a daughter of the Marquis d'Agrain, the first President of the Parliament of Dijon during the Revolutionary period. In 1819 he entered the Seminary of St. Sulpice, and was ordained as Priest in 1825. He commenced active work in the Church at Lyons, and was such a faithful worker that he had frequent offers of promotion, all of which, for a long time, he refused. He was a born soldier, as well as a devout son of the Roman Catholic Church; and, in 1834, he received the Grand Cross of the Legion of Honour from Louis Philippe, for services rendered to the Orleans dynasty during an attempted rising in Lyons. The Queen of France and the Church Dignitaries again urged promotion, but he declined these proffered honours, and came to Canada in 1839. He had not been long in Canada ere honours were again pressed on him, and, it is said, the Governor-General, Lord Sydenham, was anxious for his promotion. He, however, declined the offers, and in 1847 he worked night and day among the Irish emigrants, who were being decimated by the typhoid out-

able and courteous in his manners. His sudden change of demeanour towards Dr. Ryerson was a matter of surprise and regret to the Members of the Council, as it was wholly unexpected. He may have felt wounded at being, in some respects, placed in a false position by his opponents in the press, and by Dr. Ryerson's keen criticism on his unnecessarily misunderstanding of what he attacked; for Dr. Ryerson felt both surprised and hurt at the changed attitude of his former courteous friend, the Bishop. He, no doubt, felt it due to the Chief Superintendent of Education to account for the change in their official relations; and this he did, in a Letter addressed to Dr. Ryerson, dated the 1st of May, 1852, and in his Letter to the Hon S. B. Harrison, Chairman of the Council of Public Instruction, dated the 26th of the same month. There was, nevertheless, in both of these Letters, a latent spirit of resentment, which may have influenced him in expressing himself in the almost dictatorial and dogmatic spirit, in which these Letters were written—a spirit which, I am sure, was as alien to his feelings, as they were to his nature. In his Letter to Dr. Ryerson, of the 1st of May, 1852, he said :—

"All my previous intercourse with you and the Council of Public Instruction has been polite and Christian, and sometimes tolerant to an extent that I have been required to justify."

---

break. He was seized with the disease, and it was only by his removal to the healthy area that his life was saved. On his partial recovery he proceeded to France, and was present in Paris in 1848, during the terrible days of the barricades. His brother was killed in the fight at the Faubourg St. Antoine barricade. He was invited to enter the French Parliament, in succession to his brother, as representative for Upper Loire, but he declined the honour. As soon as his health was quite restored Pope Pius IX. urged him to take the Bishopric of Toronto. He accepted the honour, and the Pope conducted the consecration in person. In 1859 the late Archbishop Lynch was appointed Coadjutor Bishop of the Diocese, and in 1860 Bishop Charbonnel resigned his charge, returned to France, and entered the Order of Capuchins, Province of Lyons, in which he continued till the time of his death, 25th of March, 1891. He was made titular Bishop of Sosopolis in 1869, Archbishop of the same place in 1881. During the time he was in charge of the Toronto Diocese he introduced the Christian Brothers, and the Sisters of St. Joseph to Ontario. He founded the House of Providence and other charitable institutions, and completed St. Michael's Cathedral."

CHAPTER VIII.

THE CONTROVERSY WITH BISHOP CHARBONNEL, 1852.

In his Letter of 1st May, 1852, Bishop Charbonnel quoted the Canons of the Roman Catholic Council of Baltimore, "sanctioned," as he stated, "by the Supreme Head of our Church, one and universal." The Canons quoted by the Bishop were as follows :—

Council Prov. Balt. I., Canon XXXIV.—Whereas very many youth of Catholic parents, especially among the poor, have been and still are, in many parts of this Province, exposed to great danger of losing their faith, and having their morals corrupted, from the want of proper teachers, to whom so important a trust can be safely confided ; we judge it indispensably necessary to establish schools, in which youth may be nurtured in the principles of faith and morals, while they are instructed in literature.

Canon XXXV.—Since not unfrequently many things are found in the books which are generally used in the Schools, in which the principles of our faith are impugned, our dogmas falsely expounded, and history itself perverted : on account of which the minds of the young are imbued with errors, to the terrible loss of their souls ; zeal for religion, as well as the proper education of youth and the honour itself of the American Union, demand that some remedy be provided for so great an evil. Therefore we determine, that there shall be published for the use of Schools, as soon as possible, books entirely expurgated from errors and approved by the authority of the Bishops, and in which nothing may be contained which might produce enmity or hatred to the Catholic faith.

Council Prov. Balt. IV., Canon VI.—As it appears that the system of public instruction, in most of the Provinces, is so devised and administered as to encourage heresies and gradually and imperceptibly to fill the minds of Catholic youth with errors, we admonish pastors that, with the utmost zeal, they watch over the Christian and Catholic education of Catholic youth, and to take especial pains lest such youth use the Protestant version of the Scriptures, or recite the hymns or prayers of Sectaries. It must be carefully provided, that no books or exercises of this kind be introduced in the Public Schools, to the danger of faith and piety.

Now these Canons, the Bishop adds, "are the perfect expression of our sentiments."*

After referring approvingly to the policy of Archbishop Murray, whom he characterized as "the Dove of Dublin,"† in successfully resisting the Regulation which—

Required that in all the Schools for the Education of the Poor in Ireland, the Bible, without notes, should be read in the presence of all the pupils of the Schools, and that the Catechism, and all books of that kind, should be excluded.

The Bishop further urged that, as in the case of the Irish Schools which, through the influence of Archbishop Murray, had been made "more acceptable to the Catholics," so the Government here should give the Roman Catholics of Upper

---

* In connection with the foregoing extracts from the Canons of the Baltimore General Council, it is interesting to quote the later ones of that Council, of a very different spirit, as interpreted by Cardinal Satolli, in his Letter to the Archbishops assembled in New York, in November, 1892, viz.:—
"II. Where there is no Catholic School at all, or when the one that is available is little fitted for giving the children an education in keeping with their condition, then the Public Schools may be attended with a safe conscience, the danger of perversion being rendered remote by opportune remedial and precautionary measures, a matter which is to be left to the conscience and judgment of the Ordinaries.—(*No. 198, page 103.*)

† In the year 1845 I went to Dublin to master the details of the Irish Education Office system of Administration and Management. While there, I frequently met Archbishop Murray, who was one of the Commissioners of National Education, (as was Archbishop Whately). He was a most apostolic looking man, gentle, kind and courteous. I also accompanied Dr. Ryerson on his visit, while in Dublin, to Archbishop Whately—the very opposite, in appearance and manner, to Archbishop Murray. He was, indeed, very courteous; and, as Dr. Ryerson wished to introduce as much of the Irish National School System as was suitable into our Upper Canada School arrangements, he received many useful hints, as well as several very excellent suggestions, from the Archbishop. During my daily visits to the Education Department in Dublin, I formed a most agreeable acquaintance with the Right Hon. Alexander Macdonell—a relative of Bishop Macdonell, of Kingston. That this feeling was reciprocated by Mr. Macdonell, is shown by the following extract from Dr. Ryerson's Letter to me, dated, "Paris, August 23rd, 1855," in which he said : "Chief Justice Robinson, (with whom and Captain Lefroy we breakfasted in London,) told me that Mr. Macdonell, of the National Board in Dublin, mentioned you to him in very high terms." I also formed a pleasant friendship with Dr. Robert Sullivan, (Principal of the Dublin Normal School,) with the Professors and Masters, viz.—Rev. Mr. McGauley, Mr. John Rintoul and Mr. T. U. Young—the latter a son in-law of Wilderspin, and an active promoter of the system of that noted man. I also met many other distinguished men at the time,—Commissioners of Education, and others.
In a letter, addressed by Dr. Ryerson to the Provincial Secretary, on the 22nd of July, 1857, he thus referred to this personal matter : "On my recom-

Canada a system which would be equally "acceptable" to them. He concluded his letter as follows:—

I have said that, if the Catechism were sufficiently taught in the family or by the Pastor, so rare in this large Diocese ; and if the Mixed Schools were exclusively for secular instruction, and without danger to our Catholics, in regard to Masters, Books and companions, the Catholic Hierarchy might tolerate it, as I have done in certain localities, after having made due enquiry.

Otherwise, in default of these conditions, it is forbidden to our faithful to send their children to these Schools, on pain of the refusal of the Sacraments :* because the soul and heaven are above everything ; because the foot, the hand, the eye, occasions of sin, ought to be sacrificed to salvation, because, finally, Jesus Christ has confided the mission of instruction, which has civilized the world, to no others than the Apostles and their Successors to the end of time.

It is their right, so sacred and inalienable, that every wise and paternal

---

mendation, Mr. J. G. Hodgins relinquished his salary for a year, went home to Dublin at his own expense, and devoted a year to the careful study of the whole mode of conducting the System of Education in Ireland, in all the details of each of the seven Branches of the great Education Office in Dublin, and returned to Canada in 1846, with the highest testimonials of the Irish National Board of Education."

In response to this Letter, the Provincial Secretary stated that His Excellency the Governor-General-in-Council had fixed my salary at £500 per annum ; and then added the gratifying information that " His Excellency has further been pleased to direct that Mr. J. G. Hodgins, the present Deputy Superintendent of Education, be allowed, from the 1st of July, 1857, an addition to his salary of £500, the sum of £50 per annum during his tenure of that office—in consideration of his long and laborious services in connection with the establishment of a new Department"—that of Education.

NOTE.—I duly received this "good service allowance" of $200 a year until 1869, when it was stopped on the occasion of a motion in the House of Assembly, by the Hon. Edward Blake. It was restored some years later, but ceased entirely in 1889.

It is now forty years since I received this gratifying recognition of services rendered from 1844 to 1857. It was the only favour which I ever received from any of the many Governments under which I have continuously served in the same Department for over fifty-two years.—J. G. H.

* Quite a modification must have been made in the Canons of the General Council of Baltimore, as interpreted and explained by Cardinal Satolli in his letter to the Roman Catholic Archbishops, in November, 1892. The explanatory interpretation of the Canon, as quoted by Bishop Charbonnel, is as follows:

"V. We strictly forbid anyone, whether Bishop or Priest, and this is the express prohibition of the Sovereign Pontiff, through the Sacred Congregation, either by act, or threat, to exclude from the Sacrament, as unworthy, parents who choose to send their children to the Public Schools. As regards the children themselves, this enactment applies with still greater force."—(*No. 198, page 104, Conf. Tit. VI., Cap. I., II., Tit. VII.*)

NOTE.—The other paragraphs of this remarkable Letter of Cardinal Satolli are considerate and conciliatory, and may be inserted hereafter.—J. G. H.

Government has made laws respecting instruction only in harmony with the teaching Church—the Bishops united to their supreme and universal Head; and this right is so inviolable, that of late, as well as in former times, in France, in Belgium, in Prussia, in Austria, as in Ireland, the Bishops, with the Pope, have done everything to overthrow, or modify, every School, or University, System opposed to the mission given by Jesus Christ to His sacred College, "Go ye, therefore, teach all nations," etc.

On this part of the Bishop's letter, Dr. Ryerson replied as follows:

The avowal with which your Lordship's letter concludes,—containing an expression of sentiment, and a statement of facts which I have often seen ascribed to the Authorities of your Church, but which I have never before seen so broadly and explicitly avowed by any of its dignitaries,—an avowal which I could not have credited, did it not appear over your Lordship's own signature.

It is here clearly claimed that the Pope and Bishops of the Roman Catholic Church are the only persons authorized by God himself to direct the education of youth, and, therefore, that all others undertaking that work are invading the prerogative of God; that all legislation on the subject must have the sanction of 'the Bishops with the Pope;' and that they have done, and will do, all in their power to overthrow or modify every system of Public Instruction, from the School to the University, which is not under their control. Such being your Lordship's sentiments and intentions, I am glad that you have frankly avowed them.

Your Lordship's last Letter shows that the claims set up by your Lordship are not merely for "religious liberty and equal rights," but for the absolute supremacy and control on the part of your Bishops, with the Pope, in our System of Public Instruction. . . . But I doubt whether such efforts will meet with much sympathy from a large portion of the Members of the Roman Catholic Church, as I am persuaded they will not from the people of Upper Canada at large. I can appeal to the history of the past in proof of my acting towards the Roman Catholic Church in the same spirit as towards any other Church; but I must be unfaithful to all my past precedents, as well as to the trust reposed in me, and the almost unanimous feeling of the Country, if I should not do all in my power to resist—come from what quarter it may—every invasion of "the blessed principles of Religious Liberty and Equal Rights," among all classes of the people of Upper Canada.—(*Letter to Bishop Charbonnel, 12th of May, 1852.*)

In his Letter to the Hon. S. B. Harrison, Chairman of the Council of Public Instruction, dated the 26th of May, 1852, the Bishop was even more explicit as to the official influence which had been brought to bear upon him, requiring him to answer for his Christian and courteous liberality. He said:—

"All my precedents with you, the Reverend Doctor, and the Council of Public Instruction, have been polite and Christian, and, sometimes of a tolerance, for which my Church has made me responsible."

Bishop Charbonnel had abundant evidence of the fairness and courtesy of Dr. Ryerson in his treatment of the supporters of Separate Schools. This he admitted in his Letter of the 27th of June, 1851, quoted on page 54, *post*. He even complimented Dr. Ryerson on his "sincere liberality." Nothing, therefore, could have been easier, (had he not been acting under adverse influences,) or more practical than to have continued his own courteous and friendly conduct, and, from time to time, to have conferred with Dr. Ryerson, in that same friendly spirit, on the whole subject, before entering into an unpleasant correspondence with him; and, as was supposed, with the view of discharging an onerous duty, which the Baltimore Council, or other authority, had evidently imposed upon him as Bishop.

By conferring personally with Dr. Ryerson he could have ascertained the exact conditions upon which the grants, and what grants, were available for Separate Schools,—the relation of these Schools to the Municipal Councils, and to the Public School System. He could also have ascertained what were the causes, if any, which operated against Separate Schools; what Text-Books were authorized, and various other details in regard to the practical working of our School System, which were evidently unknown to him. Such an enquiry would have shed a flood of light on the whole question for the Bishop, and would have greatly simplified his treatment of it, should he, after such enquiry, have felt it necessary to enter into official and even unfriendly correspondence on the subject. All this would have been very easy for him to have done, as, up to this time, the relations between the Bishop and the Chief Superintendent were most friendly, and most propitious for intercourse of such a nature. But, as the Bishop had been called upon by the authorities of his Church, as he stated, to "justify" his hitherto "polite and Christian" intercourse with Dr. Ryerson, he, therefore, felt himself called upon, without any preliminary enquiry, to enter upon a controversy, which was so much regretted, rendered doubly unpleasant from the fact that he frequently assumed that to be "law," and consequently "justice," which was neither the one or the other, but often the reverse.

This fact, and their superior local knowledge of the principles of our School Law, added point to the criticisms of writers in the press on the Bishop's course, and greatly prolonged and intensified the discussion. It also brought into the hostile field writers, on the Bishop's side, who lacked the literary skill, courtesy, and gentlemanly bearing of the Bishop. Besides, for want of the necessary practical information on the subject, their efforts only tended unnecessarily to complicate the whole question, and, by added bitterness to the discussion, to render the satisfactory settlement of the question the more protracted and difficult.

I make the foregoing remarks with sincere regret, for my personal intercourse with Bishop Charbonnel was always most pleasant. He even did me the unexpected favour of saying and writing some very kind things in regard to certain of my official proceedings, which he thought were both fair and courteous. He was a man of generous impulses, and, in the best and highest sense, an accomplished and enlightened man of the world.

That Dr. Ryerson felt very keenly the changed attitude of Bishop Charbonnel, may be gathered from the following extract of his Letter, in reply to the Bishop, in May, 1852:—

> Your Lordship refers to the friendly and cordial character of the intercourse which has taken place from time to time between your Lordship and the other Members of the Council of Public Instruction, including myself. I can assure your Lordship that the feelings of respect and pleasure attending that intercourse could not have been greater on your part than on mine, and I, therefore, felt greatly surprised, pained and disappointed, when I read your Lordship's letter of the 24th of March last, denouncing that whole System of Public Instruction which I had understood your Lordship to be a Colleague in promoting; attacking the princi-

ples on which I have acted during the whole period of my official connection with that System; impugning the motives of its founders, reflecting upon the character of the people of Upper Canada, and advocating that which would be subversive of their hitherto acknowledged rights of local self-government.

TORONTO, 12th of May, 1852.   E. RYERSON.

The matter complained of by the Bishop chiefly arose, not by operation of the School Law itself, but apart from, and often outside of, that law altogether. Thus his complaint of the smallness of an apportionment to a Separate School was due to his want of knowledge, that it was caused, not so much by a non-observance, or violation, of the law; but, in almost every case, from the smallness of the attendance of children at the School. The use also of Goldsmith's History of England was the voluntary act of the Separate School Trustees themselves, for the book was neither imposed upon, nor authorized as a Text-Book in, the Schools by any official authority whatever.

In reply to a demand that Municipal Councils should be required to provide Houses for Separate, as for Public Schools, and that they should not provide Houses for Public Schools, without also providing them for Separate Schools, Dr. Ryerson, in his Letter to Bishop Charbonnel, of March, 1852, said:—

I have observed, with regret, that demands for exemptions and advantages have recently been made on the part of some advocates of Separate Schools which had not been previously heard of during the whole ten years of the existence and operations of the provisions of the law for Separate, as well as Mixed, schools. I cannot but regard such occurrences as ominous of evil. It is possible that the Legislature may accede to the demands of individuals praying, on grounds of conscience, for unrestricted liberty of teaching—exempting them from all school taxes, with a corresponding exclusion of their children from all Public Schools—leaving them perfectly free to establish their own Schools at their own expense; but I am persuaded the People of Upper Canada will never suffer themselves to be taxed, or the machinery of their Government to be employed, for the building and support of Denominational School-houses, any more than for denominational places of worship and clergy. . . .

TORONTO, 13th of March, 1852.   E. RYERSON.

In further reply, to Bishop Charbonnel's Letter of the 24th of March, 1852, Dr. Ryerson said:—

But if, according to your Lordship's advocacy, a Municipality must be compelled to tax themselves to provide Separate School-houses for Religious Persuasions, in addition to Public School-houses, there may be a high degree of "civil liberty" secured to certain Religious Persuasions, but a melancholy slavery imposed upon the Municipalities. The liberty of teaching, any more than the liberty of preaching, by any Religious Persuasion, has never been understood in Upper Canada to mean the right of compelling Municipalities to provide places of teaching, any more than places of preaching, for such Religious Persuasion. Such liberty, or, rather, such despotic authority, possessed by any Religious Persuasion, is the grave of the public Municipal liberties of Upper Canada.

TORONTO, 24th of April, 1852. E. RYERSON.

Dr. Ryerson, in his Letter of reply to Bishop Charbonnel, of the 12th of May, 1852, also said:—

The people and Legislature of Upper Canada have repeatedly repudiated the claim, that the authority and Officers of the law ought to be employed to impose and collect taxes for any Religious Denomination. E. R.

CHAPTER IX.

THE SEPARATE SCHOOL LEGISLATION OF 1846–1850.

IN the first draft of School Bill submitted to the Government by Dr. Ryerson, in 1846, he simply copied the provisions of the Act of 1843, relating to Separate Schools, as they stood in that Act.—(See page 45, *post*.)

In 1847, he submitted a draft of Bill for the Establishment and Maintenance of Common Schools in Cities and in Towns corporate. In this Bill, he sought to modify the Separate School provisions of the former Acts, and to give them a less positive form. His explanation of this change is as follows:—

"There is one provision in this Act, on which I desire to offer a few words of explanation, as its nature and objects have been misapprehended. I refer to the power which it gives to the School authorities of each City and Town to establish Denominational or Mixed Schools, as they may judge expedient. It has not, perhaps, occurred to those who have commented on this clause, that a similar provision, under a much more objectionable form, has been incorporated into each of the three Common School Acts for Upper Canada, which have been passed since the Union of the Provinces, in 1840.* It has been provided, in each of these Acts, that any ten householders of any School Section can demand a Separate School, and a portion of the School Fund to support it. I have never seen the necessity for such a provision, in connection with another section of the Common School Law (of 1843), which provides that "no child shall be compelled to read any religious book, or attend any religious exercise contrary to the wishes of his parents or guardians;" and, besides, the apparent inexpediences of this provision of the law, it has been seriously objected to as inequitable — permitting the Roman Catholic Persuasion to have a Denominational School, but not granting a single Protestant Persuasion the same privilege. It has been maintained, that all Religious Persuasions should be placed upon equal footing "before the law;" that, although several Protestant Persuasions may be agreed as to the translation of the Scriptures, which should be used, they are not all agreed as to the kind and extent of the religious instruction which should be given in a School—the very object contemplated in the establishment of a Separate School; and, therefore, each Protestant Persuasion should be placed upon the same footing as the Roman Catholic Persuasion. This is the case under the provisions of this City and Town School Act (of 1847), and, therefore, the authorities of no Religious Persuasion have opposed, or petitioned, against it, as some of them did against the previous School Act. But, the City and Town Common School Act does not give the power to any one Religious Persuasion, much less to any ten householders of it [as did the Acts of 1843 and 1846], to demand a Separate School : that power is taken from all Religious Persuasions alike, and given to the Public School authorities, appointed by the elected representatives of each Town or City.—(*Dr. Ryerson's Annual School Report of 1847, page 23.*)

The course of events, in regard to Separate School Legislation, up to the end of 1850, is thus briefly narrated by Dr. Ryerson, in his Letter to the Hon. George Brown, dated the 28th of December, 1858, as follows :—

. . . The provision for Separate Schools was made in the 55th and 56th sections of Mr. Hincks' School Act, 1843, and by re-enacting the same clauses in the 32nd and 33rd sections of the School Act of 1846. The draft of the last Act was prepared by myself, at the request of the Government. . . .

---

* *i.e.*, in September, 1841 ; December, 1843, and May, 1846.

In 1847, I submitted the draft of the Act for the better organization of Schools in the Cities and Towns of Upper Canada. The provision for Separate Schools was made in the 3rd clause of the 5th section of that Act, as follows:—

"It shall be the duty of the Board of Trustees of each City and Town, *Thirdly*, to determine the number, sites and description of Schools which shall be established in each City or Town, and whether such Schools shall be Denominational or Mixed."

This last phrase of the clause was omitted in the Act of 1850, the former part of the clause fully comprehending it.

EPISODE OF THE DISALLOWED SCHOOL BILL OF 1849.

During these years, from 1846 to 1849, a persistent, but not very influential, agitation originated in the Bathurst District against the School Law and the Chief Superintendent of Education. It was taken up and championed by the Hon. Malcolm Cameron, who was originally from that District, although, at the time, a Member of the Government, representing the County of Kent. The result was, that a draft of School Bill, prepared by Dr. Ryerson, and sent to the Provincial Secretary on the 23rd of February, 1849, was entrusted by the Government to Mr. Cameron,—the Hon. Francis Hincks being absent in England. Referring to this matter, Dr. Ryerson, in a Letter to me from Montreal, said:—

As to the immediate objects of my coming, it is well that I did come. The Inspector-General, (Hon. F. Hincks,) expressed himself very glad that I had come. . . . I understand that the School Bill is wholly Mr. Malcolm Cameron's.

MONTREAL, 27th of April, 1849.   E. RYERSON.

In a Letter to the Hon. James Leslie, Provincial Secretary, Dr. Ryerson said:—

I have been informed, upon authority which I cannot doubt, that the [Cameron] School Bill has been chiefly drafted by a person, who has, during the last three years, been writing in a District newspaper against myself,—a person who, as Chairman of the Education Committee of the Bathurst District Council, has put forth three Council documents reflecting upon myself,—the only Municipal Council documents of the kind which have appeared in Upper Canada. . . .

TORONTO, 12th of May, 1849.   E. RYERSON.

Further, in a Letter addressed to the Hon. Robert Baldwin, Attorney-General, in July, 1849, Dr. Ryerson said :—

> I am credibly informed that Mr. Cameron stated to a leading Member of the Opposition, that he had adopted my suggestions in reference to the Bill, . . . [and yet] Mr. Cameron told the Rev. H. J. Grasett (Rector of St. James', Toronto), that he (Mr. Cameron) had not read my communication respecting it.
> TORONTO, 14th of July, 1849.   E. RYERSON.

In his Letter to the Provincial Secretary, already quoted, the 12th of May, 1849, Dr. Ryerson adds :—

> I now submit to the Governor-Gereral in Council, that nearly every section of the Common School Bill, which is not contained in the present Act, or in the draft of School Bill which I submitted to the Government in February last, is obviously theoretical, cumbrous, intricate, expensive and inefficient.

The whole of the proceedings, relating to the School Bill, took place in Montreal, at the time of the burning there of the Parliament House, on the occasion of the passage of the "Rebellion Losses Bill," which had produced a popular outburst. After the excitement had subsided, it was found, on examination, that, not only had many objectionable features been introduced into the School Bills, as passed, but that also omissions of sections, relating to Separate Schools, had, without notice, been made. This naturally created a strong feeling of resentment on the part of the Roman Catholics; and they naturally demanded that the injustice, thus done to them by the Government, would be remedied. In consequence of this state of feeling, Dr. Ryerson felt it to be desirable that the confidence thus lost should be restored. In a Letter to me, he thus stated what it was proposed to do in the matter :—

> I am happy to say that the (Malcolm Cameron) School Bill of last Session is upset. The Members of the Government—even the Governor-General—have personally examined into what I stated in my Letter to Mr. Baldwin, of July last, and have come entirely into my views. Mr. Cameron is now out of office. . . . Mr. Hincks said, that he concurred in every sentiment in my Letter to Mr. Baldwin, and in regard to the whole matter. . . . The Government desire to bring in a new Bill, to be given into his hands, . . . when prepared. . . .
> MONTREAL, 29th of December, 1849.   E. RYERSON.

The result was, that Dr. Ryerson was requested to prepare a new and comprehensive School Bill, which would embrace all of the best features of the preceding School Acts, and any improvements which time and experience had shown to be desirable and necessary. Nevertheless, the leading newspapers of the day unwisely justified this surreptitious proceeding, of Mr. Cameron, on the ground that the proposed remedy would be a new concession to the Roman Catholics; and, on the appearance of the proposed School Bill of 1850, the Nineteenth section of it was vigorously attacked. In reply to these attacks, Dr. Ryerson, in a letter to *The Globe* newspaper of Toronto, replied as follows:—

You say that when the present party, (Baldwin-Lafontaine Government,) came into power, (1848,) "the Common School System was free from sectarian elements, but they have introduced the wedge, which threatens to destroy the whole fabric."

By these statements . . . you represent the provisions for Protestant and Roman Catholic Separate Schools, in certain cases, as of recent introduction, and peculiar to the present School Bill of 1850, when it is a fact that the same provision was introduced into the School Bill of 1841, and was also re-introduced by Mr. Hincks in his School Bill for Upper Canada of 1843. . . . The provision [of the Act of 1843 was retained,] and in the same words in the School Bill, which the Hon. W. H. Draper introduced, and had passed, in 1846. The provision, therefore, which you represent as "fatal," has existed, [even in a more extended form,] from the beginning of the present School System, in 1841,—was formally introduced by the Reform Government, [in a modified form,] into the School Act of 1843, . . . was concurred in by the same gentlemen, when they were in opposition . . . at the time when it was brought forward by the leading members of the Conservative party in 1846.

Toronto, 27th of July, 1854. E. Ryerson.

In continuing his narrative of the School Legislation of 1841-1847, Dr. Ryerson, in his Letter to the Hon. George Brown, of the 28th of December, 1858, said:—

Such was the state of the law in regard to Separate Schools, and my course in respect to it, when, in 1849, an Act was passed, under the auspices of the Hon. Malcolm Cameron, a Member of the Government, just after the burning of the Parliament House in Montreal, and a few hours before the close of the Session; an Act which I considered so objectionable that I preferred resigning office to acting under it, and which I was authorized to set aside; and, at the same time, to prepare the draft of another Act to replace it—a draft which became the School Act of 1850, containing the provisions of the School Acts of 1846 and 1847, with such modifications and additions as experience had suggested. . . . The Act of 1849 contained no provision for Separate Schools; it also abolished the provisions of the previous Act which authorized Clergymen to act as Visitors of Schools. . . . Mr. Baldwin and Mr. Hincks stated that they had never examined the Bill of 1849 before it passed; and it never came into operation. . . .

In the original draft of the 19th Section of the School Act of 1850, I proposed to place the authority for establishing Separate Schools upon the same footing as that on which it had been placed in Cities and Towns by the Act of 1847—namely, to leave it in the hands of the Township Council, as it had been left in the hands of the City or Town Board of Trustees. . . .

INCIDENTS OF THE PASSING OF THE NINETEENTH, OR SEPARATE SCHOOL, SECTION OF THE ACT OF 1850.

In continuation of his Letter to the Hon. George Brown, of December, 1858, Dr. Ryerson said —

The authorities of the Roman Catholic Church, having had their suspicions and fears excited by the unexpected and unnoticed omission of the Separate School clauses from the Act of 1849, had Representatives, both clerical and lay, in attendance, to watch the nature and progress of the School Bill of 1850, and they protested against the provisions of the 19th Section, as originally introduced. Several leaders of the high Episcopalian party were also in attendance to get a clause, providing for Church of England Separate Schools, introduced into the Bill. An Amendment to the 19th Section was concerted and agreed upon by the clerical Roman Catholic and high Episcopalian parties, by which any twelve Members of either Church could demand a Separate School in any School Section of Upper Canada. . . . The leaders on both sides of this new combination were very active, and, in the course of a few days, boasted that they would have a majority of fourteen or twenty votes against the Government, on the 19th Section of the Bill. A copy of the Amendment of the combinationists was procured for me, and I was informed of the probable defeat of the Government on the question. I saw, at once, that the proposed Amendment, if carried, would destroy the School System; and, in order to break up the combination and save the School System, I proposed to amend the 19th Section of the Bill, so as to secure the right of establishing Separate Schools to the applicants, as provided in the School

Acts of 1843 and 1846, only substituting twelve heads of families for ten freeholders or householders. This was acceptable to the authorities of the Roman Catholic Church, who said, that they did not wish to oppose the Government of Messrs. Lafontaine and Baldwin, unless compelled to do so; and they then advised all the Roman Catholic Members of the House to vote for the Government section of the Bill, as amended. When the question came up in Committee of the whole House, the leader of the high Church combination, who was not aware of the counter movement, rose to move the famous Amendment which was to defeat, if not oust, the Government; but he was surprised to find that not one of the Roman Catholic Members rose to vote for it, and only six or eight Episcopalians standing up, "few and far between," in its behalf, to the great amusement of the other Members of the House. On Mr. Hincks moving the Section, as amended, it was carried without a division, and it constitutes the 19th Section of the Act of 1850.

The 19th Section of the Common School Act, as introduced, and as passed, is as follows. The substituted words in the Section, as finally passed, are in italics:—

ORIGINAL DRAFT OF THE 19TH SECTION.

(The words struck out are in Italics.)

"It shall be *lawful for the Municipality of any Township, if it shall judge expedient,* to authorize the establishment of one or more Separate Schools for Protestants, Roman Catholics, or Coloured People, and in any case it shall prescribe the limits of the Divisions or Sections for such Schools, and shall make the same provision for the holding of the first meeting for the election of Trustees of each such Separate School, as is provided in the fourth Section of this Act, for holding the first School meeting in a new Section: Provided always, that each such Separate School shall go into operation at the same time with alterations in School Sections, and shall be under the same regulations in respect to the persons for whom such School is

"*It shall be the duty of the Municipal Council of any Township, and of the Board of School Trustees of any City, Town, or Incorporated Village, on the application, in writing, of twelve or more resident heads of families,* to authorize the establishment of one or more Separate Schools for Protestants, Roman Catholics, or Coloured People; and, in such case, it shall prescribe the limits of the Divisions or Sections for such Schools, and shall make the same provision for the holding of the first meeting for the election of Trustees of each such Separate School, or Schools, as is provided in the fourth Section of this Act, for holding the first School meeting in a new School Section: Provided always, that each such Separate School shall go into operation at the same time with alterations in School Sections, and shall be under the same regulations in respect to

Separate School Legislation, 1846-1850.

permitted to be established, as are Common Schools, generally: Provided, secondly, that none but Coloured People shall be allowed to vote for the election of the Trustees of the Separate School for their children, and none but the parties petitioning for the establishment of, or sending children to a Separate Protestant or Roman Catholic School, shall vote at the election of Trustees of such School: Provided, thirdly, that each such Separate, Protestant or Roman Catholic School *shall be entitled to share in the School Fund, according to the number of children of the religious class or persuasion attending such School, as compared with the whole number of children of School age in the Township; and the Separate School for children of Coloured People shall share in the School Fund, according to the number of such children of School age resident in such School Section for Coloured children, as compared with the whole number of children of School age resident in the Township:* Provided, *fourthly,* that the Trustees of the Common School Sections, within the limits of which such Separate School Section, or Sections, have been formed, shall not include the children attending such Separate School, or Schools, in their return of children of School age residing in their School Sections.

the persons for whom such School is permitted to be established, as are Common Schools, generally: Provided, secondly, that none but Coloured People shall be allowed to vote for the election of Trustees of the Separate School for their children, and none but the parties petitioning for the establishment of, or sending children to a Separate Protestant or Roman Catholic School, shall vote at the election of Trustees of such School: Provided, thirdly, that each such Separate Protestant, or Roman Catholic, *or Coloured, School shall be entitled to share in the School Fund according to the average attendance of pupils attending each such Separate School (the mean attendance of pupils for both summer and winter being taken), as compared with the whole average attendance of pupils attending the Common Schools in such City, Town, Village, or Township:* Provided, *fourthly, that no Protestant Separate School shall be allowed in any School Division, except when the Teacher of the Common School is a Roman Catholic, nor shall any Roman Catholic Separate School be allowed, except when the Teacher of the Common School is a Protestant*: Provided, *fifthly,* that the Trustees of the Common School Sections, within the limits of which such Separate School Section, or Sections, shall have been formed, shall not include the children attending such Separate School or Schools in their return of children of School age residing in their School Sections."

The 19th Section of the School Act of 1850, as thus amended, passed unanimously.

In a Circular to School Trustees, dated the 12th of August, 1850, Dr. Ryerson thus explains the nature and object of this 19th Section of the School Act of that year:—

The provision of the 19th Section, as far as it relates to Separate Protestant and Roman Catholic Schools, is substantially the same as that contained in the 55th and 56th Sections of the School Act of 1843, and in the 32nd and 33rd Sections of the School Act of 1846, with the exception, that the present Act imposes more effective restrictions and conditions in the establishment of such Schools than either of the former Acts referred to. Under the City and Town School Act of 1847, the establishment of Separate Schools in Cities and Towns was at the discretion of the Municipalities, and not at that of the applicant parties. No complaint having been made against this provision of the law, even in Cities and Towns, it was, at first, proposed to extend the application of the same principle and provision to Township Municipalities; but, objections having been made to it by some (both Protestant and Roman Catholic) Members of the Legislature, the provision of the former School Act was re-enacted,— requiring, however, the petition of twelve heads of families, instead of ten inhabitants, as a condition of establishing a Separate School; and aiding it upon the principle of average attendance, instead of at the discretion of the Local Superintendent, as under the former Acts. But, notwithstanding the existence of this provision of the law, since 1843, there were, last year, but thirty-one Separate Schools in all Upper Canada,—nearly as many of them being Protestant as Roman Catholic; so that this provision of the law is seldom acted upon, except in extreme cases, and is of little consequence for good or for evil,—the law providing effectual protection against interference with the religious opinions and wishes of parents and guardians, of all classes, and there being no probability that Separate Schools will be more injurious in time to come than they have been in time past. It is also to be observed, that a Separate School is entitled to no aid beyond a certain portion of the School Fund for the salary of the Teacher. The School-house must be provided, furnished, warmed, books procured, etc., by the persons petitioning for the Separate School. Nor are the patrons and supporters of a Separate School exempted from any of the Local Assessments or rates for Common School purposes. The law provides equal protection for all classes and denominations; if there be any class, or classes, of either Protestant or Roman Catholics, who are not satisfied with the equal protection secured to them by law in Mixed Schools, but wish to have a School subservient to Sectional Religious purposes, they should, of course, contribute in proportion, and not tax a whole community for the support of sectarian interests.—(*Chief Superintendent's Circular to Township Councils, dated the 12th of August, 1850.*)

In a Circular to City and Town Board of School Trustees, in regard to this 19th Section, dated the 8th of October, 1850, Dr. Ryerson said:—

. . . This provision of the Act . . . is no new provision, but one which has existed upwards of seven years,—since the commencement of our present Common School System. It has clearly been intended, from the beginning, as a protection of the minority against any oppressive or invidious proceedings on the part of the majority, in any School Division, in addition to the ordinary provision of the Act, prohibiting the compulsory attendance of any child upon a religious exercise, or reading a religious book, to which his parents or guardians shall object. The existence of so few Separate Schools (only about thirty-one in all Upper Canada, and nearly one-half of them Protestant) shows that the provision for their establishment is rarely acted upon,—as the Local School Authorities seldom find occasion for it. And as there can be no Separate School in a School Division, unless the Teacher of the Mixed School is of a different Religious Persuasion from the applicants for such Separate School, the Local Board of Trustees can always, if they think proper to do so, make such a selection of Teachers as will prevent the establishment or continuance of Separate Schools.—(*Chief Superintendent's Circular to Boards of School Trustees, dated 8th October, 1850.*)

THE FIRST TORONTO SEPARATE SCHOOL CASE IN 1851.

A difficulty occurred later on, in 1850, which necessitated the interference of the Chief Superintendent of Education, in favour of the Roman Catholic Separate School Trustees of the City of Toronto. In his Letter to the Hon. George Brown, written in December, 1858, Dr. Ryerson thus states the nature of that difficulty, and the remedy for it, as follows:—

In the latter part of 1850, certain Roman Catholics applied for a second Separate School in the City of Toronto. The Board of School Trustees rejected their application, upon the ground that the 19th Section of the School Act of 1850 did not require them to permit the establishment of more than one Separate School in the City. The applicants applied to the Court of Queen's Bench for a Mandamus to compel the Board of School Trustees to grant their request. The Court decided that—

According to the letter and grammatical construction of the Act, a City, or Town, was only a School Section, and the Trustees could not, therefore, be compelled by law to grant more than one Separate School, whatever might have been the intention of the Legislature. . . .

Dr. Ryerson then goes on to say that—

The [Roman Catholic] supporters of the Ministry of that day . . sought a Legislative remedy for a defect in the law, and applied in the proper quarter for that purpose. Mr. Hincks declined taking their complaint into consideration without consulting me,—I being then absent in the United States and England, making the first selection of books for the Public Libraries, and arrangements for procuring them. On my return in June, 1851, Mr. Hincks gave me the papers, and referred the Roman Catholic Bishop, [Charbonnel,] and Vicar-General, [Macdonell,] to me. I could not for a moment admit the Draft of the Bill they had prepared; but stated frankly, that I had not intended to deprive them of any rights as to Separate Schools which had been conferred on them by the Act of 1846; that I had never anticipated, or thought of, the construction of the 19th Section of the Act, which had been put upon it by the Court of Queen's Bench; that, by the Act of 1846, Cities and Towns were divided into School Sections as well as Townships; that the City of Toronto, under that Act, was divided into fourteen School Sections, in each of which there might be a Separate School, according to the conditions of that law. But, I asked them, as there were now no School Sections in the Cities and Towns, whether the right of having a Separate School in each Ward would not be sufficient? They answered in the affirmative; whereupon, I wrote a Draft of an Act for that purpose, and they expressed their entire satisfaction with it.*

By request, I afterwards met the greater part of the Members of the House, at an appointed time, and explained to them the position of the Separate School question, and what I thought best to be done under the circumstances. The Honourable John Ross brought into the Legislative Council the Bill, of which I had prepared the Draft. It soon passed both Houses, and became law.

[The Upper Canada Members voting for it were: Messrs. Baldwin, Bell, W. H. Boulton, Hincks, J. A. Macdonald, Meyers, Prince, Sherwood, and

---

* In a Letter to Dr. Ryerson, from Bishop Charbonnel, written in June, 1851, he said: "Very Rev. and Dear Doctor, I regret very much not to "be able to attend the meeting [of the Council of Public Instruction] this "morning; I leave to-day for London; but I will be back for the solemn "ceremony of Wednesday [2nd July—the day on which the corner-stone of "the Normal School Building was laid, and at which the Bishop was present "and took part in the ceremony].

"I see, with full hope, that the redress of the wording of the clause in "behalf of the City Catholic Separate Schools [Toronto] is in your hands and "heart; and, if Canada East has for Superintendent a Doctor *Meilleur*, owing "to the sincere liberality of our Government, and its Superintendent for the "West, our condition for the Education of our dear children will become good "and *better*.

"Respectfully and devotedly, yours in Christ,
"†ARMANDUS, Fr. My. R. C. Bp. of Toronto.
"TORONTO, 27th of June, 1851."

Stevenson—9. Lower Canada Members, 16; total, 25. Those opposed to the Bill were: Messrs. Hopkins, Mackenzie, McFarlane, J. C. Morrison, James Smith, and J. Wilson—7, all from Upper Canada.]

The operation of this Act was confined to Cities and Towns; its very wording shows that it was no innovation, and no concession; but a restoration of rights previously enjoyed. The title of the Act was:—

An Act to Define and Restore Certain Rights to Parties therein mentioned, 14 and 15. Vic., Cap. III., received the Royal Assent on the 30th of August, 1851.

Whereas it is expedient to remove doubts, which have arisen in regard to certain provisions of the Nineteenth Section of the Upper Canada School Act of 1850; and, Whereas, it is inexpedient to deprive any of the parties concerned of rights which they have enjoyed under preceding School Acts for Upper Canada: Be it therefore enacted, etc., That each of the parties applying, according to the provisions of the said Nineteenth Section of said Act, shall be entitled to have a Separate School in each Ward, or in two or more Wards united, as said party, or parties, shall judge expedient, in each City, or Town, in Upper Canada: Provided always, that each such School shall be subject to all the obligations and entitled to all the advantages imposed and conferred upon Separate Schools by the said Nineteenth Section of the said Act.

UNREST AND UNCERTAINTY—MR. W. L. MACKENZIE'S BILL, 1851.

These two untoward circumstances—the unauthorized omission of all provision for Separate Schools in Mr. Cameron's School Bill, of 1849, and the inability of the Trustees to establish more than one Separate School in the City of Toronto, as decided by the Court of Queen's Bench, in 1851, acted unfavourably upon the leaders of the Roman Catholic Church, and created a feeling of distrust and uncertainty on their part.

What also kept this feeling of suspicion and unrest, on the part of the Roman Catholics authorities, alive, was the constant efforts of prominent members of the House of Assembly, from 1851 to 1856, to repeal the 19th Section of the School Act of 1850. Generally, these gentlemen contented themselves with the introduction of a brief Bill, simply declaring that—

"The Nineteenth Section of the School Act of 1850 shall be, and is hereby, repealed."

Mr. W. L. Mackenzie, however, in his Bill of August, 1851,*

---

* Mr. Mackenzie moved this Bill as an amendment to the Act given above. It was rejected by a vote of 26 to 5.

gives his reasons for doing so, in the preamble. The extract from the preamble is interesting, from the fact, that it embodies the "popular" objection then urged against the existence of Roman Catholic Separate Schools in Upper Canada, and gives specific reasons for this objection. First, he declares—

1st. That the establishment of Sectarian, or Separate, Schools . . . is a dangerous interference with the Common School System of Upper Canada, and, if allowed . . . cannot reasonably be refused to . . . other Religious Denominations.

2nd. That if it is just that any number of Religious Sects should have Separate Common Schools, it is no less reasonable that they should have Separate Grammar Schools, Colleges and Professorships in the Universities.

3rd. That it is unjust in the State to tax Protestants, in order to provide for the instruction of children in Roman Catholic doctrines, or to tax Roman Catholics for the religious education of youth "in principles averse to the Church of Rome."

4th. That the early separation of children at School, on account of the creeds of their parents, or guardians, would rear nurseries of strife and dissension, and cause thousands to grow up in comparative ignorance, who might, under the Common School System, obtain the advantages of a moral, intellectual, literary and scientific education.

5th. That the repeal of the Nineteenth Section of the Upper Canada School Act, passed in 1850, would discourage Sectarian education, and be productive of peace, harmony and good-will in Upper Canada.

THE SEPARATE SCHOOL QUESTION FROM 1841 TO 1851.

We thus see, that from 1849 there were two potent influences at work to excite fears, and to disturb the harmony and comparative quiet which had prevailed in Upper Canada during the preceding six or eight years, on the subject of public education. Even on the part of Roman Catholics, there was little or no desire to agitate for the promotion, or extension, of Separate Schools during these years. This, Dr. Ryerson points out with evident satisfaction, in his second letter to Bishop Charbonnel, written in April, 1852, as follows:—

The Common School System . . . of Upper Canada . . . has been in operation for ten years; which was cordially approved of and supported by the late lamented Roman Catholic Bishop Power; which was never objected to, as far as I know, by a single Roman Catholic in Upper

Canada, during the life of Bishop Power, that excellent Prelate and patriot, . . . I . . . still adhere to my frequent unqualified expressions of admiration at the opposite course pursued by your honoured and devoted Predecessor, Bishop Power ; . . . I may note the facts that . . . the only Roman Catholic Member of the Legislative Assembly elected in Upper Canada, [Hon. J. Sandfield Macdonald,] has repeatedly declared himself opposed to the very principle of Separate Schools ; and that the only County Municipal Council in Upper Canada, in which a majority of the members are Roman Catholics, has adopted resolutions against the Section of the School Act, which permits the establishment of Separate Schools, under any circumstances. The facts that, out of 3,000 Common Schools, not so many as fifty Separate Roman Catholic Schools have ever existed or been applied for, in any one year, in all Upper Canada, and that the number of such Separate Schools had gradually diminished to less than thirty, until within the last twelve months,* and that, during ten years, but one single complaint has been made to this Department of any interference with the religious faith of Roman Catholic children ; and that not a Roman Catholic child in Upper Canada is known to have been proselyted to Protestantism by means of our Public Schools ;—these facts clearly show the general disinclination of Roman Catholics in Upper Canada to isolate themselves from their fellow-citizens in School matters, any more than in other common interests of the Country, and the mutually just, Christian and generous spirit in which the School, as well as other common affairs of the Country, have been promoted by Government, by Municipal Councils, and by the people at large, in their various School Sections. The exceptions to this pervading spirit of the people of Upper Canada, have been "few and far between ; " and, in such cases, the provision of the School Law, permitting the establishment of Separate Schools in certain circumstances, has been made use of, and just about as often by a Protestant, as by a Roman Catholic, minority in a School Municipality. But the provision of the law for Separate Schools was never asked, or advocated, until since 1850, as a theory, but merely as a protection, in circumstances arising from the peculiar social state of neighbourhoods, or Municipalities. I always thought the introduction of any provision for Separate Schools, in a popular System of Common Education like that of Upper Canada, was to be regretted and inexpedient ; but finding such a provision in existence, and that parties concerned attaching great importance to it, I have advocated its

---

* The following Table shows the number of Protestant and Roman Catholic Separate Schools reported, since 1847 :—

Year 1847	.	.	.	41 Separate Schools of all kinds.
" 1848	.	.	.	32 " " "
" 1849	.	.	.	31 " " "
" 1850	.	.	.	46=21 Roman Catholic and 25 Protestant.
" 1851	.	.	.	20=16 Roman Catholic and 4 Protestant.

continuance—leaving Separate Schools to die out, not by force of legislative enactment, but under the influence of increasingly enlightened and enlarged views of Christian relations, rights and duties, between different classes of the community. I have, at all times, endeavoured to secure to parties desiring Separate Schools, all the facilities which the law provides—though, I believe, the legal provision for Separate Schools has been, and is, seriously injurious, rather than beneficial, to the Roman Catholic portion of the community, as I know very many intelligent Members of that Church believe, as well as myself. I have as heartily sought to respect the feelings and promote the interests of my Roman Catholic fellow-citizens, as those of any other portion of the community; and I shall continue to do so. . .

TORONTO, 24th of April, 1852.   E. RYERSON.

Such was the brief yet comprehensive survey of the state of educational affairs in Upper Canada, when, as events proved, the untoward influences and proceedings to which I have referred (on pages 47 and 55), produced their effects, both on the popular leaders of the day, and on the authorities of the Roman Catholic Church in Upper Canada. From that time forward, each party "set its camp in hostile array." The policy of the leading newspapers of that time, and the aggressive, yet practically futile, efforts of Members of the Legislature, from 1851 to 1856, to repeal the Separate School provisions of the Law, naturally excited, and kept alive, on the part of the Roman Catholic authorities, the suspicions and fears entertained by them, as mentioned by Dr. Ryerson.

The result of all this unrest was the commencement of an agitation and conflict, of more or less intensity, which lasted until the passage of the Roman Catholic Separate School "Finality Act," (as it was called,) in 1863. Then, a season of comparative quiet and tranquility prevailed for a time; and the "Finality Act," of 1863, became the basis of the Legislation in the British America Act of 1866, which secured to the Roman Catholics of Upper Canada the right to have Separate Schools under that New Constitution of the New Dominion.

CHAPTER X.

INCIDENTS OF THE SEPARATE SCHOOL CONTEST FROM 1852 TO 1855.

I SHALL, in this Chapter, trace the progress of events which finally led to the adoption, by the Legislature, of the first complete Upper Canada Separate School Act of 1855,—the "Taché Act."

Few, of the present day, can realize the extent and bitterness of the contest which ended, for a time, in the final passage of the Taché Separate School Act. The brunt of the battle fell upon Dr. Ryerson. He was the *bête noir* of the promoters of Separate School Legislation;—and that, because, as guardian of the integrity of the Public School System of Upper Canada, he refused to assent to any measure which he conscientiously believed would militate against the success and prosperity of that System. He was, from his very position, as Chief Executive Officer of the Education Department, and as practically an arbiter between two opposing forces, the target at which both parties aimed their arrows. What added to his difficulty, in dealing with this somewhat intricate and delicate question, was the fact, that the Government of the day,—very wisely and properly,—referred all parties dealing with this question to him. Sir John Macdonald refused, in his pleasant, courteous way, all consideration of details of Separate School Legislation, until the parties concerned had first consulted the Chief Superintendent of Education in regard to them. If approved and recommended by him, Sir John was prepared to consider any question proposed to him on its merits. In this way, parties, desiring modifications in the legislation affecting Separate Schools, had to submit their proposals to the Chief Superintendent, with whom they were sure to have them discussed with fairness, but also with a clearness of perception as to their effect and purpose, which might not always be apparent to those who proposed them.*

Nevertheless, Dr. Ryerson, in thus discharging his duty, was exposed to a double fire;—on the one side, from the champions of Separate Schools, who charged him as being personally hostile to their rights and interests; and, on the other side, by open and covert attacks, as the betrayer of the cause which he was bound to defend, and as a tool in the hands of the Hierarchy, for the promotion of their alleged unpatriotic and selfish ends.

Thus attacked, Dr. Ryerson was not slow in returning the fire of his opponents. He had to defend himself from the attacks of a powerful press, who reiterated the charge, over and over again, that he was untrue to the cause of unsectarian Education, and for making, (although he only carried out in the least objectionable form,) the concessions in favour of Separate Schools, which had their origin in the Hon. Mr. Day's Common School Act of 1841, and which were embodied, in a less objectionable form, in the Hon. Mr. Hincks' Act of 1843.†

There was another circumstance, already referred to, which tended still further to excite the hostility of the combatants on both sides against Dr. Ryerson, especially, when the studiously passive attitude of the Government prevented a successful attack being made upon it. And that was, as I have already observed, the practical and prudential policy of the Leaders of

---

* The Hon. Senator R. W. Scott, the promoter of the Roman Catholic Separate School Bills of 1860, 1861, 1862 and 1863, thus narrates his experience of Dr. Ryerson, in conferences with him on the subject of Separate Schools:— "It is due to his, (Dr. Ryerson's,) memory to say that, I found him always ready to meet the wishes of the minority,—that he exhibited no prejudice, or bigotry; that, had larger concessions been sought for, Dr. Ryerson would not have thrown any obstacle in the way."—(*Hansard Report of Hon. R. W. Scott's Speech in the Senate, on the 4th of April, 1894.*)

† On this point, the Hon. R. W. Scott, in his speech, (already referred to,) said:—" There was a strong feeling prevailing with (Roman) Catholics that he, (Dr. Ryerson,) was hostile to the (Separate School) Act. People believed that he was always decidedly against Separate Schools." . . . Speaking of the "appeal" Section in the Act of 1863, Mr. Scott said that, "it was simply based on the idea that the Chief Superintendent was not friendly to the Separate School System, which was a mistake, because he was sincerely anxious to do what was really fair to make the law workable."—(*Speech in the Senate, on the 4th of April, 1894.*)

the Government for the time being—Robert Baldwin, Francis Hincks, John A. Macdonald, or John Sandfield Macdonald—to pass no School Bill, nor entertain any measure relating to elementary Education in Upper Canada, which had not been examined, modified and approved by the Chief Superintendent of Education.

It can easily be understood that, under such circumstances, a great deal of correspondence and conferences, between promoters of Separate Schools — clerical and lay, chiefly the former — took place with Dr. Ryerson, during these educationally stirring times. Having enjoyed the strong personal friendship and unbounded confidence of Dr. Ryerson, I was cognizant of all the proceedings, conferences, and correspondence which took place in this noted controversy. I was often present at his confidential conferences with various parties,—for he felt it to be desirable, although not always necessary, to have a third person present at these conferences.

CHAPTER XI.

CLAIM FOR ADDITIONAL GRANTS TO SEPARATE SCHOOLS.
—PRESSURE ON THE GOVERNMENT IN 1852.

In 1852, a claim for an increased apportionment to Separate Schools was pressed upon the Government—as the apportionment on the basis of attendance at the Separate Schools did not supply sufficient funds for their support. In dealing with this demand, as raised by Bishop Charbonnel, Dr. Ryerson wrote to him, as follows:—

In regard to the alleged injustice done to Roman Catholics, in the distribution of School moneys, so frequently asserted by Your Lordship, there is one circumstance which I may mention, in addition to the facts and reasons I have given, (in this Letter,) in reply to Your Lordship's statements and claims. The Board of School Trustees, in the City of Toronto, have caused a very careful inquiry to be made into the census returns and tax rolls of the City, in order to ascertain the comparative amount of taxes paid by Roman Catholics and Protestants. The result of that inquiry is, that while one-fourth of the entire population of the City is returned as Roman Catholics, a fraction less than one-twelfth of the taxes is paid by them.* . . . It is, therefore, clear that no class of the population is so much benefited by the General School Taxes, in proportion to what they pay, as Roman Catholics; and hence assuming—what the people and Legislature of Upper Canada have repeatedly repudiated—that the authority and Officers of Law ought to be employed to impose and collect taxes for any Religious Denomination, the sums of School Money which would be payable, when apportioned upon the basis of property, to Roman Catholic Separate Schools, would be much less than what the School Act now allows such Schools, upon the basis of the attendance of pupils. Of all classes in the community, the Roman Catholics have the strongest reason to desire the System of Mixed Schools; and every effort to urge them to apply for Separate Schools, so far as it succeeds, imposes upon them additional pecuniary burdens, at the same time that it must inflict upon them losses and disadvantages to which they are not now subject.

TORONTO, 12th of May, 1852. E. RYERSON.

Notwithstanding these facts, a strong pressure was brought to bear upon the Government of the day, demanding that additional aid should be provided for the Roman Catholic Separate Schools. This demand was communicated to Dr. Ryerson, at the time, by the Hon. Francis Hincks, (who had then charge of the Educational Legislation of the Government), in a Letter, written from Quebec, as follows:—

(*Confidential.*)—The Roman Catholics, (I understand,) are preparing a Bill, which will be passed. It is clear that we must do something. Better abolish the 19th Section [of the Common School Act of 1850] at once, than render it a mockery, as in cases where there are Free Schools. Again, it would not do to share the tax where Free Schools are established. We must decide to do something, and I think we are disposed to do it where Free Schools are established. A separate column should be placed in the roll, and the parties to state whether they desire their share of tax to be

---

* The Trustees of the Roman Catholic Separate Schools in Toronto claimed £1,150 for their Schools; and in reporting upon this demand, the Committee of the Board of School Trustees state that—"From a recent return, Your Committee find that the total *annual value* of the taxable property in the City amounts to £186,983 5s.:—of this, the proportion held by Roman Catholics is £15,750 10s. The total net amount of school tax for last year, at $2\frac{1}{2}$d. in the pound, was £1,800: the net proportion contributed by the Roman Catholic inhabitants was £156 10s."—(*Report of Free School Committee of Board of School Trustees for the City of Toronto, dated 19th May, 1852.*)

given for such School. They might participate proportionately in the Government grant. Where there are Free Schools, the Assessors will generally be Protestants. There is no danger of fraud. The [Roman Catholic] people will be able to act independently and indirectly, and will, perhaps, support the Free Schools, if fairly conducted. The plan is worth trying. If we refuse this, we will probably get worse. Write to me on this point.

QUEBEC, August 9th, 1852. F. HINCKS.

THE BELLEVILLE SEPARATE SCHOOL CASE, 1852.

The immediate cause of all this trouble and difficulty was a Separate School case, which occurred in Belleville in 1852, and, incidentally, the case of Chatham, to which Bishop Charbonnel had referred in his second Letter to Dr. Ryerson, of the 7th of March, 1852.

In a Letter to the Hon. A. N. Morin, Provincial Secretary, dated the 17th of April, 1852, Dr. Ryerson discussed these two cases. The object of these cases of appeal, he said, was:—

To compel the Local School Municipalities to apply a portion of all the School moneys they might raise towards the cost of the erection and repairs of Separate School-houses, as well as to the salaries of Separate School Teachers,—a provision that was never contemplated by the School Act, and a demand that was never before made, since I have been connected with the Department.—(*Return of Correspondence to the House of Assembly, 1851-1852, page 34.*)

Dr. Ryerson's reply to the foregoing Confidential Letter of the Hon. Mr. Hincks, was written on the 26th of August, 1852. In it he enclosed a draft of School Bill,—the fourth Section of which was designed to meet the cases of the Belleville, Chatham and other Separate Schools.

The Belleville case led to a law suit, with a view to determine the question raised. It appears that in establishing "Free Schools" in that place, the property of Roman Catholics and Protestants alike, as ratepayers, were assessed for the support of these free Schools. Dr. Ryerson, in a published Letter on the subject, states the case as follows:—

The Roman Catholic supporters of Separate Schools, claimed a share of all the moneys raised by the Municipality, as well as of the Legislative apportionment, in proportion to the average attendance of pupils at their

School, as compared with the attendance at the Common Schools; but the Board of Common School Trustees in Belleville refused to pay them any more than a Legal share of the School Fund,—that is, a share (according to the average attendance of pupils) of the Legislative Grant, and a sum equal to it, raised by the Town Corporation, but not a share in any additional sum, or sums, raised by tax for School purposes. I was appealed to, and interpreted the law, as above stated,—adding, that it was voluntary with any local Corporation whether they would allow Separate Schools to share in all the School Funds provided by local tax, or only in what the Act defined as the School Fund. The Roman Catholic Trustees instituted legal proceedings to recover a share in the School moneys to which they had contributed as ratepayers, and they failed. A new element of agitation was thus furnished. . . . And, the case of the Roman Catholic supporters of the Separate School in Belleville was viewed as one of hardship, (such as was said could not be experienced by the Protestants of Lower Canada,) and was certain to lead to one or two results, either of which would render the establishment or continuance of Free Schools impossible.

The one result was the giving to the supporters of Separate Schools the right to share in all School moneys raised by the Municipality, as well as paid to it,—which would prevent Municipal Councils from doing anything at all, as they would not be tax collectors for any Religious Denomination whatever.

The other result was, the limiting of the power of local Councils to collect a sum equal to the Legislative apportionment, and no more,—which would, of course, render Free Schools impossible.

To avoid both of these evils,—to leave Roman Catholics no ground for complaint,—to afford full scope for the establishment of Free Schools, where the people might wish to establish them, I recommended that, on proper notice, given before February in each year, the supporters of Separate Schools should be exempted from paying any Municipal School Rates whatever, but be empowered to collect their own School Rates, and examine their own Teachers, and that they should be also precluded from sharing in any Municipal moneys, unless a Municipality chose to levy and collect their School Rates for them. . . .

These suggestions, for the solution of the Separate School difficulty in Belleville, and others elsewhere, were embodied in the fourth Section of what was designated as the "Supplementary School Bill of 1853."

The suit of the Belleville Separate School Trustee against the Town Council, was not decided until early in 1853. The decision in that case was given by Chief Justice Robinson, and was concurred in by Mr Justice Burns. It was to the effect,

CLAIM FOR ADDITIONAL GRANTS.

that no Mandamus against the Town Council would be granted, as it was the opinion of the Chief Justice that—

> As the School Act of 1850 now stands, what a Separate School, established under the 19th Clause, is entitled to share in, is the sum apportioned by the Chief Superintendent out of the Government Grant, and a sum . . . raised by local assessment to meet that Grant,—raised, I mean, for the payment of Teachers generally, and not upon an estimate for any specific purpose.

In his Letter to the Hon. Mr. Hincks, (to which I have referred on page 63,) accompanying the Draft of the Supplementary School Bill of 1852-3, Dr. Ryerson said, in regard to the fourth Section:—

> This Section proposes to relieve the parents and guardians sending children to Separate Schools from paying any School tax whatever, and then allowing them to share with the other Schools according to average attendance of the same Municipality in the Legislative School Grant alone. In case such a provision were adopted. 1st, There would be no provision in the School Law requiring a public Municipal tax for Denominational Schools, and all opposition and clamour against it would cease. 2nd, There could be no complaint from any quarter that the supporters of a Separate School paid more or less than they received from the School Fund. 3rd, All the inhabitants of a Municipality, except those who might choose to send their children to a Separate School, could proceed with their School interests, as if no other class of persons were in existence. 4th, The Teachers of Separate Schools would be relieved from appearing before the County Board of Public Instruction for examination, and thus the last vestige of possible agitation between the supporters of Separate Schools and the Municipal authorities, in relation to the subject at all, would be removed. Then the Section does not, any more than the 19th Section of the existing law, give the persons who petition for, and send children to, the Separate Schools, control over all the Roman Catholics, or Protestants, of the Municipality; but only over those of the religious persuasion of the Separate School, who choose to support it.—(*Return of Correspondence on Separate Schools, printed by order of the Legislative Assembly, 1852-1855, page 21.*)

This draft of Bill, sent to Mr. Hincks, in August, 1852, was transferred by him to the Hon. Attorney-General Richards, who made some modifications in it, of which Dr. Ryerson did not approve.

On the 6th of September, 1852, Mr. George Brown introduced

a Bill into the House of Assembly, "to repeal such clauses of the Common Schools Acts of Upper Canada, as authorize the establishment of Sectarian Schools endowed with the Public Money." This Bill was never pressed to a vote, and was "discharged" on the 4th of June, 1853.

In November, 1852, Dr. Ryerson went to Quebec to confer with the Government in regard to the Supplementary School Bill, then in the hands of the Hon. W. B. Richards, Attorney-General, and other matters. In a private Letter to me, written while there, on the 11th of November, 1852, he said:—

> The School Bill, (except the Separate School fourth Clause, and the Clauses prepared by Mr. Joseph C. Morrison,) was introduced into the House of Assembly on Saturday night, and the Attorney-General wishes me to stay until it is disposed of. . . . In redrafting the Separate School fourth Clause, the Attorney-General thought that he was carrying my views into effect. The Hon. John Ross, Solicitor-General, told him that he, (Mr. Ross,) was sure that the Clause did not embrace my views. They both now agree with me; and I am to prepare the Bill, (as so agreed upon,) immediately after my return to Toronto.
>
> QUEBEC, 11th of November, 1852.   E. RYERSON.

In January, 1853, Archbishop Turgeon wrote to Bishop Charbonnel, as follows:—

> I am happy to tell Your Lordship, in answer to your Letter of the 1st instant, that the Hon. A. N. Morin . . . assured me that himself and his Colleagues were in the firm resolution to give the (Roman) Catholics of Upper Canada the same advantages which the Protestants in our part of the Province enjoys.*
>
>   + P. F. TURGEON, Archbp. of Quebec.
> QUEBEC, 11th of January, 1853.

The Bill, when revised and recast by Dr. Ryerson, was sent to Attorney-General Richards; and Mr. Richards, in reply, said:—

> (*Private.*)—Herewith you have a copy of the School Bill, as I think we can introduce it. I have consulted with our friends as to the fourth Section. We have altered it, in some respects, from the draft you sent; but I believe I have retained those portions which embody the principle to which we had all assented. . . .
>
> QUEBEC, 14th of February, 1853.   W. B. RICHARDS.

---

* From the "Life of Archbishop Lynch, by H. C. McKeown," 1886, pages 292, 293.

After the Bill had been introduced into the Legislature, the friends of Separate Schools pressed the Government still further to give coherence and stability to their System of Separate Schools, by authorizing the establishment of Boards of Separate School Trustees in Cities and Towns. The Attorney-General then sent the following Telegram to the Chief Superintendent of Education :—

Is there any objection to allow Trustees of Separate Schools in Cities and Towns to form a General Board to manage their own Schools. If not, telegraph at once ; if there are objections, write at length, immediately.
QUEBEC, 20th of April, 1853.   W. B. RICHARDS.

Dr. Ryerson telegraphed that there were objections; that he would write to-morrow. On the morrow, he replied at length, as requested. I give the main points of his Letter, as follows :—

1. It is a new demand. It was never before mooted, much less admitted. . . . It involves the introduction of principles which have never been admitted into [the Separate School portion of] our School System. . . . Why this new demand ? if it is not to avoid conditions which have been heretofore required in regard to the establishment and existence of Separate Schools.

2. It has been a principle maintained in every successive School Law of Upper Canada, that there should be no Roman Catholic, or Protestant, Separate School in any School division, or ward, of a City, or Town, except where the Teacher was of a different religious faith from the applicants. But, if there be a City, or Town, Board of sectarian School Trustees, the Common School Board may employ ever so many Teachers in the ward Schools of the same faith of the advocates of the Sectarian Schools, yet it will not prevent the establishment and support out of the public revenue of Sectarian Schools in these very wards. This is placing Sectarian Schools upon a totally different foundation from that on which they have always stood ; it is the introduction of a system of Sectarian Schools without restriction, and almost without conditions, as it is proposed to relieve the Teacher employed in them from all examination. . . .

3. Such a Board could establish as many Sectarian Schools as they please, and without requiring any public certificates of qualification from the Teachers employed. Such a Board can recognize the Teacher, or Teachers, of every private School kept by persons of their Religious Persuasion. . . . Thus such a Board in Toronto might recognize and claim public aid for every child taught in the convents. . . .

4. A large portion of the public mind is chafed at the perpetuation of, and provision for, Separate Schools in any form ; but I have endeavoured,

(during my late provincial tour,) to render this provision tolerable, by stating that no new principle would be introduced, but only the modified application of a principle already recognized and acted upon under successive Acts of Parliament.* I should deplore the revulsion which I fear will take place in the public mind, should a new and unfair provision be made, and fresh facilities be provided for the multiplication of Sectarian Common Schools,—the symbols and instruments of growing mischief in the country, from the proceedings adopted and the spirit inculcated during the last year.

5. I think the safest and most defensible ground to take, is a firm refusal to sanction any measure to provide, by law, increased facilities for the multiplication and perpetuation of Sectarian Schools, [but to intimate] a readiness to remedy any injustice, or hardship, which the operations of the existing law may be conceived to involve, but to do nothing more.

TORONTO, 21st of April, 1853.   E. RYERSON.

The following Letter was written by Attorney-General Richards to Bishop Charbonnel,—as given on page 293 of the "Life of Archbishop Lynch, by H. C. McKeown," 1886:

I hope that the provisions of the [fourth Section of the Supplementary School] Bill will be such as to prevent future disputes and differences. As I said to you personally, I have endeavoured, [in that Bill,] to give the Separate Schools in Upper Canada the same rights and powers that the Dissentient Schools in Lower Canada have.

QUEBEC, 30th of May, 1853.   W. B. RICHARDS.

As the Bill was being moved into Committee of the whole House, on the 3rd of June, 1853, Mr. George Brown, seconded by Mr. W. L. Mackenzie, moved—

That it be an instruction to the said Committee, that they have power to make provision in the said Bill, for the repeal of such sections of the

---

* As to the nature of the conferences with various parties at the County School Conventions of 1852-1853, to which Dr. Ryerson here refers, he thus explains his proceedings at them, in his Special Report, laid before the Legislature in 1858:—"In the winter of 1852 and 1853, I made an official tour of Upper Canada, and held, by appointment, a Public School meeting in each County,—having previously prepared the first draft of the Supplementary School Act of 1853. On the provisions of that draft of Bill, I consulted the most intelligent and experienced men in School matters in the several Counties, and especially on the clauses of the fourth section of the Act. I think I am warranted in saying, that those intelligent men of all parties whom I consulted, without reserve, unanimously agreed to those clauses of the Separate School Section; but were also strongly of the opinion, with myself, that no further concession in that direction should be made under any circumstances, or could be made without endangering the whole National School System, and violating individual and municipal rights." . . .

School Acts of Upper Canada now in force, as authorize the establishment and continuance of Separate Schools, and for the removal from the said Supplementary Bill of all recognition of any portion of the community in a sectarian capacity.

This motion was lost by a vote of 11 yeas to 46 nays. Mr. David Christie then moved, seconded by Mr. John Langton:—

That the words, "and also to make provision that, in the management of any Common School, which derives any portion of its support from the funds of the Province, there shall be no teaching, or other practice, permitted, which can, in any way, do violence to the religious feelings and opinions of any child, or of the parent, or guardian, of any child attending such Common School," be added at the end thereof.

This motion was lost by a vote of 16 yeas to 42 nays. On the final passage of the Bill, on the 7th of June, 1853, the Upper Canada vote stood as follows:—Yeas: Messieurs Cameron, Dixon, Hincks, McDonald, (Cornwall,) McLachlin, Patrick, Richards, Ridout, Rolph, Sherwood, and Wright, (East York): 11. Nays, (all Upper Canada Members,) viz.: Messieurs Brown, Burnham, Christie, (Wentworth,) Crawford, Ferguson, Gamble, Lyon, Mackenzie, Malloch, Seymour, Shaw, Smith, (Frontenac,) Smith, (Durham,) Stevenson, Street, White, and Wilson: 17.

The following is an analysis of the fourth Section of the Supplementary School Act, relating to Roman Catholic Separate Schools, which received the Royal Assent on the 14th of June, 1853:*—

1. Subscribers to an amount equal to the School Rates for the support of a Separate School, are relieved from the payment of such Rates for Public Common Schools.

2. Each Separate School to share in the Legislative Grant, but not in the Municipal Assessment.

3. Exemption from School Rates only to extend to the period of sending children to the Separate School.

---

* The Home District Council, on the 1st of July, 1853, petitioned against this Separate School provision in the Supplementary School Act. The Petition expressed "deep regret" at having discovered in this Supplementary School Act, that "the principle of Separate Schools is again recognized. . . . No one denomination should be preferred before the other, . . . and no facilities should be given for the establishment of Sectarian and Separate Schools, etc." The Petition is signed by Mr. Joseph Hartman, M.P.P., and by Mr. J. Elliott, County Clerk. Other Councils sent in similar Petitions.

4. Return of names of supporters of Separate Schools, and the names of the children sent, to be sent by the Separate School Trustees, to the Local Superintendent of Schools, half-yearly; also the amounts subscribed.

5. The Local Superintendent shall send the names of supporters of Separate Schools reported to him to the Clerk of the Municipality; and the Clerk shall omit such names from the Assessment Roll, except in case a rate for a School building had been imposed before the return to the Clerk of such names.

6. The provisions of the 13th Section of the School Act of 1850, shall apply to Trustees and Teachers of Separate Schools, (*i.e.*, in regard to penalties for false returns.)

7. Separate School Trustees shall be a Corporation, with power to assess for Separate School Rates, or collect Subscriptions.

8. Subscribers to, or supporters by rates, of Separate Schools, shall not vote for Public School Trustees.

CHAPTER XII.

SECOND APPEAL TO THE GOVERNMENT—RENEWED DEMANDS OF BISHOP CHARBONNEL.

SOME time after the passing of the Supplementary School Act of 1853, fresh demands on behalf of Separate Schools were made, chiefly in private Letters to the Hon. Francis Hincks, by Bishop Charbonnel. The Editor of *The Globe* newspaper, referring, in that paper, to this Supplementary School Act, thus addressed Dr. Ryerson:—

And did this third concession to the claimants of Separate Schools satisfy them? Was your oft-repeated assurance realized, that "the existence of the provision for Separate Schools" in the national system prevented "oppositions and combinations which would otherwise be formed against it?" On the contrary, the separatists only advanced in the extent of their demands, and became more resolute in enforcing them. The very next year, the matter was again brought to a crisis—a general election came on—Bishop Charbonnel pressed his demands—and Mr. Hincks consented to bring in yet another Sectarian School Act.

In his fifth Letter to the Hon. George Brown, of December 31st, 1858, Dr. Ryerson thus replied to these remarks of the Editor:—

I have (already) shown that, while the Act of 1853 removed all grounds of complaint of personal hardship by supporters of Separate Schools, and thus granted what they professed to desire, it involved "no strengthening of the sectarian element," but facilitated and secured the extension of Free Schools. Bishop Charbonnel himself professed to be satisfied with the Act of 1853. So much so, that in a *"Pastoral Address on the Upper Canada Supplementary School Act of 1853,"* dated Toronto, *9th July, 1853*, he commenced with the following words :

Owing to the equity of our Legislature, dearly beloved brethren, the Catholic minority of Upper Canada are to enjoy, for the education of their children, the same advantages enjoyed by the Protestant minority of Lower Canada.

It is true that Bishop Charbonnel . . . receded from his previous official acceptance of that Act, and put forth new complaints and demands. He did so through the public papers, and he did so in private Letters to Hon. Mr. Hincks.

SECOND TORONTO CASE—SEPARATE SCHOOL DIFFICULTIES IN TWO WARDS.

The cause of most of these new demands appear to have originated chiefly in the City of Toronto. First, there was a complaint of a Separate School difficulty in St. David's Ward, then in St. James' Ward,—which were dealt with specifically by the Chief Superintendent of Education, as they arose. That of St. David's Ward was brought before the Chief Superintendent of Education, by the Hon. John Elmsley, to whom he replied, as follows :—

It appears from your statement that, in the Public School of St. David's Ward, six Teachers are employed, and only one of them is a Roman Catholic; and, as I understand, he is not the Principal of the School. The question then is, whether, under such circumstances, the twelve heads of families are entitled to a Separate School? I think they are. . . . It is clear that, in each of the Common Schools referred to, [in the Act of 1850, 19th Section,] the law assumed the existence of but one Teacher. . . . I do not think, therefore, that the employment of one Roman Catholic among several teachers of a Common School in St. David's Ward, precludes the Roman Catholic heads of families, whom you represent, from having a Separate School, if they desire it.

TORONTO, 30th of August, 1853. E. RYERSON.

The character of the various complaints and demands, made by Bishop Charbonnel, at this time, may be gathered from the following Letter, which the Hon. F. Hincks wrote to Bishop Charbonnel, as given in the "Life of Archbishop Lynch, by H. C. McKeown," 1886, pages 293, 294 :—

I have learned with much regret from your Letter of yesterday, [2nd of August, 1853,] that a fresh difficulty has arisen regarding your Schools in Toronto. Believe me, my attention will be promptly given to the subject of the grant, with a view to find a remedy, if there be any attempt to obstruct a law honestly intended by the Government to heal up wounds which were most injurious to the peace of society. . . .
QUEBEC, 3rd of August, 1853. F. HINCKS.

Shortly afterwards, Mr. Hincks wrote the following Letter to Dr. Ryerson, on the subject of these complaints :—

(*Confidential.*)—I spoke to you about the new difficulty with Bishop Charbonnel before leaving Toronto, and am sorry to find that the Government is likely to get into very serious embarrassment regarding a question which I had hoped was happily settled. . . . This vexed question nearly upset the Government last Session. Judge Richards can tell you that I do not magnify its importance.

Note, that if by any means you refuse, practically, the Separate Schools, we are just where we were ; and the fight has to come off with the same parties, as it would have had to come before the Legislature of last Session. Bishop Charbonnel will petition, and demand, legislation. His Bill will have the support of all, or nearly all, of the Lower Canada Members ; and, then, what is the Government to do ? I assume, of course, that the Government refuses to bring in any Bill. Perhaps the Government might be broken up on that point, but suppose it is not ? If we, Upper Canadians, insist in opposing such a Bill, we will, at all events, be beaten in Lower Canada, and then Messrs. Morin and Drummond, etc., will certainly resign, and we shall get gentlemen of the Cauchon School and of the Upper Canada Tories to govern the country for longer than you imagine. If, again, our Lower Canadian Colleagues support the Bill as an open question, which they would insist, probably, in doing, and carry it, then, what would our position be ?

I cannot speculate on what I would do in such a case, but you will at once see the embarrassment ; and I can assure you few things would grieve me more than the danger of meddling with our Upper Canada School System, which is so admirably worked out by you.

Your influence at present, I need not say, is all that you can well desire. You have had proof of it ; and I may say to you, in the strictest confidence, however, that, for several weeks, we have been in a position of not a little embarrassment in arranging our University Senate, because I

SECOND APPEAL TO THE GOVERNMENT.

would not listen to your being proscribed. I must, in justice, say that the objection to you is not within the Government. It is external, in part. . .

I have put all the points of embarrassment in the other case before you, with a view of ascertaining whether you can aid in settling this affair quietly. I cannot but look upon the action of the Toronto School Trustees in appointing Teachers, (as they have done,) as intended to thwart, indirectly, the Separate School Trustees. Now, I feel it is a wise policy to let them try our late (Supplementary) Bill fairly. I confess I do not see my way clearly. The effect of not appointing Roman Catholic Teachers would be to proscribe them. Pray, however, think over the matter and give me your views, confidentially, as soon as possible. You will see, and feel, all my embarrassment, and I am certain you will try and help me out of it, if you can.

QUEBEC, 18th of August, 1853.   F. HINCKS.

In reply, an intimation was given by Dr. Ryerson to Mr. Hincks, that the matter would be carefully considered, and, that in submitting a draft of Bill "to make further provision for the Grammar and Common Schools of Upper Canada," next year, two or three Sections would be added to meet some local difficulties which had been experienced in carrying out satisfactorily the fourth Section of the Supplementary School Act of 1853, relating to Separate Schools.

In the "Life of Archbishop Lynch, by H. C. McKeown," 1886, the following Letter, written by Vicar-General Cazeau to Bishop Charbonnel, is given on page 294 :—

I have seen Mr. Hincks. Your School question vexes him very much. He will write strongly to Mr. [Ryerson], to make him interpret the Law in such a way as to do justice to (Roman) Catholics. If the Law is not interpreted as necessary, a new one shall be enacted, in order to require imperiously that the (Roman) Catholics of Upper Canada shall be treated with the same liberality as the Protestants of Lower Canada, and thus justice shall be obtained.

QUEBEC, 18th of August, 1853.   C. F. CAZEAU, V.G.

THIRD SEPARATE SCHOOL DIFFICULTY IN THE CITY OF TORONTO, 1854.

Most of the Separate School difficulties which arose occurred in the City of Toronto. This, Dr. Ryerson stated, in a Letter to Hon. John Elmsley, in reply to some complaints, (in regard to the making of certain School Returns,) which he brought before Dr. Ryerson early in 1854. Dr. Ryerson said :—

In this City alone, throughout all Upper Canada, has difficulty arisen, such as your Letter indicates—showing clearly that it has arisen from the disposition and objects of the parties concerned, rather than from anything difficult in the provisions of the law. I know not how these provisions can be plainer; but no legal provisions are plain when efforts are made to employ them for other than their obvious and legitimate objects.

TORONTO, 10th of May, 1854. E. RYERSON.

The difficulty, in this case, was the refusal of the Treasurer, or other Officer, of the City Council to refund certain School Rates collected by mistake, or in error, from Separate School supporters, during the year 1853, owing to some objection to certain returns made by the Separate School Trustees. The matter having been referred to the Finance Committee of the City Council, Dr. Ryerson addressed a Letter to Mr. Angus Morrison, the Chairman, urging the Committee to accede to the demand for a refund of the taxes. He said:—

Under the circumstances, [of defective, or incomplete, returns,] I think you will agree with me, that it is hardly fair, and not doing "as we would be done by," to take advantage of any alleged technical omissions in the first half-yearly returns of the Separate School Trustees, made within a few days after the passing [of the fourth Section] of the [Supplementary School] Act (of 1853), requiring them [to make these returns]. . . . I think it but equitable that the law should be administered in the same spirit in regard to the Trustees and supporters of Separate Schools,—whatever may be our opinion of the expediency, or inexpediency, of establishing such Schools.

TORONTO, 20th of May, 1854. E. RYERSON.

Notwithstanding the intimation to the Hon. Mr. Elmsley, on the 11th of May, that, in regard to the point of his complaint, the law was "clearly in his favour, and that there could be little doubt, or difficulty, in his obtaining a speedy remedy," yet, on the 25th of that month, Dr. Ryerson was made responsible for this very difficulty, with the authorities of the City of Toronto. In his Letter to Hon. Mr. Elmsley, he said:—

In to-day's issue of a newspaper organ of your Church, published in this City, called the *Catholic Citizen*, I am assailed for having, from vile motives, introduced this provision of the Act, [in regard to returns]; whereas, the fact is, that, although I prepared and recommended the general provisions of the fourth Section of the Supplementary School Act, it so happens that the restrictive words—

"Nor shall said exemption extend to School rates, or taxes imposed, or to be imposed, to pay for School-houses, the erection of which was undertaken, or entered upon, before the establishment of Separate Schools."

Were not submitted, or suggested, by me, but were suggested by the late Hon. Attorney-General, (now Judge,) Richards,—than whom no man in Canada could desire more anxiously what was most liberal, as well as just, towards his Roman Catholic fellow-citizens. And the circumstance that this clause of the Act, so vehemently exclaimed against by the newspaper organ referred to, originated in a mind the least liable to be charged with, or suspected of, intolerance against Roman Catholics, and was approved of by the Roman Catholic, as well as other, Members of the Government and Legislature, is an ample refutation of the insinuations referred to, and a sufficient proof that the provisions of the fourth Section of the Supplementary School Act were conceived in the spirit and interest of the utmost fairness and liberality to all parties concerned.

TORONTO, 25th of May, 1854. E. RYERSON.

RENEWED AGITATION BY BISHOP CHARBONNEL—THE TACHÉ ACT FORESHOWED.

Notwithstanding these efforts of Dr. Ryerson to remove difficulties and to answer objections, as they arose, a movement was set on foot to obtain further legislation, more favourable than ever, for Separate Schools. In a Letter from Dr. Ryerson to Bishop Charbonnel, in August, 1854, he thus referred to this movement:—

During some months past, your Lordship has been pleased several times to attack me personally by name—attacks which have been often repeated and variously enlarged upon by the newspaper organs of your Lordship. . .
I am quite aware that these attacks upon me, in connection with the provisions of the law in regard to Separate Schools, were designed to influence the recent elections; and for that very reason I thought it proper not to notice them until after the elections—that your Lordship might have every possible benefit of them, and that I might not give the slightest pretence for a charge that I interfered in the elections. . . . I may remark, that when public men have said that they will advocate granting the same privileges to the Roman Catholics in Upper Canada as are enjoyed by Protestants in Lower Canada, they are quite right, and say no more than I have said from the beginning,—no more than I have sincerely intended,—no more than each succeeding administration has intended,—no more than the late Attorney-General (now Judge) Richards believed was fully secured to them by the Supplementary School Act for 1853; for, after he and I had gone over the several clauses of the fourth Section, (relative to Separate Schools,) of the Supplementary School Bill, he asked

me if the supporters of the Separate Schools were now placed on the same footing in Upper Canada as in Lower Canada; I replied, I believed they were in every respect,—that, in some particulars, there was a difference in the mode of proceeding in the two sections of Canada, and the payment of all School moneys by County and Town Treasurers, which did not exist in Lower Canada,—that, in regard to these peculiarities, nothing was required of the Trustees of Separate Schools, which was not required of Trustees of Public Schools, with the single exception that, in the semi-annual returns of the former, the names of children and their parents or guardians were included, with the amounts of their School subscriptions, in order that it might be known whom to exempt from the payment of Public School Taxes. But I desired the Attorney-General to examine for himself the provisions of the two laws in regard to Separate Schools. At his request, I took the School Law of Upper Canada, as existing and as proposed, and he took the School Law of Lower Canada, and went over the provisions, clause by clause, relative to Dissentient Schools, while I referred him to the corresponding clauses of the School Laws of Upper Canada; and after he had finished, he said the equality in the two cases was perfect, and he was prepared to defend it. After this examination, and with this conviction, the Attorney-General, with the concurrence of his Colleagues, brought the Bill before the Legislative Assembly, and it was passed.

TORONTO, 26th of August, 1854. E. RYERSON.

In his fifth letter to Hon. George Brown, written in December, 1858, Dr. Ryerson thus specifies these complaints, made about this time, (1854,) and which led to the further proposed legislation in the Taché Act. The chief complaint was:—

That the money paid to Separate Schools was apportioned and paid by the Local Superintendents in Townships, and by the Board of Common School Trustees in each City or Town; that the apportionment of it was sometimes partial; and the payment of it often delayed under various pretences, to the great inconvenience and vexation of Trustees of Separate Schools; and it was urged that, as the Chief Superintendent of Education in Lower Canada apportioned and paid the School money to the Trustees of Dissentient Schools, so should the same officer in Upper Canada apportion and pay the School moneys to Separate Schools.

In the same letter to Mr. Brown, Dr. Ryerson said:—

As to this complaint, I believed it frivolous, as in the cases adduced to justify it, the Trustees of Separate Schools had not complied with the conditions and requirements of the law, and the Secretary of their Board in Toronto had refused to do so, and yet demanded the money otherwise payable to the Separate Schools; that I believed it was desired to place me in a position in which continued complaints could be made against me to the Government, and I be at length compelled to yield to their demands.

Mr. Hincks thought otherwise, and pressed me to undertake the task of apportioning and paying the money to Separate Schools, as did the Superintendent in Lower Canada, and did not leave it to the Local Superintendents and Boards of Common School Trustees. . . .

In a Letter to the Attorney-General, Dr. Ryerson refers to the complaint which had been made, as to the former mode of paying School moneys to the Separate School Trustees. He said :—

Some time last summer, the late Inspector General, (Hon. F. Hincks), communicated with me on this subject, and suggested whether I could not undertake to distribute and pay the School Grant to Separate Schools, as this would be satisfactory to the complaining parties. I expressed my conviction, that this would not satisfy Bishop Charbonnel—that I was satisfied he had ulterior objects in view—that his object was to get a measure by which the Catholic population, as a Body, would be separated from the Public Schools, and the Municipalities made tax-gatherers for the Separate Schools. But, in deference to Mr. Hincks' wishes, and as he had done so much to aid me in my work, and to promote the Public School System, and seemed to think it would be satisfactory, I consented to undertake the task proposed, although I had expressed strong objection to it in my printed Report for 1852.—(*Letter to the Hon. John A. Macdonald, dated, Toronto, 2nd April, 1855. Correspondence, etc., printed by the House of Assembly, 1855, page 52.*)

Dr. Ryerson took with him to Quebec the draft of Bill of September, 1854, to which he referred. In a private letter to me, dated at Montreal, the 10th of the same month, he said :—

I arrived at Quebec yesterday morning, and left last evening, having done all that could be done in the circumstances, [change of Ministry]. I gave the Hon. Mr. Hincks the draft of Bill, after having shown it to Mr. John [afterwards Mr. Justice] Wilson, of London, Mr. John Langton, and Mr. John W. Gamble. Mr. Hincks will see to it, the same as if he were in office. . . . Mr. Hincks has received a letter from Monsignor Joseph Eugene, the Roman Catholic Bishop, of Bytown, very much in the style of Bishop Charbonnel's first threatening Letter to me. Mr. Hincks' reply is a masterpiece, and it brought the Bishop to his senses. . . . The whole will be published. The Ministry having resigned, Sir Allan Macnab was sent for, by Lord Elgin, to form a Ministry. . . . He has agreed to carry the measures to which the Ministry were pledged ; and Mr. Hincks has promised him (Sir Allan) his support, and that of his friends. . . . I afterwards conversed upon the whole affair with Mr. Hincks and Lord Elgin. There is a perfectly good understanding between Sir Allan and Mr. Hincks. . . . Publish my Letter to Bishop Charbonnel, of the 26th of August, as was intended.

MONTREAL, 10th of September, 1854. E. RYERSON.

With a view to expedite the passage of the Bill sent to Mr. Hincks, Dr. Ryerson went to Quebec the next month, so as to confer with the Macnab Ministry on the subject. In a private Letter to me from Quebec, he said:—

I think that the short School Bill will be introduced, and passed, before the adjournment. This subject is committed to the present, and the late, Attorney-General. I went over the Bill with them to-day. They entirely approve of it. Mr. [now Sir John] Macdonald is to confer with Mr. Morin on the Separate School clauses of it, until after which, he does not wish me to leave.

QUEBEC, 28th of October, 1854.　　　　　　　　E. RYERSON.

In October, Dr. Ryerson again wrote me a private Letter, as follows:—

The Government approve of my draft of the School Bill. Even Mr. Morin—(the guardian of Roman Catholics in the Government)—has expressed himself satisfied with what I have recommended. I have got them to bring it in immediately, and to have its provisions apply to this year; and, for which, I am much indebted to Mr. Hincks.

QUEBEC, 31st of October, 1854.　　　　　　　　E. RYERSON.

Dr. Ryerson thus continues the narrative of these events, in his fifth letter to Hon. George Brown, dated December, 1858:—

In 1854, I submitted a draft of a short Bill, which was passed and became the Act 18 Vic., Chap. 142, intituled: "*An Act to make Further Provision for the Grammar and Common Schools of Upper Canada.*"

In connection with the draft of that Act, I submitted separately the drafts of three clauses, to remove the ground, or pretext, of the three complaints now made; and these three sections contained the *ultimatum* of what I was willing to do in regard to Legislation on the subject of Separate Schools—since in the Letter enclosing them, dated 6th September, 1854, I remarked as follows to Mr. Hincks:—

I think our next step must be, if further Legislation be called for, to take the sound American ground of not providing for, or recognizing, Separate Schools at all. In this we should have the cordial support of nine-tenths of the people of Upper Canada; while, in the course now pursued, the more you concede, the more you contravene the prevalent sentiment of the Country, and the greater injury you are inflicting upon the great body of the parties for whom Separate School are professedly demanded, but who have not, as far as I am aware, any safe and adequate means of speaking for themselves, or even of forming a judgment.

In his Letter to the Hon. F. Hincks, of the 6th of September, 1854, Dr. Ryerson said:—

The following Sections relate to Separate Schools, and, without undermining our General System, provide for all that, even the ultra, advocates of Separate Schools profess to demand, and all I think the Country can be induced to give. [Then follows the explanation of the three Sections proposed in 1854.] These three Sections relieve the Trustees of Separate Schools from making any return, or including any item in any return whatever, not required of other Trustees; leave the applicants for Separate Schools to do anything, or nothing, as they please; but do not permit them to make the Municipal Council their School-tax Collector, nor give them the Legislative School Grant, except in proportion to the average number of children they teach.

These Sections of draft of Bill in 1854 were in the following terms:—

VI. And be it enacted, That so much of the 4th Section of the Act, 16 Vic., Chap. 185, as requires each supporter of a Separate School to subscribe, or pay, a certain sum, in order to be exempted from the payment of the Public School Rates, and so much of the said Section of said Act as requires the Trustees of a Separate School to include, in their semi-annual returns, a statement of the names of the children attending such School, or of the names of parents, or guardians, sending children to such School, or of the sum, or sums, subscribed or paid by each of the supporters of such School, shall be, and is hereby repealed: Provided, always, that the supporters of a Separate School, or Schools, in order to be entitled to exemption from the payment of any Public School Rates for any one year, as authorized by the said 4th Section of the Act, 16 Vic., Chap. 185, shall, on, or before, the first day of February, of such year, communicate in writing, with their names and places of residence, to the Clerk of the Municipality in which such Separate School, or Schools, are situated, a declaration to the effect, that they are supporters of such Separate School, or Schools.

VII. And be it enacted, That the Trustees of Separate Schools, elected in each of the Wards of any City, or Town, in Upper Canada, shall have authority to unite, during their pleasure, into one Joint Board of Trustees, for the management of the several Separate Schools in such City, or Town.

VIII. And be it enacted, That the Chief Superintendent of Schools for Upper Canada shall have authority to determine the proportions of the Legislative School Grant, which may be payable, respectively, according to law, to Public and Separate Schools; and shall have authority to pay the sums thus apportioned in such manner as he shall judge expedient, upon the conditions, and at the time prescribed by law: Provided, always, that such returns shall be made to him, and in such manner, by all parties concerned, as he shall require, to enable him to decide upon the amount, and payment of said sums.—(*Correspondence on Separate Schools, page 24, printed by order of the Legislative Assembly, 1855.*)

In the Letter to the Hon. George Brown, of the 31st of December, 1858, already quoted, Dr. Ryerson said :—

It will be seen above that my Letter, enclosing a draft of a short School Bill to Mr. Hincks, and three clauses relating to Separate Schools, on the mode of paying School money to them, was dated the 6th of September, 1854. A few days after, Mr. Hincks resigned office, and the Sir Allan Macnab administration was formed. In the meantime, Bishop Charbonnel was most active in writing to Members of the Government and the Legislature, impugning me, complaining of the law, and enlisting other Roman Catholic Bishops with him.

The following Letters will show the nature of the influence which was thus being used, in 1854, to promote the passage of a purely Roman Catholic Separate School Bill.

In September, 1854, Vicar-General Cazeau, of Quebec, thus writes to Bishop Charbonnel, (as given on page 295 of the " Life of Archbishop Lynch, by C. H. McKeown ") :—

All the Lower Canadian Ministers will be maintained in the [Sir A. N. Macnab] Cabinet. I do not deceive myself in telling your Lordship that they agreed, as a condition of their alliance with Sir Allan, that justice should be done to your (Roman) Catholics about Separate Schools.

QUEBEC, 11th of September, 1854.   C. F. CAZEAU, V.G.

Bishop Phelan of Kingston, in a Letter, (quoted on page 295 of the " Life of Archbishop Lynch, by C. H. McKeown," 1886,) addressed to Bishop Charbonnel, said :—

I have a Letter from our Attorney-General, (Hon. John A. Macdonald), in which he promises that he will pass a Bill that will be satisfactory to us all. Notwithstanding all his promises, I still feel anxious to see that some action should be taken on our School Bill [of 1854].

QUEBEC, 11th of September, 1854.   C. F. CAZEAU, V.C.

Dr. Ryerson, in the foregoing Letter to the Hon. George Brown, already quoted, further states that :—

Among the extracts of correspondence that Bishop Charbonnel afterwards published, are the following, which I quote from the Toronto *Mirror*, of July 18th, 1856 :—

From Vicar-General Cazeau to Bishop De Charbonnel :

It has been resolved, in the Council, that Justice should be done to the Separate Schools. Sir Allan hastened to tell me that he had always been favourable to them; and I replied, that your Lordship had always relied on him.

QUEBEC, 28th of December, 1854.   C. F. CAZEAU, V.G.

SECOND APPEAL TO THE GOVERNMENT.

In a Letter written by Bishop Phelan, in January, 1855, as given in Mr. C. H. McKeown's "Life of Archbishop Lynch," (1886,) the Bishop said:—

I have delayed writing to you until I had an interview with the Attorney-General, (Hon. John A. Macdonald,) who assures me that he has had prepared a Bill for us in Upper Canada. He says he gave it to the Hon. A. N. Morin, a (Roman) Catholic in communication with the Right Rev. Dr. De Charbonnel, The Chief Superintendent read it attentively, and said nothing against its provisions.*

KINGSTON, 8th of January, 1855.   + PATRICK PHELAN, Bp. of Carrhoe.

Soon after writing the foregoing Letter, Bishop Phelan expressed his doubts in regard to Dr. Ryerson's silence, and addressed the following one to Bishop Charbonnel:†—

I assure you I have my misgivings about the new School Bill as unobjecable to ——, (Dr. Ryerson,) and, therefore, I earnestly requested the Attorney-General, (Macdonald,) to send us a copy of it, that we might send it back to him, with our remarks on the margin of it.

KINGSTON, 16th of January, 1855.   + PATRICK PHELAN, Bp. of Carrhoe.

From the Bishop of Bytown to Bishop De Charbonnel:

Your protestation reached me here in the midst of the bush. I signed and sent it immediately to Bishop Phelan; were it lost, send me a duplicate. We ask merely, and only, for the law which rules Lower Canada. Go to Quebec, if you can, for you are, amongst us, the most able to treat the School Question with the Government.

BYTOWN, 2nd of March, 1855.   + JOS. EUGENE, Bp. of Bytown.

DOCUMENTS SUBMITTED, BY THE ROMAN CATHOLIC BISHOPS OF UPPER CANADA, TO THE GOVERNMENT, IN 1854.

The following documents were submitted to the Government, in 1854-55, by the Roman Catholic Bishops of Kingston, Toronto, and Bytown (Ottawa):—

1. Comparative Table of Legislation on Separate Schools in Upper and Lower Canada.

2. Draft of a School Bill for Upper Canada, prepared by the three Roman Catholic Bishops of Kingston, Toronto, and Bytown, (Ottawa,) in 1854-55.

---

* To whom this Letter was written is not stated—most likely to Bishop Charbonnel. There must have been some misapprehension in regard to Dr. Ryerson reading a Separate School Bill, apparently for the first time, and making no objection to its provisions. This was entirely contrary to his usual practice in such cases.

† "Life of Archbishop Lynch, by C. H. McKeown," 1886, page 296.

1. *Comparative Table of Legislation on Separate Schools in Upper and Lower Canada, Prepared by the Roman Catholic Bishops of Kingston, Toronto, and Bytown (Ottawa).* *

IN UPPER CANADA.

Dissenters must		For having Separate Schools, be *twelve* heads of families; apply *to* and be authorized *by* persons opposed to them.	
Separate School Supporters	Cannot	Have a Separate School where a Catholic teaches a Common School, nor provide by themselves for the Election of Trustees	A.† 19th Section.
		Nor elect for Trustee a Clergyman having no Property	A. 5th Section.
	Must	Contribute to the Common School Buildings and Libraries	A. 27th Section, B.† 4th Section.
Separate School Trustees	Cannot	Be less than 21 in Toronto	A. 22nd Section.
		Exercise the same powers as the Common School Trustees	A. 19th Section, B. 1st Section.
		Circumscribe their Schools wherever they like	A. 19th Section.
		Receive their shares from the Chief Superintendent, and apply to him for any case they like	A. B. Here and there.
		Nor receive any share according to population	B. 4th Section.
		Avail themselves of the Municipal Assessment and Collecting	ditto.
	Must	Take a census during the greatest heat and cold	ditto.
		And twice a year the names of Parents and Pupils, with daily attendance	ditto.
		The names of Subscribers to Separate Schools, having no child thereat	ditto.
		And the amount of their Taxes, even unknown	ditto.
		Collect Taxes from Parents and Subscribers	ditto.

Separate Schools Are visited by Clergymen of different faith   A. 32nd Section.

---

* I have the Original of this Comparative Table and Draft of School Bill, as proposed, in 1854 and 1858, by the three Bishops named, in my possession.—J. G. H.

† N.B.—" A." means the Upper Canada School Act, of 1850; "B." the Supplementary School Act, of 1852.

SECOND APPEAL TO THE GOVERNMENT. 83

From those penalties general dissatisfaction of Dissenters, who cannot have either Separate Schools, or the money due for them; witness Toronto, Hamilton, London, St. Catharines, etc., etc.

IN LOWER CANADA.

Dissenters may	In any number whatever, heads of families or not, establish Separate School, without petition *to*, or authorization *from*, persons opposed to them	A.* 26th Section, B.* 18th Section.
	Have Separate Schools even where a Dissenter teaches the Common School	
	Keep Common School Buildings for themselves, far from being obliged to contribute to Common School Buildings or Libraries	A. 26th Section.
	Elect for Trustee a Clergyman having no property	B. 6th Section.
Separate School Trustees.	Are only six in Quebec and Montreal, larger Cities than Toronto	A. 43rd Section.
	Have all the same powers as the Common School Trustees	A. 26th Section.
	Circumscribe their Schools as they like	B. 18th Section.
	May apply to the Chief Superintendent for any case, and receive from him their shares in all School Funds	A. 26th Section, B. 18th Section.
	On easy Reports and Certificates	A. 27th Section, B. 18th Section.
	According to their population in Quebec and Montreal, and wherever they are pleased with the Municipal Assessment, and Collecting	A. 26th and 43rd Sections.
	If not, they provide for both, and get shares according to attendance	B. 18th Section.
	Cannot be visited by Clergymen of Rome	A. 33rd Section.

From those liberal clauses working liberally, full satisfaction of Protestants.

For further particulars, see the Pamphlet of Angus Dallas, just published, entitled: "*The Common School System; its Principles, Operation and Results.*" Toronto: Thompson & Co., Printers, Queen Street East. †

---

* N.B.—"A." means the Lower Canada School Act, 9 Vict., Chap. 27; "B." 12 Vict., Chap. 50.

† (NOTE.—I have referred to this and other Pamphlets in a subsequent Chapter.—J. G. H.)

In the Letter to the Hon. George Brown, of the 31st of December, 1858, already quoted, Dr. Ryerson proceeds:—

Bishop Charbonnel proceeded to Quebec, a few days after which I was officially telegraphed to proceed there also. I was there shown the "protestation" against the Upper Canada School Law, signed by Bishop De Charbonnel and two other Roman Catholic Bishops.* I went over the "protestation," item by item, first with the Attorney-General for Upper Canada (Hon. John A. Macdonald), and then with the Attorney-General for Lower Canada (Hon. A. N. Morin), and showed that the statements as to the inequality of the law in regard to Separate Schools in Upper and Lower Canada were unfounded; and I examined the (Bishop's) Draft Bill, clause by clause, and maintained that it was inadmissible, and not at all in harmony with the professed objects proposed, but an invasion of the rights of the people and Municipalities of Upper Canada. It was then proposed that I should meet Bishop De Charbonnel, with the two Attorneys-General. I did so, and afterwards Bishop De Charbonnel and myself, (by request), discussed the question alone; but, after hours of discussion, we were where we began. I refused to concede any more than I had proposed in the three clauses addressed to Mr. Hincks, on the previous September, and he refused to accept those clauses, or state his demands.

After several days, I returned from Quebec, supposing that I had, at least, satisfied the Law Officers of the Crown of the justice of our Separate School Law, as it was, and having the firm belief that no Separate School legislation would take place that Session.

But, that I might leave no means in my power unemployed to maintain the integrity of our School System, and that I might place on record the substance of what I had stated verbally at Quebec, I addressed, on my return to Toronto, a letter to the Hon. Attorney-General John A. Macdonald, dated Toronto, 2nd April, 1855, "on the Roman Catholic Bishops' comparative Table of Legislation on Separate Schools, and draft of a new School Bill for Upper Canada." In that Letter, of over seventeen printed pages, octavo, I discussed—

1. Bishop Charbonnel's statements respecting the School Laws of Upper and Lower Canada, in regard to Separate Schools.

2. The nature of demands made in Bishop Charbonnel's Draft of Bill.

3. Course of proceeding which I have pursued, and which Bishop Charbonnel has pursued, towards me, in respect to Separate Schools.— (*See Correspondence on Separate Schools, printed by order of the Legislative Assembly in 1855, pp. 39-55.*)

---

* It is published in the Official Correspondence on Separate Schools, (pp. 34-37,) with a Draft of Bill annexed, printed by order of the Legislative Assembly, 1855.

DR. RYERSON'S CRITICISM OF THIS TABLE, AND HIS REPLY TO THE STATEMENT OF THE ROMAN CATHOLIC BISHOPS.

In his Letter to Attorney-General Macdonald, written on the 2nd of April, 1855, Dr. Ryerson made an elaborate reply to the statements in this Table. His opening paragraph was as follows:

The statements contained in this "Comparative Table of the Legislation on Separate Schools," are the same as those which were delivered by Bishop Charbonnel at the "Catholic Institute" in Toronto, and published in the *Catholic Citizen*, in July, before the last general elections, and afterwards shown by me to be wholly incorrect, in a Letter addressed by me to the Bishop, and published in the Toronto papers, dated the 26th of August, 1854.

The preliminary statement of the three Bishops, to which Dr. Ryerson refers, and their Draft of Bill, are as follows:—

1. *Preliminary Statement of the three Roman Catholic Bishops.*

The only efficient remedy to that inveterate wound in a country which wants, above all, union and peace for its progress and prosperity, is to repeal clauses 19 of the School Act, of 1850, and 4 of the Supplementary Act, of 1853, of Upper Canada; to place Separate Schools for everything under only one Official, not opposed to Separate Schools, and give them an equal share in all School Funds. On that principle, and on the Legislation of Lower Canada, is framed the following project of a School Bill [for Upper Canada]:—

2. "*An Act to better define certain Rights to parties therein mentioned, as drafted by the three Bishops.*

Whereas, the Clauses of the School Acts on Separate Schools in Upper Canada do not secure all that is granted to the dissenters in Lower Canada,

I. Be it enacted, That the Clause 19 of the 13 and 14 Vict., Chap. 48, and Clause 4 of the 16 Vict., Chap. 185, be, and are, repealed.

II. That in any School Section, when the arrangements for the Common School shall not be agreeable to any number whatever of dissidents, those dissidents may signify, in writing, to the Chairman of the Board of Common School Trustees, their will of having one or more Separate Schools, and give in the names of three Trustees, freeholders or not, elected by a majority at a public meeting, convened by three heads of families of the same School Section, and held according to the clauses 4 and 5 of the School Act of 1850: Provided, that no Member of those dissidents shall be allowed to vote at any Common School election within the School Section in which their Separate School shall be established. (*So it is in Lower Canada, see 9th Vict., Chap. 27, Section 26.*)

III. That the said Trustees, by the only fact of the said signification and election, shall form *de facto* a Corporation under the name of   , having all the same rights and powers, as defined and extended in Common School Acts of Upper Canada and in this Act, subject to the same duties and penalties as the Board of Common School Trustees, such as defined in the clauses 12 and 13 of the School Act of 1850, with the exception that they will be exclusively accountable to the only one Official appointed *ad hoc* for copies, reports, etc.: That Board also shall be renewed partly at each Annual School Meeting, as provided by the clause 3 of the School Act of 1850. (*So it is in Lower Canada; see Lower Canada Act.*)

IV. That in localities divided into Wards, each Ward this year, within two months after the passing of this Act, and every year after, on the second Wednesday of January, shall elect one fit person to be a Trustee of one or more Separate Schools, and hold office until his successor be elected at the ensuing year, or himself may be re-elected, if he consent thereto ; that those Trustees shall form one Corporation, under the name of   , having the same rights, subject to the same duties and penalties as mentioned in the preceding Clause III., with the same exception that they will be accountable, for such conditions as may be required, exclusively to the only official appointed for the superintendence of Separate Schools ; and that any majority of the Members present, at any meeting regularly held, at which there shall be an absolute majority of the Members of the Board, may validly exercise all the powers of the Corporation.—(*So it is in Lower Canada, see 9th Vict., Chap. 29, Section 5.*)

V. That the said Trustees may circumscribe their Separate Schools as they like, (*so it is in Lower Canada, 12th Vict., Chap. 50, Section 18,*) receive children of their faith from other School Sections, (*so it is in Lower Canada, 9th Vict., Chap. 27, Section 29,*) and qualify Teachers for their Separate Schools, until they have a Separate Normal School.

VI. That the said Trustees shall be entitled to receive from their said special Superintendent, on a report such as required by him, such sums out of the Government Grant, out of all the taxes for School and Library purposes, and out of any Provincial, or Municipal School Funds, as proportionate to the population they represent, according to the last official census, (*so in Lower Canada, 9th Vict., Chap. 27, Section 26; 12th Vict., Chap. 50, Section 18,*) provided that those sums shall be expended for School purposes : Provided, also, that should any Municipal Corporation refuse to pay any portion of those sums, either the Chief Superintendent shall deduct a sum, equal to the deficiency, from the apportionment of the current and following years, until full payment, or the Secretary of the Board shall refer the case to the Superior Court, who will judge of it, and shall order the payment by all legal means.

VII. That such of the provisions of the Common School Acts of Upper Canada, as are contrary to the provisions of this Act, shall be, and are hereby, repealed.

VIII. That generally all words and provisions of this Act, doubts and difficulties arising about it, shall receive such large, beneficial and liberal construction as will best ensure the attainment of this Act, and the enforcement of its enactments, according to their true intent, meaning, and spirit. —(*So in Lower Canada, 9th Vict., Chap. 27, Section 55.*)

IX. That the present Act shall take effect from the first of January of this year, 1855."

We, the undersigned, hereby declare that nothing short of the above will satisfy the conscientious convictions of the Catholics of this Province.

     + PATRICK PHELAN, Bp. of Carrhoe, Adm't. Apostolic.
(*No date* + ARMANDUS FR. MA., Bp. of Toronto.
given.) + JOS. EUGENE, Bp. of Bytown.

In his Letter to Hon. Attorney-General John A. Macdonald, dated the 2nd of April, 1852, and published in the "*Correspondence*," laid before the House of Assembly, in 1855, Dr. Ryerson thus analyses the provisions of this Bill, as proposed by the three Bishops:—

This Draft of Bill is the first document that Bishop Charbonnel has printed, stating explicitly what he and his Colleagues demand. This document speaks for itself; and no private professions, or disclaimers, as to what is, or is not, desired, or intended, will be of any value, in the face of what is here summarily and deliberately demanded as necessary to "satisfy the conscientious convictions of the Catholics of this Province."

The professed object of Bishop Charbonnel's statements and Draft of Bill, is to secure to the Roman Catholics in Upper Canada what is enjoyed by Protestants in Lower Canada; but the provisions of the Draft of Bill itself would confer upon Roman Catholics in Upper Canada what is not enjoyed by Protestants in Lower Canada, or in any other civilized country. Under the pretence of assimilating the School Law of Upper Canada to that of Lower Canada, in regard to Separate Schools, an attempt is made to place the property of every Protestant in Upper Canada, the power of every Municipality, and the School Fund itself, in subjection to the promoters of Separate Schools, without their being subject to any of the restrictions and obligations to which Separate Schools in Lower Canada and Public Schools in Upper Canada are now subject. An analysis of the provisions of this Draft of Bill will more than justify this assertion.

1. The first feature of this Draft of Bill that I shall notice, is, that which relates to the accountability, or rather non-accountability of Separate School Trustees, and the conditions of their claims upon the School Fund.

The third and fourth Sections provide a special Superintendent for Separate Schools, to whom alone they are to make returns, and such returns only as he may require ; and, on 'a report, such as (the sixth Section prescribes) required by him,' are Provincial and Municipal School Funds to be paid to Separate School Trustees, and that, according to the last official census of the population. Now, every one of those provisions is contrary to the School Law of Lower Canada. Here is a special Superintendent for Separate Schools, which does not exist in Lower Canada ; here is no provision as to the kind of returns, or when the returns shall be made, or how attested, all of which are prescribed by the School Law of both the Canadas, and are not left to any one man, and especially a man chosen to promote a special object. Nothing is prescribed as to the length of time Schools shall be kept open, in order to share in the School Fund, or how conducted, or any inspection. Under such provisions, there might be one Separate School in a Township, or City, that School not kept open more than three days in a year, nor contain more than three pupils, and yet, according to the Separate School ratio, the Trustees of it receive several hundred pounds of the School Fund ! It is also here provided that all the money thus to be given to Separate Schools, shall be paid to the Trustees, and that without any personal responsibility, on their part, as to the expenditure of this money ; whereas, the School Law of Upper Canada does not permit any part of the School Fund to be paid into the hands of School Trustees at all, but to legally qualified Teachers alone, on the written orders of Trustees.

2. The second feature of this Draft of Bill, which I notice, is, that it annihilates the individuality, and individual right, of choice on the part of the members of the Religious Persuasion of the Separate Schools.* The second Section provides that 'any number whatever of dissidents,' in a Municipality, may establish a Separate School ; the third section makes three persons signified by themselves *de facto* a Corporation ; and the sixth Section makes them the representatives of the whole population, according to the last census, of the persuasion to which they belong. Thus, any

---

* This idea of the right of individuals, and of independent action on the part of the supporters of Separate Schools, assumed, as a matter of course, by Mr. Hincks, in his Letter to Dr. Ryerson, of the 9th of August, 1852, also runs through the whole of Dr. Ryerson's writings, in regard to the Separate School question. He points out that a different and opposite principle is prominent in the legislation of those who promote Separate Schools. Thus he says : "The second proviso [in the Acts prepared under the auspices of Col. Taché, in 1855, and of Mr. R. W. Scott, in 1860-1863] is, that the Roman Catholics, as a body,. shall be defined as supporters of Separate Schools, and thus, by law, be excluded from the Common Schools." This was in the first project of the Taché Bill referred to,—thus depriving every Roman Catholic of the right, or liberty, of choice as to whether he would support a Common, or a Separate, School ; and also depriving every Roman Catholic parent of the right, or liberty, of choice, as to whether he would send his children to the Common, or Separate, School.—(*Dr. Ryerson's* "*Remarks on the Separate School Agitation*," *February, 1865, page 18.*)

three Priests, or any other three Members of such Persuasion, can erect themselves into a Corporation, to represent and control the whole population of that Persuasion in a Municipality, and claim and receive into their own hands School moneys of every kind, according to the numbers of such Persuasion, as certified by the last official census, though nine-tenths of such Persuasion might wish to remain, and have their children educated with other classes of their fellow-citizens. No such monstrous provision exists in the School Law of Lower Canada. In the Section of the Act there, authorizing the dissentients to receive a portion of the assessment, on their protesting against the assessment adopted by the Commissioners, (Section 18, of the Act, 12th Vict., Chap. 50,) it is only the parties making the representation that are included, and they only receive what they themselves pay to the Collector. The law there does not make the last official census the basis of distribution ; much less does it ignore individual right of choice. So the School Law of Upper Canada recognizes individual rights ; deals with each individual for himself, and does not ignore, or proscribe, him from the Public Schools, and all the privileges connected with them, except at his own request.

3. The third feature of this Draft of Bill, (for which, see pages 85-87, *ante*,) is, that it transfers all the Common School property of Upper Canada from its present occupiers to the Trustees of Separate Schools. The seventh Section repeals all the Provisions of the present "Common School Acts of Upper Canada" that "are contrary to the provisions of this Act"; and the third Section gives to the Trustees of Separate Schools all the rights and powers, which the 12th and 13th Sections of the School Act of 1850 give to the present Trustees of Common Schools ; and the 12th Section of that Act includes the possession, and control, of all Common School property in Upper Canada. Truly, this is a very ingenious and modest provision to "satisfy conscientious convictions !" And this is far from being all ; for,

4. A fourth feature of this Draft of Bill is, that it gives the Trustees of Separate Schools unrestricted power to tax all property in Upper Canada,—not only that which belongs to the supporters of Separate Schools, but that which belongs to every Protestant and every Roman Catholic in Upper Canada ! The present Upper Canada School Law makes the Trustees of Separate School Corporations, and gives them the same power in the management of their own Schools, and in respect to all persons for whom such Schools are established, as is possessed by the Trustees of Common Schools, but the "conscientious convictions" of Bishop de Charbonnel, and his Colleagues, require much more. They claim by the 3rd Section of this Draft of Bill, "all the same rights and powers" which the 12th Section of the School Act of 1850 gives to the Common School Trustees. These "rights and powers," thus claimed, are not restricted to any class, or classes, of persons, but are absolute and universal. The only

7

restriction on them is that which is contained in the 13th Section of the same Act,—a Section imposing a fine of Five pounds upon a Trustee convicted of "knowingly signing a false report,"—a Section of no effect in connection with the other provisions, which relieve Separate Schools of all inspection, create for them a special Superintendent of their own, and with no obligation, to make any returns, except such as he may require from them. The 9th, 10th, 11th, 14th, 18th, 29th and 31st Sections of the School Act of 1850, (13th and 14th Vict., Chap. 48,) and the 4th, 5th, 6th, 9th, 10th, 11th, 12th, 13th and 17th Sections of the Supplementary School Act of 1853, (16 Vict., Chap. 185,) impose various restrictions and obligations upon Trustees in regard to the exercise of the large powers which the nineteen clauses of the 12th Section of the School Act of 1850 confer upon them,—thus preventing them from levying any rate upon the supporters of Separate Schools; requiring semi-annual returns; limiting their applications to Councils, etc., etc.; but the 3rd Section of this Draft of Bill discards all these restrictions and obligations, and demands for the Trustee Corporations to be created, absolutely, and without restrictions, all the "rights and powers," as well as all the property, which the 12th Section of the School Act of 1850 confers upon Common School Trustees, the ninth clause of which Act authorizes them "to apply to the Municipality of the Township, or employ their own lawful authority, as they may judge expedient, for the raising and collecting of all sums authorized in the manner hereinbefore provided, to be collected from the freeholders and householders of such Section, by rate, according to the valuation of taxable property, as expressed on the Assessor's, or Collector's, Roll." Here is no restriction as to persons, or property; all are subject to the taxing power of the Separate School Trustees,—whom this Draft of Bill makes the sole School Trustees! And, in this connection, it is also to be observed that the proviso in the 2nd Section of this Draft of Bill allows none but dissentients to vote at the election of these Trustees. This is also the provision of the present law; but the present law restrains the acts of the Trustees thus elected, to the property and persons of the dissentients. This Draft of Bill, however, while it restricts the elective franchise to a particular class, gives the Trustees elected by that class, power over all the taxable property of all classes of freeholders and householders in the Section! Nor is this all, for—

5. A fifth feature of Bishop de Charbonnel's Draft of Bill is, that it gives the Trustee Corporations it creates, equal power over the Municipal Councils as over individuals. The ninth clause of the 12th Section of the School Act of 1850, above quoted, gives the Trustees power to apply, at their pleasure, to the Municipality, to impose School rates; and the 18th Section of the same Act makes it the duty of such Council to levy and collect the amount of rates thus applied for, from all the taxable property of the Section concerned; and the 6th Section of this Draft of Bill requires

the Special Superintendent to pay the amount of such taxes, or, from the Chief Superintendent, if the Municipality fails to do so. Thus is every Municipality in Upper Canada, as well as the School Fund, subjected to the discretionary demands of Separate School Trustees. Nor is even this all, for—

6. A sixth feature of this Draft of Bill is, that it ties the hands of all Public School Trustees, (were any to exist,) from doing anything for their own School without doing also as much for the Separate Schools; for the 6th Section of this Draft of Bill requires "all taxes for School and Library purposes," as well as "any Provincial and Municipal Funds," to be paid to the Trustees of Separate Schools, in proportion "to the population they represent, according to the last official census." Thus, whatever might be done by any parties for the erection of Public School-houses, or the support of Public Schools, they could not raise a penny by taxes, even from themselves, without dividing it with the Trustees of Separate Schools, who are not subject to corresponding obligations,—who may do nothing whatever,—and who are to receive, not in proportion to their taxable property, but in proportion to population, though the ratio of that population may be three times that of the taxes they pay, as is the case even in the City of Toronto.*

I might remark upon other minor features of this Draft of Bill, and show its operations in other aspects; but the six features I have exhibited sufficiently prove that it contemplates the complete destruction of our Public School System, and the subjection of the School Funds, Municipalities and property, and the whole population of Upper Canada, to a Religious domination, such as is without a parallel in any age, and is incompatible with the free government or liberties of any Country. I doubt whether the ingenuity of man could devise, under meeker pretensions, and in fewer words, the destruction of the Educational Institutions and the constitutional liberties of a whole people, and their prostrate subjection under the feet of a Religious Denomination. The authors of this Draft of Bill must have presumed marvellously upon their own powers, and upon the simplicity of the Members of the Legislature. I am persuaded that no person will more promptly recoil from and repel such a measure than the great body of the Roman Catholic Members of the Legislature, and of the community, who will be grieved, and ashamed, to see the worst imputations of their opponents exceeded by the monstrous propositions

---

* The Trustees of the Roman Catholic Separate Schools in Toronto, in 1852, claimed £1,150 for their Schools; and, in reporting upon this demand, the Committee of the Board of School Trustees state that—"From a recent return your Committee find that the total annual value of the taxable property in the City amounts to £186,983 5s.:—of this, the proportion held by Roman Catholics is £15,750 10s. The total net amount of School tax for last year, at 2½d. in the pound, was £1,800; the net proportion contributed by the Roman Catholic inhabitants was only £156 10s."

covertly involved in what is demanded by Bishop Charbonnel, and his Colleagues, under the pretext of " satisfying their conscientious convictions."

The Members of the Legislature now have the issues of the whole question before them ; and they, as well as the people of Upper Canada at large, will understand their rights, their interests, and their duty.— (*Letter to the Hon. Attorney-General John A. Macdonald, dated the 2nd of April, 1855. Correspondence printed by order of the House of Assembly, 1855, pages 46-49.*)

CHAPTER XIII.

THE TACHÉ SEPARATE SCHOOL BILL OF 1855.

THE just yet severe criticism which the Draft of the Separate School Bill,—which was practically the ultimatum of the three Bishops of Kingston, Toronto, and Bytown,—called forth from Dr. Ryerson, and others, prevented its being submitted to the Legislature at that time. It was, however, re-submitted to the Government in 1858, apparently without any modification, notwithstanding Dr. Ryerson's adverse criticism of it. (See Dr. Ryerson's private Letter to me, of the 30th of January, 1858, pages 121, 122, *post*.) The duty of preparing a less crude and sweeping measure was, apparently, entrusted to the Hon. L. T. Drummond, M.P.

This Drummond Bill was introduced into the Legislative Council by the Hon. Sir E. P. Taché. In his fifth Letter to the Hon. George Brown, dated the 31st of December, 1858, Dr. Ryerson thus refers to the circumstances under which this Taché Bill was submitted to the Legislature :—

This Letter, (*i.e.*, the one addressed to the Hon. John A. Macdonald, Attorney-General, on the 2nd of April, 1855,—with the exception of the two telegrams, which I will give presently,) was the last Letter I wrote to any Member of the Government, (at that time,) on the Separate School Law. . . .

Then, as to the sequel. About the middle of May, six weeks after I had returned from Quebec, a Separate School Bill was introduced by Sir E. P. Taché into the Legislative Council, repealing all preceding Separate School provisions of the law, and substituting one Act in place of them, including

The Taché Separate School Bill of 1855.

the three clauses, which I had transmitted to Mr. Hincks in the previous September. That Bill was professedly designed to assimilate the Separate School Laws of Upper and Lower Canada, and was, upon the whole, drawn up with great fairness,—imposing upon the supporters of Separate Schools several forms and requirements which had never before been imposed upon them, and simply because such forms and requirements had been imposed upon the supporters of Dissentient Schools in Lower Canada. But the Bill contained a provision, (which I had always resisted,) to compel the Municipalities to be tax-collectors for Separate Schools, and for giving Separate Schools an undue share of School money; and also another provision for establishing Separate Schools of every kind, without limit, such as would have divided the Protestant population into endless parties, and destroyed the School System. The Hon. L. T. Drummond, Attorney-General for Lower Canada, is said to have prepared this Bill, while Col. Taché introduced it into the Legislative Council,—there being then, (as was stated,) no Upper Canada Member of Government in the Council.

As to the manner and instruments of preventing that Bill from passing in its original form, and striking out its objectionable clauses, the following facts will show. My first intelligence of the Bill was by the Telegram, of which the following is a copy, addressed to me by Mr. J. W. Gamble, M. P. :—

"QUEBEC, May 18th, 1855,—To DR. RYERSON,—Are you aware of provisions of Government Bill, relation Separate Schools, introduced into the Legislative Council? Copy mailed your address to-day.
"J. W. GAMBLE."

To the above I replied forthwith :—

"To J. W. GAMBLE, Esq ,—I have not seen the Bill, and know nothing of it."

On receiving a copy of the Bill from Mr. Gamble, I addressed the following Telegram to the Hon. Attorney-General John A. Macdonald, Quebec:—

"Have seen Mr. Taché's Separate School Bill. High Church Episcopalians alone are gainers. All others are losers. In the 14th Section, the person should be of religious persuasion of Separate School. It should be so worded as not to include Municipal Council Assessment. Why not restrict the 2nd Section, and the whole Bill, to Roman Catholics alone?
"TORONTO, May 19, 1855.   "E. RYERSON."

After further considering the Bill, I addressed the following Telegram to the Hon. Attorney-General Macdonald, Quebec :—

"Mr. Taché's Roman Catholic Separate School Bill, amended as suggested, and confined to Catholics, is harmless. Otherwise destroys School System. Any ten persons, using name of any Persuasion, can avoid paying all School taxes by complying with forms of Bill, and adopting, as their's, any Lady's, or other, School, to which they send, or subscribe, a few shillings, or pence.
"TORONTO, May 22nd, 1855.   "E. RYERSON."

To the foregoing, I received the following reply:—

"To Rev. Dr. Ryerson, Toronto,—I agree with you, and will make alterations as you suggest.

"Quebec, May 22nd, 1855. "John A. Macdonald."

What influence the above Telegrams had in striking out the worst features of the Bill, and especially when the Attorney-General afterwards amended the Bill, as they suggested, the reader can easily judge.

The Taché Bill passed the Legislative Council on the 21st of May, but not without the following Protest from the Hon. James Crooks, of Flamboro', Father of the Hon. Adam Crooks, Q.C., the first Minister of Education for Ontario:—

DISSENTIENT:

Because the settled policy of every Government is to provide that all of the subjects live in amity and good-fellowship, one with another, and that whatever differences may exist among them, as to forms of Religion, or any other matter, it is deemed good policy that the youth, as far as possible, be brought together at Public Schools for Education at an early period of life, leaving to their Parents, or other Guardians, the duty of instructing them in the forms of Religion they profess, and the principles of the Christian Religion.

That following out these judicious principles, the Imperial Government have erected and endowed a number of [Queen's] Colleges in Ireland, [one each in the Provinces of Ulster, Munster, and Connaught.] Some Professors of Religion, not Protestant, are there successfully employed, and heretofore with perfect success: Whereas, by passing the present Bill, the asperity of feeling, one towards another, engendered by different forms of Religion, is perpetuated, and the policy of the Imperial Government set at naught.

JAMES CROOKS.

Legislative Council, 21st of May, 1855.

The Taché Bill, as it passed the Legislative Council, was sent down to the House of Assembly, and, on the 22nd of May, it was moved by the Hon. John A. Macdonald, Attorney-General, West, seconded by the Hon. William Cayley, that the Bill be read a first time. In amendment to this motion, Mr. George Brown, seconded by Mr. Joseph Hartman, moved that it be read that day six months. The votes of the Upper Canada Members on this motion were: Brown, Christie, Delong, Fraser, Gamble, Hartman, Langton, Lumsden, Mackenzie, Mathewson, Merritt, Patrick, Rankin, Rolph and Wright (15), and Darche and J. B. E. Dorion, of Lower Canada; total, 17. The Upper Canada nays were: Bowes, Larwill, Powell, Cayley, Church, Clarke, Crysler, J. A. Macdonald, R. McDonald, Sir A. Macnab, John Ross, James Ross, Shaw, H. Smith, Southwick, Spence, Stevenson (16). Lower Canada nays, 45; total, 61.

On a vote for a "call of the House" on the same day, to consider the Bill, the Upper Canada yea votes were: Aikens, Brown, Christie, Delong, Fraser, Gamble, Hartman, Langton, Lumsden, Mackenzie, Merritt, Patrick, Rankin, Rolph and Wright (15), and 6 Lower Canada yea votes, viz.: Bellingham, Darche, DeWitt, J. B. E. Dorion, A. A. Dorion and Papin; total, 21. The Upper Canada nay votes were: Bowes, Cayley, Church, Clarke, Larwill, J. A. Macdonald, R. McDonald, Sir A. N. Macnab, Powell, John Ross, James Ross, Shaw, H. Smith, Spence and Stevenson (14), and 41 Lower Canada nay votes; total, 55. The following is a copy of the Taché Bill, as passed:

THE TACHÉ SEPARATE SCHOOL BILL OF 1855, (18 VICT., CHAP. 131.)

Whereas it is expedient to amend the laws relating to Separate Schools in Upper Canada, *so far as they affect the Roman Catholic inhabitants thereof:* (*b*) Be it therefore enacted by the Queen's Most Excellent Majesty, by and with the advice and consent of the Legislative Council, and of the Legislative Assembly of the Province of Canada, constituted and assembled by virtue of, and under the authority of, an Act passed in the Parliament of the United Kingdom of Great Britain and Ireland, and intituled, *An Act to reunite the Provinces of Upper and Lower Canada, and for the Government of Canada,* and it is hereby enacted by the authority of the same, as follows:—

I. The Nineteenth Section of "*the Upper Canada School Act of* 1850," and the Fourth Section of "*the Upper Canada Supplementary School Act of* 1853," and all other provisions of the said Acts, or of any other Act, inconsistent with the provisions of this Act, are hereby repealed, *so far only as they severally relate to the Roman Catholics of Upper Canada* (*b*). [13 and 14 Vict., Chap. 48, § xix. 14 and 15 Vict., Chap. 111. 16 Vict., Chap. 185, § iv., repealed.]

II. Any number of persons, not less than *five heads of families, being freeholders, or householders, resident within any School Section, of any Township, or within any Ward of any City, or Town,* (*a*) *and being Roman Catholics,* (*b*) may convene a public meeting of persons desiring to establish

(*a*) Amended in the Legislative Council.
(*b*) Amended in the House of Assembly.

a Separate School *for Roman Catholics* (*b*) in such School Section, or Ward, (*b*) for the election of Trustees for the management thereof.

III. A majority of the persons present, *not less than ten in number,* (*b*) *being freeholders, or householders,* (*a*) *and being Roman Catholics,* (*b*) at any such meeting may elect three persons, *resident within such Section,* (*a*) to act as Trustees for the management of such Separate School, and any person, *being a British subject,* (*b*) may be elected as such Trustee, whether he be a freeholder, or householder, or not.

IV. A notice addressed to the Reeve, or to the Chairman of the Board of Common School Trustees, in the Township, City, or Town, in which such Section is situate, may be given by all persons *resident within such Section, being freeholders, or householders, and being Roman Catholics,* (*b*) favourable to the establishment of such Separate School, whether they were present at such meeting or not, declaring that they desire to establish a Separate School in such School Section, and designating, by their names, professions, and places of abode, the persons elected, in the manner aforesaid, as Trustees for the management thereof.

V. Every such notice shall be delivered to the proper Officer by one of the Trustees so elected, and it shall be the duty of the Officer receiving the same to endorse thereon the date of the reception thereof, and to deliver a copy of the same, so endorsed and duly certified by him, to such Trustee.

VI. From the day of the date of the reception of every such notice, the Trustees therein named shall be a Body Corporate under the name of "The Trustees of the Roman Catholic Separate School, for the Section Number   , in the Township, (City, or Town, *as the case may be,*) in the County of   ."*

VII. *If a Separate School, or Separate Schools, shall have been established in more than one Ward of any City, or Town, the Trustees of such Separate Schools may, if they think fit, form an union of such Separate Schools,* (*b*) and, from the day of the date of the notice in any public newspaper, published in such City, or Town, announcing such union, *the Trustees of the*

---

* In the original 6th and 8th Sections of the Bill, as introduced into the Legislative Council, the words "Episcopalian," and "Jewish, Coloured," etc., "as the case may be," were inserted. In the "Rough Draft of a Bill," the corresponding words used were "Denominations," and "Denominational Schools." The word "Episcopalian" was, in each case, altered in the Legislative Council to "Protestant." In the House of Assembly, all of these words were struck out. The 7th Section, as printed in the original Bill, was struck out in the House of Assembly. It was as follows : "VII. Persons favourable to the establishment of Separate Schools, shall elect one person only to be a Trustee for the management of one, or more, Separate Schools in each Ward of every City, and Town, in Upper Canada, divided into Wards ; and every Trustee so elected shall form a Body Corporate, under the name of the Trustees of the Roman Catholic, *Episcopalian,* [altered to "Protestant,"] *Jewish, Coloured,* School, etc., *as the case may be,* [struck out in the Council,] Separate School for   Ward of the *City, Town,* Village, as the case may be, of   , in the County of   . (See Mr. Elmsley's Letter, page 117, *post.*)

several Wards shall, *together,* (b) form a Body Corporate, under the *title* (b) of "The Board of Trustees of the Roman Catholic *United* (b) Separate Schools for the City, (*or* Town,) of   , in the County of   ."

VIII. All Trustees elected, and forming a Body Corporate under this Act, shall have the same power to impose, levy and collect, School Rates, or Subscriptions, upon, and from, persons sending children to, or subscribing towards, the Support of Separate Schools, and all other powers in respect of Separate Schools, as the Trustees of Common Schools have and possess under the provisions of the Acts hereinbefore cited in respect of Common Schools; and they shall also be bound to perform all duties required of, and shall be subject to all penalties provided against, the Trustees of Common Schools ; *and Teachers of Separate Schools shall be liable to all penalties provided against Teachers of Common Schools.* (b)

IX. All Trustees elected under this Act shall remain in office until the second Wednesday of the month of January next, following their election, on which day in each year an Annual Meeting shall be held, commencing at the hour of ten of the clock in the forenoon, for the election of Trustees for Separate Schools theretofore established ; but no Trustee shall be re-elected at any such Meeting without his consent, unless after the expiration of four years from the time when he went out of office.

X. All Trustees elected under this Act shall allow children from other School Sections to be received into any Separate School under their management, at the request of the parents, or lawful guardians, of such children, *provided such children, or their parents, or guardians, are Roman Catholics; and no children attending such School shall be included in the return hereafter provided to be made to the Chief Superintendent of Schools, unless they shall be Roman Catholics.* (b)

XI. A majority of the Trustees in any Township, or Village, or of the Board of Trustees in any Town, or Village, elected under this Act, shall have power to grant Certificates of Qualification to Teachers of Separate Schools under their management, and to dispose of all School Funds of every description coming into their hands for School purposes.

XII. Every person *paying rates, whether as proprietor, or tenant,* (a) who on or before the first day of February of any year, shall have given notice to the Clerk of the Municipality in which any Separate School is situated, that he is a *Roman Catholic, and a* (b) supporter of such Separate School, shall be exempted from the payment of all rates imposed, *within such Ward, or School Section,* (b) for the support of Common Schools, and of Common School Libraries, for the year then next following, *and every Clerk of a Municipality, upon receiving any such notice, shall deliver a Certificate to the person giving the same, to the effect that such notice has been given, and showing the date of such notice ;* (a) but any person who shall fraudulently give any such notice, or shall wilfully make any false statement therein, shall not secure any exemption thereby, but shall, on the contrary, be liable to a penalty of Ten Pounds currency, recoverable, with costs, before any Justice of the Peace, at the suit of the Municipality interested: *Provided always, that nothing herein contained shall exempt any such person from paying any rate for the support of Common Schools, or Common School Libraries, or for the erection of a School-house, or School-houses, which shall have been imposed before such Separate School was established.* (b)

XIII. Every Separate School established under this Act shall be entitled to a share in the Fund annually granted by the Legislature of this Province for the support of *Common* (b) Schools,* according to the average number of pupils attending such School during the twelve next preceding months, or during the number of months which may have elapsed from the establishment of a new Separate School, as compared with the whole average number of pupils attending† School in the same City, Town, Village, or Towhship: Provided always, that no Separate School shall be entitled to a share in any such fund unless the average number of pupils so attending the same be fifteen or more, (periods of epidemic, or contagious, disease excepted: *Provided, also, that nothing herein contained shall entitle any such Separate School within any City, Town, Village, or Township, to any part or portion of School moneys arising or accruing from local assessment for Common School purposes within any such City, Town, Village, or Township,* (a) *or the County, or Union of Counties, within which such Town, Village, or Township, is situate: Provided, also, that if any Separate School shall not have been in operation for a whole year at the time of the apportionment, it shall not receive the sum to which it would have been entitled for a whole year, but only an amount proportional to the time during which it has been kept open.*(b)

XIV. The Trustees of each Separate School shall, on or before the thirtieth day of June and the thirty-first day of December of each year, transmit to the Chief Superintendent of Schools for Upper Canada a correct statement of the names of the children attending such School, together with the average attendance during the six next preceding months, or during the number of months which may have elapsed since the establishment thereof, *and the number of months it shall have been so kept open,* (b) and the Chief Superintendent shall thereupon determine the proportion which the Trustees of such Separate Schools will be entitled to receive out of such Legislative Grant,‡ and shall pay over the amount thereof to such Trustees, and every such statement shall be verified under oath, before *any*

---

* After the word "Schools," the following words were struck out in the House of Assembly: "and in any fund arising from any other source whatsoever, set apart for Common School purposes."

† After the word "attending," the words, "the Common," were also struck out.

‡ After the word "grant," the words, "or other fund, as aforesaid, according to law," were struck out in the House of Assembly. The words, "any Justice of the Peace," were substituted for the words "the Judge of."

Justice of the Peace (b) for the County, or union of Counties, within which such Separate School is situate, by at least one of the Trustees making the same.

XV. But the election of any Trustee, or Trustees, made under this Act, shall become void, unless a Separate School be established under his, or their, management, within two months from the election of such Trustee, or Trustees.

XVI. And no person subscribing towards the support of a Separate School, or sending children thereto, shall be allowed to vote at the election of any Trustee of a Common School in the City, Town, Village, or Township, in which such Separate School is situate.

PASSAGE OF THE TACHÉ SEPARATE SCHOOL BILL, 1855.

Several amendments were made to the Bill, as I have shown, during its passage through the House of Assembly, and these amendments, [as noted in the Bill, on pages 95-100,] having been concurred in by the Legislative Council, the Bill received the Royal assent on the 30th of May, 1855.

Speaking of the passage of the Bill by the Legislature, at this time, Dr. Ryerson, in his fifth Letter to the Hon. George Brown, of the 31st of December, 1858, said :—

. . . It is of little consequence whether Members of the Opposition, or others, prevented the Bill from passing, as originally introduced. The School System of Upper Canada is equally the property of all parties, not of one party. . . . The Government, and the Catholic and French Members of the House, could not do otherwise than listen to the remonstrances of their own friends, and especially of Members of the Church of England, which the Bill, as introduced, was adapted to conciliate and favour. But, to the honour of the Church of England, and to the honour of Canada, and especially to the honour of the Gentlemen themselves, the Episcopalians stood forward as a phalanx against the seductions presented to them by the provisions of the Bill as introduced. . . . I feel it no less my duty than pleasure, to express my own gratitude, and, I believe, that of Upper Canada generally, to Messrs. Gamble, Stevenson, W. B. Robinson, Langton, and Crawford, for the earnest and noble stand they took on that occasion as champions of the unmutilated Common School System of Upper Canada. . .

In a private Letter to me in June, 1855, Dr. Ryerson said :—

NOTE.—The 18th Section, providing for a "large, beneficial and liberal construction" of the Act, was struck out as unnecessary in the House of Assembly. The original 7th Section, relating to Ward Schools, was also struck out; so that the number of Sections in the Act was reduced from eighteen to sixteen.

I met Mr. George Brown, M.P., on the boat this afternoon. He says that the Separate School Bill underwent various changes,—all to the disadvantage of the Supporters of Separate Schools;—that the Bill, as finally passed, was quite a different Bill from the original one which we have; that the substantial debate on the subject took place at the second reading of the Bill.

HAMILTON, 8th of June, 1855.   E. RYERSON.

SIR JOHN MACDONALD AND THE TACHÉ SEPARATE SCHOOL ACT.

Mr. Joseph Pope, in his "Memoirs of the Right Honourable Sir John Alexander Macdonald," thus refers to Sir John's proceedings in regard to the Taché Separate School Bill of 1855:—

Parliament, which had adjourned on the 18th of December, 1854, re-assembled in Quebec on the 23rd of February, 1855.

. . . A Measure was passed, (during the Session of 1855,) dealing with the School System of Upper Canada. The latter was introduced into the Assembly by Mr. Macdonald, who stated that the principle of the Bill was not new, for already, under the law, Separate Schools existed in both sections of the Province, so that the people would keep only, in a more acceptable form, that which they already had. Petitions, numerously signed in Upper Canada, had urged upon the Government and Legislature the necessity for a change.* The old law provided, that, if twelve householders petitioned for a Separate School, the Municipal Council was compelled to grant it. The Bill introduced by Mr. Macdonald enacted that five heads of families could establish a Separate School; that Trustees would be elected, precisely as before. The old law was retained to this extent, that Roman Catholics might set up a School in a Protestant community, or Protestants in a Roman Catholic community, or Jews, or Coloured people, in either;† but Protestants could not dissent from Protestants, nor Roman Catholics from Roman Catholics.

Mr. Macdonald said, that he was as desirous as any one of seeing all children going together to the Common Schools, and, if he could have his own way, there would be no Separate Schools. But we should respect the opinions of others who differed from us, and they had a right to refuse to accept such Schools as they could not conscientiously approve of. It was better to allow children to be taught at School such religious principles as their parents wished, so long as they learned, at the same time, to read

---

* The majority of the Petitions from Upper Canada was against, rather than for, the Separate School Bill.—J. G. H.

† All reference to "Jews, or Coloured people," was struck out of the Bill by the House of Assembly, (see page 96, *ante*).—J. G. H.

newspapers and books, and to become intelligent and useful citizens.—(*Vol. I., pages 137, 138.*)

In a subsequent part of the "Memoirs," Mr. Pope says:—

I have already shown what was Mr. Macdonald's position in regard to the question of Separate Schools. The following quotation, from one of his speeches, delivered about this time, presents his views on the subject very clearly:—

I have called the attention of the people to the fact that the 19th Clause of the Common School Act of 1850, became law long, long before I was in the Government at all; so that the merit of it, or the blame of it, is not with me, but rests entirely with the Baldwin-La Fontaine Administration, as it was brought in under the auspices of Mr. Baldwin, particularly,—that pure, and honest, man,—of whom I always love to speak, though we were opposed in politics. And, if it be asked: why we did not repeal it, I answer, in the first place, that it is one thing to give a right, or a franchise, and another thing to deprive people of it; and, in the second place, we have the indisputable evidence of a disinterested witness,—a man who cannot be suspected of any leaning towards Popery,—I mean, the Rev. Dr. Ryerson, a Protestant clergyman himself, at the head of the Common School System of Upper Canada,—a person whose whole energies have been expended in the cause of Education,—who states deliberately to the people of Canada, that the Separate School Clause does not retard the progress, or the increase, of Common Schools; but that, on the contrary, it "widens the basis of the Common School System." If I thought that it injured that System, I must say that I would vote for its repeal to-morrow.

You must remember, also, that Lower Canada is decidedly a Roman Catholic country:—that the Protestant population of Lower Canada is a small minority, and, if Protestant Schools were not allowed there, our Protestant brethren in Lower Canada would be obliged to send their children to be educated by Roman Catholic Teachers. Now, I don't know how many Protestants, or how many Roman Catholics, I may be at this moment addressing, but I say that, as a Protestant, I should not be willing to send my son to a Roman Catholic School, while I think a Roman Catholic should not be compelled to send his to a Protestant one.

In Lower Canada, the Teachers are generally the Roman Catholic Clergy, and, of course, it is their duty to teach what they consider truth, and to guard their pupils against error. But, the system in vogue there is more liberal than even ours, in that it not only permits the establishment of Protestant Schools for Protestant children, but allows the whole Municipal machinery to be employed to collect the rates to maintain them. In discussing this subject, I have always found that, when it is fairly laid before the people, they always, by their applause, signify their approbation of the consistent course of the Government in regard to it.—(*Pages 170, 171, and 172, Vol. I.*)

CHAPTER XIV.

PRIVATE AND CONFIDENTIAL CORRESPONDENCE RELATING TO THE PASSAGE OF THE SEPARATE SCHOOL ACT OF 1855.

1. *From the Hon. John A. Macdonald, Attorney-General, to Dr. Ryerson, Chief Superintendent of Education.*

I have this day given notice of the Bill to amend the law respecting Grammar and Common Schools. The Clause relating to . . . Separate Schools has been omitted. It is not yet decided whether that subject shall be touched during the present Session, or deferred until the meeting (of the Legislature) at Toronto, in February, 1856.

The Clauses relating to Vagrant Children have likewise been omitted, as I do not wish to insert any clause that might impede the passage of the Bill. [NOTE.—This subject was again dealt with in 1862. See the Church of England Separate School proceedings of that year, in a separate Chapter.—J. G. H.]

I think it is likely that we will send the Bill to a Special Committee, as you suggest. I shall have that settled in a day or two, when I will write to you, or, perhaps, send a telegram. If a Special Committee is struck, your testimony will undoubtedly be required. . . .

QUEBEC, 2nd of March, 1855. JOHN A. MACDONALD.

2. *Telegram from Dr. Ryerson to J. George Hodgins.*

Dr. Ryerson, having been summoned to Quebec, sent the following Telegram to me while there:—

Yours received. . . . All right about Separate Schools. . . . Prepare copies of all Correspondence with Supporters of Separate Schools since 1852.

QUEBEC, 2nd of April, 1855. E. RYERSON.

3. *Letter from Bishop Phelan, (as given on pages 296 and 297 of the " Life of Archbishop Lynch, by C. H. McKeown,") to the Hon. Attorney-General Macdonald, as follows:—*

Although you informed me in your last Letter that it is, and always was, your object to enable the (Roman) Catholics to educate their youth in their own way, it does not appear, however, at present, that you intend making, at this Session, any of the amendments in the present School Act which you required me to communicate in writing to you.* If this was the case, what was the use of asking me for my views on the subject of Separate Schools? I am aware of your difficulties on this point; the Chief Superintendent of Schools for Canada West, especially being opposed to any measure that would be favourable to our Separate Schools, and consequently determined to prevent, if possible, the amendments we require. But, I trust, that neither you nor the Ministry will be prevented from doing us justice by your allowing us the same rights and privileges for our Separate Schools as are granted to the Protestants of Lower Canada. If this be done at the present Session, we will have no reason to complain; and the odium thrown upon you of being controlled by Dr. Ryerson will be effectually removed. If, on the contrary, the voice of our opponent, [Dr. Ryerson,] upon this subject of Separate Schools, is more attended to and respected than the voice of the (Roman) Catholic Bishops, the Clergy, and nearly 200,000 of Her Majesty's loyal (Roman) Catholic subjects, claiming justice for the education of their youth, surely the Ministry that refuses us such rights cannot blame us for being displeased with them, and, consequently, for being determined to use every constitutional means to prevent their future return to Parliament. This, of course, will be the disagreeable alternative to which we shall be obliged to have recourse, if full justice be not done us at this Session, with regard to our Separate Schools.

KINGSTON, 16th of April, 1855.   + PATRICK PHELAN, Bp. of Carrhoe.

This Letter, the writer of the "Life of Archbishop Lynch" states, "was sent to the Attorney-General, (Hon. John A. Macdonald,) with the concurrence of the other two Bishops of Canada West,"—*i.e.*, of Toronto and Bytown.

It will be noticed that the tone of some of these Letters, chiefly those from the Bishops, and which refer either to Members of the Government, or to Dr. Ryerson, in 1853-1855, are singularly peremptory and menacing in their tone.

In the foregoing Letter, Bishop Phelan reproaches Attorney-General Macdonald with "being controlled by Dr. Ryerson,"

---

* The "amendments" to which Bishop Phelan here refers may be those contained in the "Draft of a School Bill for Upper Canada, prepared by the three Bishops of Kingston, Toronto, and Ottawa, and intituled: 'An Act to better define certain rights to parties therein mentioned,'" accompanied by a "Comparative Table of Legislation on Separate Schools in Upper and Lower Canada," (pages 85-87, *ante*.) No other measure of the kind appears to have been submitted by the Bishop at this time. That Bill of 1854 seems to have been again submitted to the Attorney-General in 1858, as mentioned to me, in a private Letter from Dr. Ryerson, dated the 30th of January, 1858, pages 121, 122, *post*.

and warns him that, "if the voice of" this, "our Opponent . . . is more attended to and respected than the voice of the Catholic Bishops, Clergy, and" people, . . . "every constitutional means" will be used "to prevent" the return of the Ministry "to Parliament." He also refers to the Chief Superintendent as being especially "opposed to any measure that would be favourable to Separate Schools, and, consequently, determined to prevent, if possible, the amendments we require."

Language of this kind seems strange, coming, as it did, from one who, from his position, would naturally insist on those "in authority under him" discharging their duty fearlessly and conscientiously; and yet, for doing so, as no one could question, both Attorney-General Macdonald and Chief Superintendent Ryerson are spoken to, and of, in this Letter, in a manner the very reverse of just, fair, or right, and with an assumption of the power to control their free action, which neither of them could either submit to, or acknowledge.*

4. *Letter from the Hon. John A. Macdonald to Dr. Ryerson:*

The press of business . . . prevented me from writing to you before. Your official Letter, dated the 2nd of April, arrived after the other papers relative to Separate Schools had been laid before the House. —[Page 87, *ante*.]

It is just as well, as the new (Separate School) Bill, while it pleased Dr. de Charbonnel, could do no harm; and it is just as well to avoid controversy on the subject.

I was pleased to learn, by your Telegram, that this new Bill, as limited to Roman Catholics, is better than the old Law. I stated so in the House, on your authority, and said, that "no one could doubt your devotion to the cause of Common Schools; and no one could fear your over-attachment to Sectarian Institutions." George Brown and John Langton were both obliged to admit that, with the amendments I consented to, the Bill was

---

* The testimony of Senator Scott, as given on page 60, *ante*, is in striking contrast with this language of Bishop Phelan. Mr. Scott, who had to do with Dr. Ryerson in difficult and delicate negotiations, and conferences, on the Separate School question, says that he "always found him ready to meet the wishes of the minority; that he exhibited no prejudice or bigotry. . . . The idea that the Chief Superintendent was not friendly to the Separate School System . . . was a mistake, because he was sincerely anxious to do what was really fair to make the [Separate School] Law workable.—(*Speech in the Senate in 1894.*)

PRIVATE AND CONFIDENTIAL CORRESPONDENCE.   105

quite innocent; and they only voted against the passage of the Bill, as a proof of their dislike to Separate Schools on any condition. So we have got well out of that difficulty.

(There was quite a combination of parties in the House against the junction of the Grammar and Common School Boards in Cities, Towns, etc.;* and so many remonstrances were made against it by Grammar School Trustees, that I was threatened with a good deal of difficulty from both sides of the House. As there was no pressing necessity for the change, and I did not want to risk my Bill, I struck out the clauses, and we got the Bill through without difficulty. When we meet in Toronto, next Winter, we can talk over the required improvements in the School Bills at our leisure.

(Your Tour in Europe will, doubtless, suggest to you many improvements in practice and theory, which you may want the Legislature to sanction. To-day I recommended your application for leave of absence to the favourable consideration of His Excellency. . . .

(With every wish that your proposed journey may set you up again, and enable you to continue your public services in the cause of Education with undiminished vigour. I am, etc.,)

QUEBEC, 5th of June, 1855. JOHN A. MACDONALD.

5. *From the Hon. John A. Macdonald to Dr. Ryerson:*—

Our Separate School Bill, which is as you know, quite harmless, passed with the approbation of our Friend, Bishop de Charbonnel, who, before leaving here, formally thanked the Administration for doing justice to his Church.

He has, however, got a new light since his return to Toronto, and now says that the Bill won't do. I need not point out to your suggestive mind, that, in any article written by you on the subject, it is politic to press two points on the attention of the public.

First. That the Bill will not injuriously affect the Common School System. (This for the people at large.)

Second. That the Separate School Bill of 1855 is a substantial boon to the Roman Catholics. (This is to keep them in good humor.)

You see that, if the Bishop makes the Roman Catholics believe that the Separate School Bill is of no use to them, there will be a renewal of the unwholesome agitation, which I thought was allayed. I send you the Bill as passed.

P.S.—I received your Telegram.

QUEBEC, 8th of June, 1855. JOHN A. MACDONALD.

---

* This paragraph of Sir John A. Macdonald's Letter is inserted on account of the recent revival of the question in the City of Toronto. Dr. Ryerson was so strongly opposed to the union of Grammar and Common School Boards, that he provided in a later Act for the severance of such unions.

In June, 1855, after the passage of the Taché Roman Catholic Separate School Bill, Dr. Ryerson left for Europe, to purchase articles for the Educational Museum, and to make arrangements in regard to the purchase of Books for the School Libraries.

6. *Letter from J. George Hodgins to Dr. Ryerson, (in England):*

I send you by mail six copies of the first part of the Correspondence on Separate Schools. . . . The *Catholic Citizen*, of this City, has, to-day, rather a weak article ridiculing Protestants for their opposition to the Roman Catholic Separate Schools, and holding Mr. George Brown and his friends responsible for the alterations made in the Bill. . . . The Editor says that the object of Roman Catholics, in asking for the measure, was "not so much to place (Roman) Catholics in an isolated position, in an educational point of view, as to separate them from an unchristian system of Education. . . .

The *Prescott Telegraph* has a Letter in it from the Rev. E. P. Roche, Roman Catholic Priest, to Mr. Wm. Patrick, M.P.P., in reply to his statement in the House of Assembly, that he (Roche) had asked him to vote for a Special Superintendent of the Roman Catholic Separate Schools. He denies it, and attacks Mr. Patrick with bitterness, and "the bloated bigot, Dr. Ryerson,"—"playing," (as he says you do,) "with admirable tact and dexterity, his borrowed literary apparatus to the metamorphosing of bad Catholics and good Protestants into most accomplished Yankee 'know-nothings.'" I quote these extracts only to show you that another storm is likely brewing.

The *Toronto Examiner*, of yesterday, says that it is likely you have gone to Europe to "try and induce the Roman Catholics there to relax their opposition to public Education in Canada!" This paper is now apparently under Mr. W. L. Mackenzie's control.

Toronto, 28th of June, 1855. J. George Hodgins.

7. *From J. George Hodgins to Dr. Ryerson, (in England):—*

I have sent to Attorney-General Macdonald your Circular to Roman Catholic School Trustees,* and the forms prescribed under the authority of

---

* The following are the only parts of this Circular which refers to the general question of Roman Catholic Separate Schools:

You will herewith receive a copy of "An Act to amend the Laws relating to Roman Catholic Separate Schools in Upper Canada." For the provisions of this Act, I am not entitled to either praise or blame, as I never saw it until it appeared in print, after its introduction into the Legislature.

1. I have ever believed and maintained that the provisions of the law, as previously existing in respect to Separate Schools, were conceived in a kindly feeling, and were equitable and liberal. I am so persuaded still. But these provisions of the law having been complained of by Bishops of the Roman

the Roman Catholic Separate School Act of 1855. He acknowledged them on the 2nd instant, as follows:

"QUEBEC, 30th of July, 1855.—DEAR SIR,—Absence from Quebec has prevented me from answering your favour before. I am obliged for the forms for the Separate Schools, which seem well adapted for the purpose intended. The Circular to the Trustees of Separate Schools is very satisfactory. I am, etc.,—JOHN A. MACDONALD."

The published correspondence in regard to Separate Schools, has elicited no remarks from the press, so far as I have seen, except in the case of the *Hamilton Gazette.* I send the extract to you.

TORONTO, 4th of August, 1855.   J. GEORGE HODGINS.

8. *From J. George Hodgins to Dr. Ryerson, (in England):—*

I have had the form of Annual Report of the Roman Catholic Separate School Trustees to the Local Superintendent of Schools made out. I had a good deal of doubt on the subject, particularly as you yourself seemed undecided in the matter. At all events, it will test the point, as to whether these Trustees are under the same obligations, as to reporting, as are the Common School Trustees; and I think it well to maintain the right of the Local Superintendent to exercise a supervision over Separate, as over Common, Schools. I have quoted the authority,—for making the report,—to the Local Superintendent, from the Roman Catholic Separate School Act of last Session. The Departmental Regulations on the subject are absolutely necessary,—as our experience has proved to us this summer and autumn. . . . The Roman Catholic Separate School Trustees at Kingston and Belleville seem disposed not to give us the return of daily attendance of pupils at their Schools, and it is on that attendance the apportionment to these Schools is based. They make objections to do so.

In his Letter to me of the 30th of July last, [see above,] the Attorney-General approved of the forms for Roman Catholic Separate Schools.

TORONTO, 31st December, 1855.   J. GEORGE HODGINS.

Catholic Church, the new Separate School Act is the result,—an Act which confers upon members of the Roman Catholic persuasion, powers and distinctions which are not possessed by any class of Protestants in Upper Canada, and which their own Representatives would never consent to confer upon them.

2. While in our Public Schools, the religious rights and faith of pupils of all persuasions are equally protected, and while I am persuaded of the Superior advantages of those Schools in respect to both economy and all the appliances of instruction, I shall, on this very account, in addition to the obligations of official duty, do all in my power to lessen the disadvantages of those who prefer Separate Schools, and secure to them every right and advantage which the Separate School Act confers.—(*Circular, dated 15th June, 1855.*)

CHAPTER XV.

EFFECT OF THE CHARBONNEL SEPARATE SCHOOL CONTROVERSY UPON LOWER CANADIANS—NOVA SCOTIA.

AMONG the many private Letters left with me by Dr. Ryerson, is one from Mr. E. Goff Penny, of the Montreal *Herald*, (subsequently a Senator,) dated the 13th of August, 1855, and endorsed by Dr. Ryerson as : *"On the effect of the Controversy with Bishop de Charbonnel upon the Minds of French Canadians."* It is as follows :—

Having this day received from Quebec a copy of the first part of some Correspondence between yourself and Bishop de Charbonnel, I was reminded of a conversation which lately took place between myself and a Canadian friend of mine, which I think it may gratify you to read an account of.

As I know, to some extent, what are the discomforts of maintaining and exercising an opinion for oneself, and what is the satisfaction at finding that a promulgation of opinion has had its effect in a quarter, or quarters, where we supposed it impossible to make any impression, I have taken the liberty, though our acquaintance is slight, to write you a line on the subject.

My friend is a highly respectable bourgeois of Longueuil,—a man who has been engaged in business . . . but is now living upon his means. . . . He has no children ; can speak no English ; can read and write . . . and makes himself acquainted with the current events of the day, as detailed in *La Minerve*, and lately in *Le Pays*. For the rest, a person of extremely strong, unprejudiced mind, and, as far as I know, not at all affected by Protestantism, except in so far as he has no ill-feeling towards, and has considerable regard for, some of its professors. We were conversing about the local School of the Village, when he suddenly dropped the subject, by saying : "There is one man in Upper Canada whose talents I esteem above those of any other man in the Country." I asked who he spoke of. "Oh," said he, "M. Chef Surintendant Ryerson." I could not at first understand how he had acquired this high opinion of you, inasmuch as I thought it not very probable that he could have seen many of your writings. But he soon told me that his opinion was founded upon your controversy with Bishop de Charbonnel, some two or three years ago. He said that the Bishop was, in his opinion, completely confuted. But, he added, what perhaps was not quite so complimentary to you as the other portions of his discourse: "What surprises me most, is how a man, who has the reputation which Count de Charbonnel gained here, could possibly expose himself openly to be reproved for misrepresentation, and, throughout the correspondence, could exhibit such poor powers of reasoning, joined with so much ill-temper."

I said to him that the *Minerve* would never have translated the Correspondence if its effect had been anticipated,—at least if it had been anticipated that the effect it had had upon him would be general. He laughed, and said: "Oh, it was very *gauche* on their part; but some of them are so foolish that they cannot see the plainest folly, if it only come from a Bishop."

I do not think my friend very different from scores of quiet, intelligent Canadians, a little above the class of *habitants* throughout the country, so that the translation of your Correspondence, meant, of course, to damage you with the Lower Canadians, may have really had a very different effect among minds of that class, which eventually influences public opinion.

"HERALD OFFICE," MONTREAL,   E. GOFF PENNY.
13th of August, 1855.

The Hon. B. Wier, in introducing to Dr. Ryerson Mr. William Annand, M.P.P., and Editor of *The Nova Scotian*, Halifax, by Letter, added the following:—

The great question of popular Education is now exciting the minds of the people of Nova Scotia. And it seems to many of us quite impossible to overcome the difficulties and prejudices which meet us from every quarter,—more particularly with reference to the Roman Catholic portion of our people. I do not know of anyone in the Provinces so well calculated as yourself to advise a course calculated to meet the difficulty, as you have had many years' experience, and have given your time and great talents almost exclusively to the subject. We failed to carry an Assessment Bill last summer, but still hope that, during the recess, some plan may be devised to meet the obstructions which beset us. . . .

Mr. Annand will confer with you on the general subject.
HALIFAX, 8th of May, 1856.   B. WIER.

CHAPTER XVI.

RENEWED CONTROVERSY—THE BOWES' SEPARATE SCHOOL BILL, 1856.

As intimated by the Hon. John A. Macdonald, in his private Letter to Dr. Ryerson, of the 8th of June, 1855, the "new light," which, in that Letter, is spoken of, seems to have shed its power of illumination on the mind of Mr. John G. Bowes, Mayor of the City of Toronto, and also its M.P. In the Session of 1856, he introduced a Bill into the Legislature to modify the twelfth Section of the Taché Separate School Act of 1855. Dr. Ryerson was absent, in Europe, at the time, The following Letters were, therefore, addressed to him there :—

1. *Letter from J. George Hodgins to Dr. Ryerson, (in Europe):*

Mr. John G. Bowes, Mayor of Toronto, and a Member of the House of Assembly, has given notice of a Bill to modify already the Roman Catholic Separate School Act of last Session ! I do not know the nature of the Bill, but I hear that one modification proposed is to give the power of dispensation from payment of a Separate School tax into the hands of the Separate School Trustees,—that their certificate will be sufficient to exempt the parties holding it from School taxation. . . . I send you a copy of the remarks made by Mr. Bowes, in introducing his Bill. You will see also, from the enclosed, that the Hon. G. E. Cartier has made the explanatory remarks, which he promised me he would make. . . . I send you a copy of my last Letter to *The Mirror*, (Roman Catholic organ.) I trust that it will lead to a stop being put to letter writing in that paper on the part of dissatisfied Separate School parties.

TORONTO, 23rd of February, 1856.   J. GEORGE HODGINS.

The Bill, which Mr. Bowes introduced into the Legislature, was as follows :—

1. The Twelfth Section [of the Separate School Act of 1855] shall be, and is hereby, repealed.*

---

* This "twelfth Section" of the Separate School Act of 1855, will be found on page 97, *ante.*

2. Notwithstanding anything in the above-named Act, or in any other School Act, or Acts, to the contrary, every person paying rates, whether, as proprietor, or tenant, who, when required to pay his School Taxes, or Rates, shall present to the Collector a certificate, in duplicate, from the Secretary-Treasurer of the Trustees, or of any Board of Trustees, of any Roman Catholic Separate School, or Schools, that he has paid all School Rates, or Taxes, required by such Trustees, or Board, for the then current year, shall be exempted from the payment of all Rates, or Taxes, imposed for the building, or the support, of Common Schools, or Common School Libraries, for the same year ; and it shall be the duty of such Collector to retain one of the above-named certificates, and sign his name to the other, to be returned by him to the ratepayer.

2. *Letter from J. George Hodgins to Dr. Ryerson, (in Europe)*.

Mr. Joseph Hartman, M.P. for (North) York, was here to-day. He told me that the Bowes' Separate School Bill will come on in two or three days ;— that Mr. Bowes will not move that it be read, but that some one else in the House will do so, whom Mr. Bowes did not name, but that he (Mr. Bowes) will support it, and that, with Lower Canada influence, it may pass. He thinks that the editorial article in *The Mirror*, which I sent to you, is indicative of a plot which is on the *tapis* ;—that the policy of the Lower Canada Members of the Cabinet is to drive you from office ; that the School Bill which you sent to Attorney-General, (Hon. John A. Macdonald,) would have been introduced long before this only for the opposition of John A.'s Lower Canada Colleagues, and that they will not consent to its introduction. Now, therefore, is the time to stand firm, and not be driven, or cajoled, or checkmated, in this matter.

I suggested to Mr. Hartman, that it might be well for him to move for a Return of all Petitions on the Separate School question which have been presented to the Legislature, with a view to concentrate in one point all the sentiments of the Country on that subject.

TORONTO, 7th of July, 1856.   J. GEORGE HODGINS.

DR. RYERSON'S HISTORY OF THE BOWES SEPARATE SCHOOL BILL.

In his fifth Letter to the Hon. George Brown, of December 31st, 1858, (already quoted,) Dr. Ryerson thus continues his narrative of the efforts made to promote Separate School Legislation in 1856 : —

After the close of that Session of 1855, I left for Europe, and did not return until an advanced period of the next Session of the Legislature, at Toronto, when I learned that Mr. Bowes had introduced a short Bill, prefessedly to amend the twelfth Section of the Taché Roman Catholic

Separate School Act of 1855, but which, in reality, would have involved the subversion of our whole Common School System; though I do not think Mr. Bowes, (and perhaps few others,) had any idea of the scope and effect of the ingenious Bill which had been put into his hands, as he withdrew it, shortly after I pointed out to him its real character. A private Member, bringing in such a Bill, shows that the Government would not do anything on the subject; and, on my first conversations with Upper Canada Members of the Government, after my return from Europe, I learned that they intended to vote against Mr. Bowes' Bill, which they afterwards did, (when it was taken up by a Lower Canada Member,) and, for doing which, the Roman Catholic Members of the Government, and others, were denounced and excommunicated by Bishop de Charbonnel,—who thus employed the highest power of the priesthood to control Upper Canada School Legislation and Government. . . .

After the failure of Mr. Bowes' Bill in the Session of 1855, it was officially announced in the public papers, by Roman Catholic Episcopal authority, that that Bill would be brought up again, and presented at the next Session of Parliament. In view of that announcement and threat, I analyzed the Bill in my Report for 1855, and exposed its unjust and dangerous provisions to the public, as also the course of aggression which had been pursued against the people of Upper Canada by the extreme advocates of Separate Schools. It was in that connection, and with a view to such threatened agitation and aggression, that I said in my Annual Report for 1855, (written in 1856):—

But, if the parties, for whom Separate Schools are allowed and aided out of the Legislative School Grants, according to the average attendance of pupils, (which is the principle of distributing the School Grant among the Common Schools in all the Townships of Upper Canada,) shall renew the agitation upon the subject, and assail and seek to subvert the Public School System, as they have done, and endeavour to force legislation upon that subject, against the voice and rights of the people of Upper Canada, by votes from Lower Canada, and the highest terrors of ecclesiastical authority, then I submit that the true and only alternative will be to abolish Separate Schools altogether, and substitute the provisions of the National System in Ireland, in regard to united, secular, and separate religious, instruction, and extend it to Lower, as well as to Upper, Canada.— (*Annual Report for 1855, page 11.*)

A difficulty having arisen with the Trustees of the Kingston Roman Catholic Separate Schools, in regard to their returns of the attendance of pupils at the Separate Schools there, Bishop Phelan wrote to Bishop de Charbonnel on the subject, as stated on page 298 of the "Life of Archbishop Lynch, by C. H. McKeown," as follows:—

I see that Dr. Ryerson gives his own interpretation to our new School Bill, [the Taché Bill of 1855,] stating that the amendment of 1851 is repealed; but it is our Attorney-General's opinion that it is not repealed. The Doctor reads in our daily reports, the "daily attendance," instead of the "average attendance." Now our Solicitor-General, Mr. H. Smith, has blotted out the word "daily," and authorizes the Rev. Mr. Dollard to hold to this.*

KINGSTON, 11th of July, 1856.   + PATRICK PHELAN, Bp. of Carrhoe.

CHAPTER XVII.

THE BRUYÈRE-PINSONEAULT-DALLAS CONTROVERSY.

THE years 1856, 1857, and 1858 were among the most memorable in the history of Roman Catholic Separate Schools in Upper Canada,—not, by any means, for what was done in regard to them, but for what was said, by those who were the Representative champions of the cause,—*pro* and *con*.

I have already pointed out, (on page 42,) what was the character of the prolonged agitation, founded upon an unnecessary misconception of facts, in regard to the Roman Catholic Separate Schools, which was commenced by the Rev. J. M. Bruyère, (then Rector of St. Michael's Cathedral, Toronto,) in December, 1856, and was closed by Bishop Pinsoneault,—who entirely endorsed the Rev. Mr. Bruyère's proceedings,—in February, 1857.†

---

* I personally had to deal with this matter during Dr. Ryerson's absence in Europe. In my Letter to him in January, 1856, I said: "I have a reference from the Government in regard to the Rev. P. Dollard, of Kingston, and my refusal to accept the Returns of attendance at the Separate Schools there. I think I have explained matters satisfactorily to the Government." See also the last paragraph of my Letter to Dr. Ryerson, of the 31st of December, 1855, on page 107, *ante*.

† In a Letter to the Rev. J. M. Bruyère, dated the 10th of February, 1857, Bishop Pinsoneault thus addressed him:—"Concerning what you have said about Public Libraries, the question is not whether you were right or wrong, with regard to the exact number of Catholic books said to be on their shelves, but whether you had good ground for denouncing them as dangerous to faith and morals. Now, most emphatically do I endorse your sound views on this question, for we can hardly be less opposed to mixed Libraries than to mixed Education,—the same principles of faith and morals being equally involved in both systems."

One of Mr. Bruyère's objections to Dr. Ryerson's Public School Library scheme, (which was the cause of this attack upon him,) is thus stated, and replied to, by Dr. Ryerson :—

Mr. Bruyère's statement in regard to books in the Official Catalogue for Public Libraries are unfounded and contrary to fact. While he exclaims against the Histories of "infidel Hume and the sceptical Gibbon," he ought to know that neither of these works is in the "Index Expurgatorius," while Archbishop Whately's Logic and Macaulay's History are thus distinguished. He says, "D'Aubigné's History of the Reformation" is in the Catalogue,—which is not the fact. He says there is no such book in the Catalogue as "Cardinal Wiseman's Lectures,"—whereas "Cardinal Wiseman's Lectures on the Connection between Science and Revealed Religion" are on the Official Catalogue, and also Bossuet's Universal History. Mr. Bruyère likewise says, "in vain will we look in these Public Libraries for Lingard's Anglo-Saxon Church ; Gahan's Church History ; History of the Church by Reeve," when the titles of each of these three Histories are printed in the Official Catalogue ; as is also that of Lingard's History of England ; Mylius' History of England ; Fredet's Ancient History, and Fredet's Modern History !

BISHOP DE CHARBONNEL HIMSELF SELECTED ROMAN CATHOLIC BOOKS, IN 1853.

These works were inserted in the Catalogue three years ago, on the recommendation of Bishop de Charbonnel, to whom was communicated the wish of the Council of Public Instruction that he would select the Roman Catholic Histories he judged best, as the Council, on the disputed ground of civil and ecclesiastical history, intended to select a certain number of standard works on each—leaving it to what Mr. Bruyère himself calls the "good sense, honesty, and liberality of the Municipalities in Upper Canada," to procure which they might please ; and most of them have made a fair selection of Histories from both sides.

CARDINAL WISEMAN WAS ALSO CONSULTED ABOUT BOOKS IN 1851.

Nay, when in London in 1851, making selections of Library Books for examination, and arrangements for procuring them, I had, (on the strength of a letter of introduction from a high quarter,) an interview with Cardinal Wiseman, to whom I briefly explained the principles on which I proposed to promote the establishment of Public School Libraries in Upper Canada, —the avoidance of doctrinal and controversial works of any religious persuasion, as between Protestants and Roman Catholics, and the selection of the best popular works in all the departments of human knowledge, and I wished His Eminence to favour me with a list of books and their publishers, such as were approved by his Church and in harmony with the character and objects of the proposed Canadian Libraries. Cardinal Wiseman frankly replied, that nearly all the books printed and sold by Catholic publishers, were doctrinal expositions and vindications of the Roman Catholic Church, or such as related to questions between Catholics and Protestants, and, therefore, not adapted to the non-controversial and non-denominational Libraries I proposed to establish. Yet, after this, I applied to Bishop Charbonnel, . . . and inserted in the Catalogue every historical library book recommended by him, and more than the histories enumerated by Mr. Bruyère. Thus, throughout, have I pursued a fair, a kind and generous course towards Roman Catholics, and have treated them with a consideration which has not been shown to any Protestant denomination.

During the Separate School controversies of these years, three noted Pamphlets were issued, bearing on the question, including one by Mr. Angus Dallas,—a Merchant in Toronto,—under the signature of "A Protestant," in 1857, and others. The primary cause of this new movement and agitation was the issue of a Lenten Pastoral by Bishop de Charbonnel, in 1856.

SUMMARIES OF THE SEPARATE SCHOOL DISCUSSIONS, 1856-1858.

After the passage of the Taché Roman Catholic Separate School Act of 1855, there was a lull in the Separate School controversy for a time; but the issue of Bishop de Charbonnel's Lenten Pastoral, in 1856, had the effect of sounding again the tocsin of war. The Letters of the belligerents, which had, during the preceding years, been published, chiefly in the newspapers, were, in 1857,—forty years ago,—collected together into three separate pamphlets. The following titles of these pamphlets give a practical historical view of the whole controversy, and are, in fact, a literary curiosity in a way. These titles are as follows:—

1. Dr. Ryerson's Letters in reply to the attacks of Foreign Ecclesiastics against the Schools and Municipalities of Upper Canada,—including the Letters of Bishop de Charbonnel, Mr. Bruyère and Bishop Pinsoneault,—104 pages.

(NOTE.—In a prefatory word "to the Reader," in this Pamphlet, it is stated that "none of (the Authors) have been consulted; and none of them . . . are aware of the present publication,—certainly, Dr. Ryerson is not.")

2. Controversy between Dr. Ryerson, Chief Superintendent of Education in Upper Canada, and Rev. J. M. Bruyère, Rector of St. Michael's

Cathedral, Toronto, on the Clergy Reserves Funds; Free Schools *vs.* State Schools; Public Libraries and Common Schools, Attacked and Defended. Rev. J. M. Bruyère for the Prosecution; Dr. Ryerson for the Defence. To which is appended a Letter from the Right Reverend Dr. Pinsoneault, of London, C.W., to the Rev. J. M. Bruyère, on the Subject of the late Controversy with Dr. Ryerson,—108 pages.

(NOTE.—In the Introduction to this Pamphlet, it is stated that "Dr. Ryerson declined . . . to accept the invitation to join in the publication of this Correspondence; and Rev. M. Bruyère was induced to assume the whole charge of the publication."

3. Statistics of the Common Schools: Being a Digest and Comparison of the Evidence furnished by the Local Superintendents and the Chief Superintendent in their Reports for 1855, with suggestions applicable to the approaching Crisis. In a series of Seven Letters to the Honourable John A. Macdonald. By A Protestant,—56 pages.

Appended to this Pamphlet was a second one, of 23 pages, with this title:—

Suggestions on the organization of a System of Common Schools, adapted to the Circumstances and State of Society in Canada: Being a series of Three Letters addressed to the Honourable John A. Macdonald. By A Protestant,—total, 79 pages.

This Pamphlet was written by Mr. Angus Dallas,[*] in 1857. In 1858, he published a fourth Pamphlet, entitled: an "Appeal on the Common School Law; its Incongruity and Maladministration," etc.,—32 pages. Mr. Dallas was a man of a literary turn, but a legislative theorist, in matters of education.

These various Pamphlets, and those relating to the Roman Catholic Separate Schools, officially prepared by Dr. Ryerson, and printed by order of the House of Assembly, in 1855 and 1858, show what a state of educational unrest existed in Upper Canada at the time. It culminated in the determined, yet abortive, efforts, for the time, which were put forth by the Representatives of the Roman Catholic Church, in 1860, 1861, and 1862, to get a Separate School Bill passed by the Legislature.

---

[*] Appended to the Comparative Table, (prepared by the three Roman Catholic Bishops,) on pages 82, 83, *ante*, is this *Note:* "For further particulars, see the Pamphlet of Angus Dallas, just published, entitled, "The Common School System; its Principles, Operation and Results." This Pamphlet was published by Mr. Dallas in 1855.

CHAPTER XVIII.

RENEWED EFFORTS TO PROMOTE SEPARATE SCHOOL LEGISLATION, 1857-1860.

In 1857, one of the most active lay promoters of Separate Schools in Toronto, and of the Legislation of 1860-62, 63, (Hon. John Elmsley,) wrote a "confidential" Letter to Dr. Ryerson, of nearly ten foolscap pages, urging him to refer—

> The whole of the Separate School question, from beginning to end, to a Select Committee of the Legislative Assembly, . . . and to pursue that proposal until [he had] succeeded in calling the attention of the Legislature to this most important subject.

Mr. Elmsley then makes the following appeal to Dr. Ryerson, as Chief Superintendent, to comply with his request. He said:

> Your position will enable you, if you press the proposition for enquiry before a Select Committee of the House of Assembly with vigour and earnest sincerity, to obtain that most desirable end. The present Administration [Macdonald-Cartier] are, I am well aware, most unwilling to face the difficulties of this grave subject; but when the demand for investigation comes from the Chief Superintendent of Education, it cannot be withheld. Forward! then, my dear Sir, be not deterred by seeming obstacles; they must all vanish before your steady and sturdy purpose of finally obtaining your wishes.
>
> You have publicly thrown down the gauntlet; the friends of Separate Schools have caught it up, and now challenge you to the combat,—the combat of dispassionate argument,—the battle of cool investigation.
>
> Should the House of Assembly grant such a boon, you would, of course, be prepared to sustain your position by all legitimate means at your disposal.
>
> On the other hand, the friends of Separate Schools would not be behind in stating very forcibly all the grounds upon which they base their dissatisfaction with the School Laws, as they now subsist, and . . . would endeavour to counteract the effects of your Annual Reports to the Governor-General. . . .

Mr. Elmsley then goes on to say:—

> I enclose for your consideration the Draft of a Bill, which may be presented to the Legislature this Session. I have submitted it to the proper authorities placed in charge of our Separate Schools; and now await either their action, or their refusal to act, if it should be considered inexpedient to move in the matter this year. . . .
>
> This Draft of Bill comprises all Religious Denominations recognized by Law in Upper Canada. . . . We can have no kind of objection to the Law being limited to ourselves, and by the substitution of the words, "Roman Catholic," for the words, "Religious Denominations," this limitation can be very easily effected.

Among Dr. Ryerson's papers, (in my possession,) together with this "confidential" Letter from Mr. Elmsley, were two Drafts of a Separate School Bill. They have neither name nor date on them. This one Draft is headed:—

> Rough Draft of a Bill to be entitled: An Act to Repeal the Laws relating to Separate Schools, and to authorize the establishment of Schools by any of the Religious Denominations recognized by Law in Upper Canada.

This Draft had evidently been subjected to a good deal of revision by some party, or parties, for, after revision, it was reprinted, under the title of a—

> Draft of Bill, entitled: An Act to repeal the Laws respecting Separate Schools, so far as they relate to Roman Catholics, and to authorize the establishment of Schools by Roman Catholics in Upper Canada.

Twelve is the number of Sections in both Drafts of Bill, but they are very much enlarged and altered in the revised copy.

CHAPTER XIX.

CONFIDENTIAL REPORT TO THE GOVERNOR-GENERAL ON THE SEPARATE SCHOOL QUESTION IN 1858.

The belligerent character of the discussion on Separate Schools, during these last three years, (1856-1858,) no doubt induced the Governor-General, (Sir Edmund Head,) to send a confiden-

Confidential Report on Separate Schools. 119

tial Memorandum to Dr. Ryerson, in which he enumerated a number of points in regard to the Separate School question, on which he desired specific and detailed information from the Chief Superintendent. In asking for this information, Dr. Ryerson was informed that,—

His Excellency wishes it to be understood that he makes these enquiries simply for his own information, and without implying that there is any probability of change in the existing Separate School Law.

Dr. Ryerson's confidential Report to the Governor-General on the Separate School question, extends to twenty-three foolscap pages. I only give those portions of it which are not already, in substance, contained in this History. In the first part of his confidential Report he said:—

As to the actual state of the Law in Upper and Lower Canada, in regard to Separate Schools, I append a Paper, which was prepared by Mr. J. G. Hodgins, the Deputy Superintendent of Education, and printed in 1856, containing, in parallel columns, the provisions of the respective Laws in Upper and Lower Canada on Separate Schools, with notes in the margin, showing the points of agreement and difference in the provisions of the Law in each section of the Province.*

On examining this comparative view of the provisions of the Law in both sections of Canada, it will be seen that the advantage, upon the whole, is on the side of the Roman Catholics of Upper Canada. The School Laws of Upper Canada secure a protection, in religious matters, in the Public Schools that the School Law of Lower Canada does not secure to the Protestants ; nor are the Roman Catholics of Upper Canada required to express any dissatisfaction with the proceedings of the Public School Trustees, in order to be entitled to establish Separate Schools, as are the Protestants of Lower Canada. . . .

It is worthy of remark that, on the passing of each of the three Acts, (1850, 1853, and 1855,) amending the Law in regard to Separate Schools, the Roman Catholic Bishop of Toronto and the Upper Canada Roman Catholic newspaper organs expressed their entire satisfaction with them, (at the time,) but afterwards complained of them, when it was found that they did not accomplish the object predicted at the time of their enactment by some of these newspapers,—namely, "that they would deal a death-blow to the State School System." . . .

It may be asked, why is it that the provisions of the School Law, in

---

* This Comparative Table is too extensive to be inserted here. It is printed as Appendix "A," (pages 56-68,) to the "Special Report on the Separate School Provisions of the School Law of Upper Canada," etc. Printed by Order of the Legislative Assembly, 1858.

regard to Dissentients, operate so much more successfully in Lower, than in Upper, Canada ? I answer— . . .

1. It is not the wish of the Protestant inhabitants of Lower Canada to overthrow a National School System, as is avowed by the leading Roman Catholic advocates of Separate Schools in Upper Canada.

2. The supporters of Dissentient Schools in Lower Canada are, as a whole, more intelligent and more wealthy, and know better how to proceed and manage their affairs than the supporters of Separate Schools in the rural parts of Upper Canada. . . .

3. The cordial co-operation of the first Roman Catholic Bishop of Toronto, (the Right Reverend Michael Power, D.D.,) in support of the Public Schools,—before the introduction of the new counsels and feelings against them,—the greater resources, conveniences, cheapness and efficiency of the Public, over the Separate, Schools, the equal protection of the religious scruples and rights of all classes of pupils in the Public Schools, instead of their being Denominational, as they are, for the most part, in Lower Canada,—the serious disadvantage which Roman Catholics experience, and inflict upon their children, by isolating them from other classes of youth in their intellectual training and social intercourse, are all circumstances and considerations unfavourable to Separate Schools, . . . and weigh strongly with a large proportion of the most intelligent Roman Catholics. . . .

The existence of the provisions, (for Separate Schools,) at all, is clearly against the feelings of the great majority of the people of Upper Canada ; and it has been considered by numbers of most intelligent persons as inconsistent with, and dangerous to, the stability of a National System of Education. But I combated these apprehensions, . . . so that there was no agitation on the subject, when Bishop de Charbonnel, in 1852, and, after him, other Roman Catholic Clergy and their newspapers, commenced an attack upon our whole School System, . . . and demanded that the Roman Catholics, as a body, should be incorporated into a Separate organization, and receive Legislative School Grants and Municipal School Funds, according to their numbers, with a [Provincial Roman Catholic] Superintendent from among themselves,—thus claiming absolutely a large portion of Public and Municipal Revenue and local corporate powers of a vast extent, as an endowment for the exclusive teaching of the Roman Catholic Church,—a thing never mooted in respect to the Protestants of Lower Canada,—never heard of in any free country, and subversive of the right of individual liberty and choice among the Roman Catholics, and inconsistent with the rights of Municipalities, and of individual property among the Protestants. . . .

It is this double aggression by Roman Catholic Bishops and their supporters, in assailing, on the one hand, our Public Schools and School System, and invading what has been acknowledged as sacred constitutional rights of individuals and Municipalities ; and, on the other hand, in demanding the erection and support, at the public expense, of a Roman Catholic Hierarchical School System, which has aroused, to so great an extent, the people of Upper Canada against permitting the continuance any longer of the provisions of the Law for Separate Schools.

And it must be acknowledged that a combined secular, with separate religious instruction, is the only safe, just, and defensible system of National Education. . . .

In conclusion, I beg to add a word as to the interference of parties in Lower Canada with the School System of Upper Canada. . . . The feelings, habits, municipal and other institutions, of the inhabitants in each Province has been equally and exclusively consulted in their construction and development. . . .

There has been no interference in Upper Canada with the School System of Lower Canada, which has been framed and carried into effect in accordance with the wishes of the inhabitants there, and of their Representatives in Parliament.

I deprecate the interference of Bishops and Priests in Lower Canada, or of their Representatives, . . . (as has been already experienced,) with the School System of Upper Canada,—the wishes of whose inhabitants and their Representatives are entitled to no less consideration than those of Lower Canada, especially when the fundamental principle of our School System is equal and impartial protection to all Religious Persuasions, and equal educational advantages for all.

TORONTO, January, 1858.   EGERTON RYERSON.

In connection with this Report, Dr. Ryerson was summoned to Quebec by Sir Edmund Head. While there, I received from him the following confidential Letter, in regard to his visit:—

1. *Letter from Dr. Ryerson, (Quebec,) to J. George Hodgins:—*

(*Confidential.*)—I was desired to come here by the Governor-General's direction, on the Separate School business. The Roman Catholic Bishops, (Dr. Charbonnel is here,) are "moving heaven and earth" to get a Separate School Bill passed this Session ; and the Upper Canada Members of the Government are determined, if possible, to prevent anything being done on the subject until Parliament goes to Toronto.

The enclosed papers have been printed and distributed among the greater part of the Members of the Legislature. They are signed by the Roman Catholic Bishops of Toronto, Kingston, and Bytown, declaring that nothing short of the adoption of the "project" of the accompanying Bill will satisfy the conscientious convictions of (the Roman) Catholics.*

---

* From this description of the "Papers printed and distributed among the Members" of the Legislature, it would appear that they are identical with those which were presented to the Government by the three Bishops named, in 1855, and which will be found on pages 81–83 of this volume.

I am glad that they have thus committed themselves to a simple dictation as to what they really demand,—which, you will see, is an absolute control of all the taxable property of all classes of the inhabitants of Upper Canada.

I, this morning, pointed out to Attorney-General John A. Macdonald, the falsity of each particular of the accompanying comparison between the School Laws of Upper and Lower Canada, when he said they were really "frivolous, when not untrue." He was to propose to Messrs. Drummond, Cauchon, and Cartier to meet me on the same subject. I have not yet learned whether they will do so, or no.

I have insisted that all the Correspondence which I have had with parties on Separate Schools, since the 1st of January, 1853, should be laid before the House; and the Governor-General, (Sir Edmund Head,) thought it very desirable. Mr. Joseph Hartman has given a notice of a motion to that effect. I hope that you will have it prepared as soon as possible,—including everything that has passed between complaining parties and other parties and me, including my Letter [of 1854] to Bishop de Charbonnel, published in the newspaper some months since. I intend also to include in the Return the enclosed Statement, (and Draft of Blll,) with refutations of it. You can make notes on it, as it will facilitate my doing so when I get back. . . . There is a strong desire on the part of the Representatives of the English part of Lower Canada to be annexed to Upper Canada in their School System. Sir Edmund Head is very anxious for it. He highly approved of my Report on the "New Brunswick College Question;" and has sent it to the authorities of McGill College, to see if they cannot adopt something of the same kind.*

Hon. William Cayley, (Inspector-General,) has admitted to-night that I am right about the division of the Common School Grant of £50,000, between Upper and Lower Canada. Lower Canada now gets £29,000, and Upper Canada £21,000. We had a laughable discussion in regard to it, and referred the question of the interpretation of the forty-first Section of the Upper Canada Common School Act of 1850 to Judge Badgely, who had come in; and he, on Mr. Cayley's own statement of the abstract question, (putting his hand on my mouth, and not letting me state the case,) decided in my favour, as to both the £50,000 Grant, and any succeeding Grant for Common School purposes. I also found in Dr. Meilleur's School Report for Lower Canada, that he stated the same thing as I had in regard to the division of the former Grants. I showed it to Sir Edmund

---

* In August, 1854, Sir Edmund Head, then Lieutenant-Governor of New Brunswick, appointed Dr. Ryerson, with Hon. J. H. Gray, (Chairman,) Mr. (now Sir William) Dawson, (then of Nova Scotia,) Hon. J. S. Saunders, and Hon. James Brown, (of New Brunswick,) Commissioners, "to enquire into the present state of King's College, [there,] its management and utility, with a view of improving the same, and rendering that Institution more generally useful," etc. The Report, to which Dr. Ryerson makes reference, was written by him in December of that year.

Head, who said that it was practical proof of my correctness. Judge Badgely said that Dr. Meilleur's statement removes all possible doubt as to what had been done on the subject. . . .

QUEBEC, 30th of January, 1858.   E. RYERSON.

2. *Letter from Hon. John A. Macdonald to Dr. Ryerson:*—

You had better get some independent Member to move for any Report on Separate Schools which you may desire.*

TORONTO, 28th of April, 1858.   JOHN A. MACDONALD.

CHAPTER XX.

SPECIAL REPORT ON ROMAN CATHOLIC SEPARATE SCHOOLS IN 1858.

AFTER conferring with Sir Edmund Head in regard to the Confidential Report, which Dr. Ryerson had prepared, at his request, it was considered desirable that the substance of that Report, with such modifications as might be necessary, should be prepared, with a view to its being laid before the Legislature. On his return from Quebec, therefore, Dr. Ryerson prepared a "Special Report" on the Separate Schools, Text-Books, and other matters, and sent it to the Provincial Secretary on the 20th of April, 1868. The renewed agitation, in regard to Separate Schools, rendered such a Report the more necessary,—especially as an effort was then being made to obtain further legislation in favour of these Schools. Mr. Thomas R. Ferguson, M.P., had sought to counteract such efforts, by introducing, as was the habit, an abortive Bill into the House of Assembly, early in April, 1858:—

To repeal the several Acts, and parts of Acts, authorizing the establishment and maintenance of Separate, or Sectarian, Schools in Upper Canada.

---

* On the 4th of May, the House of Assembly, on motion to that effect, adopted an Address to the Governor-General, asking for "Copies of any Report, or Reports, that have been made to him by the Chief Superintendent of Education for Upper Canada, during the present year, on the subject of Separate Schools." This motion had reference to Dr. Ryerson's "Special Report on the Separate School provision of the School Law of Upper Canada," etc. This Report was laid before the House of Assembly on the 7th of May, 1858.

The measure, as was usual, was not pressed to a vote, and no legislation on behalf of Separate Schools took place in that year.

Dr. Ryerson felt, however, that it was necessary to counteract the movement which had been set on foot to obtain this legislation, and especially, to controvert the claims which had been put forth in connection with it. In the "Special Report," which he had prepared on the subject, he thus explained, (on page 15.) what he believed to be the issues involved in "this renewed controversy." He said :—

Certain Dignitaries of the Roman Catholic Church in Upper Canada, for whose members the Separate School provisions of the School Law were specially designed, have assumed, since 1852, a threefold position, essentially different from what they had ever professed.

1. They have advocated Separate Schools, (not as a protection against wrong in particular cases, but) as an institution and agency of their Church, and as a dogma of faith, and a rule of duty binding upon all their adherents, and in all places.

2. They have advocated the support of these Schools by Municipal taxation, as well as by Legislative Grant, and that according to the number of their Church population, and not according to the number of children they might teach, or even according to the number of those who might desire Separate Schools for their children,—thus leaving their own Church adherents without any right of individual choice, and the Municipalities, or Common School Trustees, without any power to levy a School rate, to erect a School-house, or furnish a School, or support a Teacher, or for any School purpose whatever, unless a corresponding sum, according to population, was given in support of the Roman Catholic Church Schools!

3. They have . . . avowed their great and ultimate object to be the destruction of the National School System of Upper Canada, and have invoked aid from Lower Canada to accomplish it.

To show that I am quite correct in my remarks in reference to the first of the positions above stated, it is only necessary to recollect the means which the Roman Catholic Bishop of Toronto, (Dr. de Charbonnel,) employed to enforce his Church teachings, when, in an official Circular, (or Lenten Pastoral of 1856,) to the Clergy and Laity of his Diocese, he said :—

"Catholic electors in this country, who do not use their electoral power in behalf of Separate Schools are guilty of mortal sin. Likewise parents who do not make the sacrifices necessary to secure such Schools, or send their children to Mixed Schools. Moreover, the Confessor who would give absolution to such parents, electors, or legislators as support Mixed Schools to' the prejudice of Separate Schools, would be guilty of a mortal sin."

I may also add, that each of the three Bills prepared and insisted upon by the authority of several Prelates of the Roman Catholic Church, involved all, and a great deal more, than is implied in the second of the above stated positions.*

Dr. Ryerson always felt an insuperable objection to the second of the foregoing demands,—that is, that the Municipal assessment and the Legislative School Grant should be apportioned "according to the number of the [Roman Catholic] Church population, and not according to the number of children they might teach." On page 13, of his Annual School Report for 1855, (written in 1856,) he said :—

I have reason to believe that it is, by extreme exertions of ecclesiastical authority that many Roman Catholics can be made to endorse the teachings, [enforced by this same authority,] against the character and cherished institutions of a great majority of the people of Upper Canada. . . . Hence the efforts to deprive them [the Roman Catholics,] of the exercise of choice, by not leaving them to express their individual wishes, from year to year, but endeavouring to include them as a body [in their demands]. . . . Hence, also, the efforts to make Municipal Councils the imposers and collectors of Rates for Separate Schools, on account of the reluctance of many of the ratepayers concerned to pay Rates for the support of Separate Schools, and, in order to avoid the contact of Church authority with them. Hence, likewise, the efforts to get apportionments for the support of Separate Schools, not according to average attendance, (which is the principle adopted in regart to Public Schools,) but according to the population in the locality of a whole Religious Persuasion. . . .

CHAPTER XXI.

ABORTIVE SEPARATE SCHOOL LEGISLATION IN 1858-1861.

EXCEPT for the correspondence in regard to Separate School matters, which took place with the Education Department, no legislation on the subject was attempted in 1859. Mr. Ferguson re-introduced his Separate School Act Repeal Bill of

---

* For one of these Bills, see *The Correspondence on Separate Schools in Upper Canada*, printed by order of the Legislative Assembly, in a Return to an Address, dated the 2nd of April, 1855. A copy of it will be found on page 85, a reference to this and the others on page 118.

1858, but only as a feint, for it was not pressed to a vote, but was dropped, In 1860, the Hon. G. W. Allan introduced a Bill into the Legislative Council, to modify the restrictions in the sixteenth Clause of the twenty-seventh Section of the School Act: 22nd Victoria, Chapter 64, but it failed to pass during that Session.

In that same Session of the Legislature, Mr. R. W. Scott, (of Ottawa,) introduced into the Legislative Assembly the first of his series of Roman Catholic Separate School Bills, which he brought in successively in the following years, 1861, 1862, and 1863. It was read a first time on the 16th of March, 1860. This Bill consisted of five Sections, and provided for the repeal of Sections numbers eighteen, twenty, twenty-three, twenty-nine and thirty-four of the Taché Separate School Bill of 1855, and the substitution therefor of other sections in their place.

In this year, (1860,) the prolonged parliamentary discussions on the Toronto University Question, and the visit of the Prince of Wales, engrossed public attention, that nothing further took place in the Legislature in regard to Roman Catholic Separate Schools.

In 1861, Mr. Scott again renewed his efforts to obtain legislation in favour of Separate Schools, and again failed to do so. On the copy of his Bill in my possession, the late Mr. Alexander Marling, LL.B., for many years Chief Clerk in the Department, and my successor in January, 1890, as Deputy Minister of Education for Ontario, has made the following notes:—

This Bill is similar in most essentials to that of the Hon. John Elmsley, (see page 117,) with the following exceptions:—

1. Mr. Scott requires a notice by the Roman Catholic Separate School Trustees annually, of the names of their supporters, upon which list the Municipal Collectors are compelled to collect their rates.

2. Mr. Elmsley permits the Municipality to allow the Collector to ascertain who are Roman Catholics, and all such are to be exempted from Common School rates, unless they object; but he also provides that the Municipality shall collect from the Roman Catholic ratepayers the same proportionate amount as from other ratepayers, from which it is clear that this amount is to go to the Separate Schools.

3. There is, indeed, a singular coincidence in the purport of the Scott and Elmsley Bills, although the words in both are different.

Mr. Marling then gives the following analysis of each Section of Mr. Scott's Bill of 1861 :—

I. The words, "Village, or Town," are added to this Section, authorizing five heads of families to call a meeting for the election of Trustees.

II. Notice to be given by one Trustee of the meeting for the election of Trustees, instead of by the Roman Catholic inhabitants favourable to the establishment of the Separate School.

III. Gives power to Roman Catholics in different School Sections to unite, as in the case of Wards of a City. (This is the same as in Mr. Elmsley's Bill.) The word "contiguous," used in this Section, is very objectionable, as too indefinite.

IV In City and Town Separate School Boards, only one Trustee is to be elected for each Ward. (The same in Mr. Elmsley's Bill.)

V. After giving a notice before March in any year, no annual notice is required to exempt ratepayers : a list of supporters of the Separate School, on the bare authority of the Trustees, is to be given to the Municipal Clerk ; and there is no provision for verifying this list ; and this list will also exempt those in "contiguous" Municipalities.

VI. This Section takes away the limitation to Separate Schools having fifteen pupils, (which Mr. Elmsley's Bill leaves in,) and gives Separate Schools a share in the Municipal Assessment, (which Mr. Elmsley also does.)

VII. This is the same as in the present Law, except as to the oath of Trustees, which is not required. (Same as in Mr. Elmsley's Bill.)

VIII. This Section obliges the Municipal Collector to collect Separate School rates. (Mr. Elmsley proposed only to permit them to do so.)

Although this Bill was introduced and read a first time, on the 23rd of March, 1861, yet it never reached a second reading, but was discharged from the Orders of the Day in the House of Assembly, on the 16th of the following May.

CHAPTER XXII.

FAILURE OF SEPARATE SCHOOL LEGISLATION IN 1862.

EARLY in the year 1862, Dr. Ryerson sought to meet the reasonable objections which had been urged against the Taché Separate School Act of 1855, in that it contained no provision authorizing the establishment of a Roman Catholic Separate School in an Incorporated Village. They could be established in a rural School Section, and in the Ward of a City, or Town, but not in an Incorporated Village. Dr. Ryerson, therefore, submitted the following Draft of Bill to the Government in the early part of March, 1862, being—

An Act to Restore Certain Rights to the Parties Therein-Mentioned, in Respect to Separate Schools.

Whereas it is expedient to restore to the parties therein-mentioned certain rights of which they were deprived by the Act [of 1855]: 22nd Victoria, Chapter 65, of the Consolidated Statutes of Upper Canada : Her Majesty, by and with the advice and consent of the Legislative Council and Assembly of Canada, enacts as follows :

1. The words, "any Incorporated Village, or Town," shall be inserted between the words, "within" and "any," in the third line of the eighteenth Section of said Act.

2. So much of the thirty-fourth Section of said Act as requires Trustees to make their Returns or Reports under oath is hereby repealed.

3. It shall be lawful for the majority of the ratepaying supporters of the Separate School, in each School Section, (in two or more School Sections,) whether in the same, or adjoining, Municipalities, at Public Meetings duly called by the Separate School Trustees of each such Section, to form such Section into a Separate School Union Section, of which union of Sections the Trustees shall give notice within fifteen days to the Clerk, or Clerks, of the Municipality, or Municipalities, and to the Chief Superintendent of Education ; and each such Separate School Union Section, thus formed, shall be deemed one School Section for all Roman Catholic Separate School purposes.

4. The twenty-ninth Section of said Act : 22nd Victoria, Chapter 65, shall be amended as follows :

After the first notice required to be given to the Clerk of the Municipality by the supporters of a Separate School Section, each subsequent annual notice required by Law to be given, of the names and residences of the supporters of a Separate School in any rural School Section, City, Town, or Incorporated Village, shall be given in writing by the Trustees of such Separate School ; but subject, in case of incorrect returns, to the penalties imposed by law on School Trustees in case of other false returns.

5. The Roman Catholic Separate Schools, (with their registers,) shall be subject to such inspection as may be directed, from time to time, by the Department of Public Instruction for Upper Canada.

Dr. Ryerson accompanied this Draft of Bill with the following explanatory memorandum. He said :—

No new principle is introduced into this Draft of Bill, nor does it contain any provision, (except those of the last Section,) which was not embraced in the Common School Acts of 1850 and 1853.

The framers of the Roman Catholic School Act of 1855 aimed to assimilate the Separate School Law of Upper Canada, with the Dissentient School Law of Lower Canada, but they were ignorant of the effect of some of the provisions of their Act, arising from the Municipal System of Upper Canada, in connection with School Sections, Assessments, etc.

The provisions of the accompanying Draft of Bill only restore to the parties concerned rights of which they were deprived by the Roman Catholic Separate School Act of 1855.

I will now advert to the specific provisions of the accompanying Draft.

1. The supporters of a Separate School cannot establish a Separate School in an Incorporated Village, nor in a Town, as such, though they may establish a Separate School in any School Section, or any Village not incorporated, and in any Ward of a [City or] Town. Such anomalies should, of course, be corrected, as the first Section of the Bill proposes.

2. Since 1856 the managers of Dissentient Schools in Lower Canada have not been required to make their Returns and Reports on oath ; nor is there any reason why the Trustees of Separate Schools in Upper Canada should be required to do so, especially as the penalties are the same for making a false Return, or Report, whether made on oath, or not, as the ordinary Trustees are not required to make their Reports, or Returns, on oath, and Separate School Trustees were not required to do so before they were required to do so by the Taché Bill of 1855. The second Section of the Bill provides to abolish this invidious and needless anomaly.

3. Two or more Common School Sections can be united into one ; nor is there any just reason why Separate School Sections should not be allowed to do the same, as is provided by the third Section of the Bill.

4. The requiring each individual supporter of the Separate School to go and notify the Clerk of the Municipality annually, imposes a needless trouble and burden, after the first such notice ; and when the School is once organized, the annual notice of the names and residences of the supporters of the Separate School is quite sufficient, as the only object of such notice is to give the Municipal Council such authentic information as to the parties and properties to be exempted from Common School Taxes, and as the Trustees are liable to a penalty if they insert any name in their notice, without the authority of the bearer of it.

5. The fifth Section has been prepared with the consent of the Heads of the parties concerned, upon the principle that Schools thus receiving public aid upon definite and periodical Returns, should be subject to such examination, from time to time, as may enable the Department which pays the money, to ascertain whether the conditions of its payment have been fulfilled.

TORONTO, March, 1862.   E. RYERSON.

THE BISHOP LYNCH APPOINTMENT EPISODE IN 1862.

In order to emphasize his desire to secure the continued co-operation of the Representative of the Roman Catholic Church in Toronto on the Provincial Council of Public Instruction, Dr. Ryerson wrote the following Letter to the Provincial Secretary on the subject, and Dr. Lynch was appointed:—

> I have the honour to submit to the favourable consideration of the Governor-General-in-Council, the appointment of the Right Reverend Doctor Lynch, Roman Catholic Bishop of Toronto, as a Member of the Council of Public Instruction for Upper Canada, in place of the Right Reverend Doctor de Charbonnel, who has removed from the country.
>
> I am happy to be able to add, that Bishop Lynch has authorized me to present his name for this appointment; and that between his Lordship and myself an entire agreement has been come to on the Separate School provisions of the Law.
>
> TORONTO, 15th of March, 1862.   E. RYERSON.

When it was known that this appointment of Bishop Lynch had been suggested to the Government by Dr. Ryerson, he was called to account, in the leading newspaper in Toronto, for it, on the ground that he had called on the Bishop to secure his influence in favour of the Government candidate in Toronto. To this charge Dr. Ryerson replied, through *The Leader* newspaper, on the 29th of April, 1862, as follows:—

> I never called upon Bishop Lynch in behalf of the Government, much less did it submit a School Bill to him. . . .
>
> In respect to what occurred between Bishop Lynch and myself, it may be proper for me to remark, that my first conversation with Bishop Lynch was to ascertain how far we were agreed, or could agree, as to the correction of acknowledged anomalies and inequalities in certain provisions of the Separate School Law, as it now exists. The Bishop had already reduced his views to writing, and on comparing his notes with mine, there was found to be little difference. It was then proposed that his Lordship should, on an appointed day of the following week, call at the Education Office, when I would have the proposed measure prepared in the form of a Bill. On the appointed day, the Bishop, with the Very Rev. Angus Macdonell, Vicar-General, of Kingston, called at the Education Office, when we considered the whole question, and agreed in our views respecting it—not involving the introduction of any new principle, but the restoration of rights and privileges which were actually enjoyed by Roman Catholics under the School Acts of 1850 and 1853, but which were taken away by

the Roman Catholic Separate School Act of 1855, prepared, though it was, by the Hon. L. H. Drummond, and under the auspices of certain Roman Catholic Bishops, but in ignorance of the working and effect of some of its provisions, arising from the nature of our Municipal Institutions.

It is but just for me to remark, that I found the views of Bishop Lynch, as also those of another Roman Catholic Bishop, [Horan, of Kingston, see his Letter, page 133,] with whom I have had communication on the subject, moderate and constitutional, appreciating the rights of citizens and the institutions of our country, as well as the interests and institutions of their own Church. In these high quarters, I must say that I heard no such pretensions or assumptions as those involved in some of the provisions of the Roman Catholic Separate School Bill, now before the Legislative Assembly, and introduced by Mr. Scott, of the City of Ottawa, who seems to have become the organ of an ultra party in the Church of Rome, that has caused much trouble on the Separate School question in Upper Canada. Mr. Scott's present Bill is very different from the moderate and reasonable one which he introduced two years ago. Some of the provisions of Mr. Scott's present Bill are unobjectionable; others are impracticable, and must cause endless disputes; others are inconsistent with rights of Municipalities and citizens, and such as, I think, no Member of the Legislature can constitutionally consent to. If Mr. Scott's Bill be pressed, I hope, for the honour and character of Upper Canada, it will be rejected by the united vote of both parties of Upper Canadian Representatives.

(NOTE.—See Mr. Scott's personal attack on Dr. Ryerson, (in regard to this Letter,) on the next page.)

Dr. Ryerson then proceeds to give a generous and a genuinely patriotic reason why the wishes of moderate and reasonable Roman Catholics should be met, in removing anomalies and impracticable provisions in the Separate School Act. He said:

I feel that I am not second to Mr. Scott himself in my desire to see every needless impediment removed to the easiest possible working of the Separate School Law.

Some months since I took the liberty to suggest to a Member of the Government, that, as this was the first Session of a new Parliament, and, as the Roman Catholics had shown as much loyal feeling and British enthusiasm as any other class of citizens, in the late apprehended collision between Great Britain and the United States, [in regard to the Mason and Slidell "*Trent* affair,"] and as the French of Lower Canada had unanimously evinced that feeling in a manner beyond all praise, and some of their Bishops had sent out the most patriotic Circulars on the subject, the Government and Parliament could very appropriately and gracefully respond to such a noble manifestation of national loyalty and patriotism, by removing all that is justly objectionable in the Roman Catholic Separate School Law ;* but the accomplishment of so just and legitimate an object is very different from perpetrating so great an act of injustice to Upper Canada, and inflicting so flagrant a wrong upon many of its citizens and institutions, as the passing of Mr. Scott's present Separate School Bill.

TORONTO, 29th of April. 1862.   E. RYERSON.

When this Letter reached Ottawa, on the 30th of April, Mr. R. W. Scott took occasion, on the next day, to raise a "question of privilege," in regard to it, and to assail Dr. Ryerson for having written such a Letter, instead of replying to one from him, which, he stated in the House, he had written to Dr. Ryerson, enclosing a copy of his Bill, two weeks before. In this statement, Mr. Scott was entirely astray. I have the copy of that Letter, and it is dated on the "26th of April, '62." Dr. Ryerson did not receive it in Toronto until the 28th, and, on the next day, (the 29th,) he, very properly, wrote the Letter in *The Leader*, which caused Mr. Scott to raise his "question of privilege." In doing so, he said :—

In his opinion, the conduct of the Chief Superintendent of Education, —a paid Officer of the Government,—in the course he had taken, was very censurable. Nearly a fortnight ago, he had sent him a copy of his Bill, with a request that he would express his views thereon. But, instead of replying to his communication, Dr. Ryerson came out in a strong Letter to *The Leader*, in which he thought proper to indulge in unwarrantable reflections on himself personally, and called on the Members of both sides of the House to throw out the Bill. He asked, if the House was, in that manner, to be dictated to by Dr. Ryerson ? . . . It really was monstrous that, in this way, the Commons of Canada should be lectured and dictated to by their salaried servant.—(*Globe Report*.)

To this gratuitous attack on Dr. Ryerson by Mr. R. W. Scott, the Hon. John A. Macdonald replied as follows :—

---

* The only response which this warm-hearted tribute to the kindness and loyalty of our Roman Catholic fellow-subjects called forth from Mr. R. W. Scott, in the House of Assembly, on the 1st of May, 1862, was the following :— " It was nothing more than a gratuitous impertinence for Dr. Ryerson to counsel that a Separate School Bill should be granted because, forsooth, the Roman Catholic Bishops wrote to the Curés to extend their hospitality to the troops which were sent to defend the country. . . . He asserted that it was an insult to the people of Canada that such language should be used by their paid officer."—(*The Globe Report of Mr. R. W. Scott's remarks on his "Question of Privilege," in the House of Assembly, on the 1st of May, 1862.*)

He thought it scarcely fair to a functionary holding the high and important position of Dr. Ryerson, for the Member for Ottawa to refer to him as he had done. It was a very proper wish for him to desire to set himself right, and he ought not to have taken the opportunity of attacking the Chief Superintendent, as he had done. If he thought that Dr. Ryerson had behaved as he ought not to have done, it was nothing but reasonable that the attention of the House should be called to the act of wrong-doing. But this course should not have been taken without due notice being previously given, in order that a full opportunity might be allowed to such functionaries to defend themselves.

So far as I have been able to ascertain, Mr. R. W. Scott never publicly made the *amende honorable* for this gratuitous and unjust attack on Dr. Ryerson,—the result of his own absurd mistake. (Privately he acknowledged it, however; see page 140.) Mr. M. C. Cameron gave him an opportunity to do so; but he remained silent, when, on the 3rd of June, 1862, (more than a month after he had made his attack,) Mr. Cameron said:

> The promoter of this Bill, on a former occasion, used very strong language in disapproval of Dr. Ryerson's conduct. He was now disposed to accept that gentleman's view, as more favourable to himself.

The "promoter" of the Bill, however, preferred to sit still, and leave to others the duty which he should have been chivalrous enough to have cheerfully performed.*

PRIVATE LETTER FROM BISHOP HORAN, OF KINGSTON.

Immediately after the conference at the Education Office with Bishop Lynch and Vicar-General Macdonell, as mentioned in the Letter, (on page 130,) Dr. Ryerson sent a copy of his Bill, " to Restore certain Rights," etc., to the Right Reverend Doctor E. J. Horan, Bishop of Kingston, for his information. In reply, Bishop Horan said:—

> I have read with attention the proposed amendments to the Roman Catholic Separate School Bill, which you were so kind as to send to the

---

* I wrote two notes to Mr. Scott early in this year, (1897,) in regard to the "finality" of the Roman Catholic Separate School Act of 1863,—and incidentally in reference to the apparent discrepancy,—which, in his Senate Speech of April, 1894, he failed to notice, or explain,—respecting the presence of two of the Roman Catholic Clergy, (instead of one,) at the conferences between him and Dr. Ryerson, settling, in 1862 and 1863, the terms of the Separate School Bills of those years. Mr. Scott had, therefore, thus another opportunity to make any statement, or explanation, he pleased, had he wished to do so; but he neither acknowledged, nor replied to, either of my Letters.—J. G. H.

Vicar-General (Macdonell) for his perusal and mine. I thank you for this mark of courtesy, and shall always endeavour to make myself deserving of it.

I fear that your proposed amendments are not sufficient, and that they would not do away with the principal difficulties we met with in establishing and maintaining our Schools.

If there is to be any legislation on this matter, as I hope there will be, it should be of a kind to set this long-vexed question at rest, by dealing with the true grievances of which Roman Catholics complain, and granting them those rights to which they have an unquestionable claim.

I have made out a draft of the points, which I consider should be embraced in any amendments to the present Law. I am aware that all is not contained in what I propose; but still, I believe, an Act containing these points would give very general satisfaction.

I should feel most happy, Rev. Sir, if your views on this subject could coincide, as I then could hope, with the help of your powerful influences, to obtain for my co-religionists a boon they have so long desired. . . . Your much obliged Servant,

KINGSTON, 22nd of March, 1862.   + E. J. HORAN, Bp. of Kingston.*

CHAPTER XXIII.

PRIVATE AND CONFIDENTIAL LETTERS IN REGARD TO THE ROMAN CATHOLIC SEPARATE SCHOOL BILL OF 1862.

THE Separate School Bill, to which Dr. Ryerson refers, in his Letter to *The Leader*, of the 29th of April, (page 130,) was introduced into the House of Assembly by Mr. Richard W. Scott, of Ottawa, on the 7th of that month. On the 26th of that month he enclosed a copy of it to Dr. Ryerson, then in Toronto, expressing a hope, in his Letter of that date that the Bill would meet with his approbation, and added, in his Letter, that he wanted the Bill " to be a finality."

Three days after writing this Letter, Mr. Scott, (on the 29th,)

---

* I knew Bishop Horan when he was Principal of the Laval Normal School. He was a most interesting man to meet and converse with. He was consecrated Bishop of Kingston, in succession to Bishop Phelan, on the 1st of May, 1858, and died on the 15th of February, 1875.

moved the second reading of his Bill, and, on the 1st of May, made an attack on Dr. Ryerson for not replying to that Letter. The Bill, having passed the second reading, was referred to a Special Committee of the House of Assembly. Its history and untimely fate is best detailed in the following private and confidential correspondence which took place in regard to it :—

(1. *Telegram from Dr. Ryerson to the Hon. John A. Macdonald* :—

Will endeavour to see you on Monday. I write a few lines this evening.
TORONTO, 11th of March, 1862.   E. RYERSON.)

2. *Letter from the Hon. John A. Macdonald to Dr. Ryerson* :

I send you a copy of the Separate School Bill, and would like to have your opinion on the subject as soon as you can conveniently send it.*
QUEBEC, 28th of April, 1862.   JOHN A. MACDONALD.

3. *Telegram from Dr. Ryerson to the Hon. John A. Macdonald* :—

Scott's Separate School Bill most objectionable and injurious. It ought, by all means, to be rejected. Have written. See my short remarks and appeal, [of the 29th of April, 1862,] against the Bill in yesterday's *Leader*.†
TORONTO, 1st of May, 1862.   E. RYERSON.

4. *Note from Dr. Ryerson to J. George Hodgins* :—

I see that I must adopt very prompt and decisive measures against Scott's Separate School Bill. I wish you would have the enclosed Telegrams written out, . . . and send them immediately to the Hon. John A. Macdonald, to my Brother William, and to Mr. Alexander Morris. Those to my Brother and Mr. Morris must be paid. I am gaining; but am getting on slower than I had expected.‡
TORONTO, May the 1st, 1862.   E. RYERSON.

---

* The successive Roman Catholic Separate School Bills introduced by Mr. Scott into the House of Assembly, are as follows :—Bill No. 69, Received and Read, 16th of March, 1860 ; Bill No. 11, Received and Read, 23rd of March, 1861 ; Bill No. 2, Received and Read, 7th of April, 1862 ; Bill No. 3, Received and Read, 27th of February, 1863—four Bills in all. The only one which became Law was that of 1863.

† This Letter will be found on page 130.

‡ Dr. Ryerson was ill in bed when he wrote this Note to me. The Telegrams, (numbers 5 and 6,) sent to Mr. William Ryerson, M.P., and to Mr. Alexander Morris, M.P., were the same as the one I sent to the Hon. John A. Macdonald.

7. *Letter from the Hon. John A. Macdonald to Dr. Ryerson:*

Private. I am truly grieved to learn of your protracted illness. I should think that change of air would do you good. The proposed visit to Quebec will be of great service to you, and I am very anxious to see you.

Mr. R. W. Scott . . . introduced the present Bill without showing it to me. Notwithstanding this, I thought it well to support the principle of his Bill, on the understanding that it should be sent to a Special Committee and made to suit me. Scott has been looked up to as the exponent of Roman Catholic views on the subject; and the Bill, when "amended to suit," will be carried through the House by him, and must be accepted by the Roman Catholics as their Bill.

You will see that Scott objected to your Letter of the 29th of April, 1862, [in *The Leader* of the 30th, page 130,] and Mr. H. M. Foley took occasion to insinuate that I had got you to write it in order to help James Patton,*—at the same time that I pretended to be a friend of the Roman Catholics. My answer to Scott was that his veracity was not impeached in any way; and that, if he chose to make a motion specifically on the subject, he might do so, on due notice, and I was ready to meet him.

I will keep back the action of the Select Committee on the Bill, in the expectation of your speedy arrival here.

QUEBEC, 3rd of May, 1862.   JOHN A. MACDONALD.

8. *Letter from Mr. William Ryerson to Dr. Ryerson:—*

I have received your Letter this morning. You object strongly to Scott's Bill. I am afraid your objections come too late. When the Bill was first introduced, I spoke to John A. Macdonald to forward to you, without delay, a copy. He promised to attend to it; but your objections, even by telegraph, were not received until the debate on the Bill had closed. Your Letter in *The Leader*, of the 29th of April, [page 130,] was not received until next day.

I was prevented by sickness from attending the House on the day when the subject was again brought up by Mr. Scott. The feelings excited against you by him are very strong. The sneers, insinuations, and charges against you, I am told, were received with laughter and cheers from both sides of the House; while but one single individual, John Hillyard Cameron, opened his mouth, or uttered one word, in your favour.†

---

* James Patton, Esq., LL.D., Vice-Chancellor of the University of Toronto, was then spoken of as a Candidate for the Legislative Council.

† The following is what Mr. John Hillyard Cameron said in the House of Assembly, on the 1st of May, 1862, in reply to Mr. R. W. Scott's attack on Dr. Ryerson:—"He regretted to see that a certain amount of feeling had been manifested against the Rev. Chief Superintendent of Education for Upper Canada; but he could not see that his conduct could, in any respect, be called blamable. He occupied the important office of Chief of the Education Depart-

The cause of such feelings are : that you have expressed, or stated, to several persons, that you had no great objection to Scott's Bill,—that, with some few amendments, it would be harmless, etc. You now say that the Bill now introduced is entirely different from the former one, or the one to which you alluded [in your Letter to *The Leader*, page 130]. All this may be true ; but your friends knew nothing of the difference ; and you have neglected to inform them, until too late. And, even now, you have not stated one point, or one clause, of the Bill to which you object, nor have you given your reasons for objecting to the Bill itself. You merely condemn the Bill *in toto*, and call upon the House to throw it out.

Your enemies, and you have many such, call you vain, insolent, pretentious, and I know not how much more ; while your friends, now committed to the principle of the Bill, have nothing to say. I greatly fear that the Bill, with some amendments, will be sustained by a large majority.

I would say more, but am unable, as I have been sick for several days. . . . I should be glad to hear from you. I shall write again as soon as I am able.

QUEBEC, May the 5th, 1862.   WILLIAM RYERSON.

9. *Letter from Dr. Ryerson, (London,) to J. George Hodgins :*

I am better than when I left home, (for change,) but I gain slowly. . . . I enclose you the first part of my reply to Mr. Scott, etc. . . . The effort to look over it has caused much pain in my head. . . . I had hoped to have been able to proceed with my remarks on the provisions of Mr. Scott's Bill, but I shall not be able to do so.

I have thought it best to have my remarks on this Scott Bill printed, but I leave it to your discretion at present.

LONDON, Ontario, 19th of May, 1862.   E. RYERSON.

10. *Letter from Dr. Ryerson, (London,) to J. George Hodgins :*

The Doctor has cautioned me against mental exertion for some time to come, but I thought I would finish the document, of which I sent you the first part, . . . but before I had written a page . . . I had to lie

---

ment of Upper Canada, and had, as such, the care of seeing that the educational wants of that section of the Province were properly attended to. A Bill had been introduced into the House by a private Member, which affected the Education Department, and which would entail changes of a very serious nature. The Rev. Superintendent had expressed his opinion on this Bill ; and was he to be punished for having done so? He felt assured, that if the Bill came up for a third reading, in a similar form to that in which it came up for a second reading, a very large number of the Upper Canada Members would oppose it."—(*Globe Report.*)

down. . . . From the reported crisis at Quebec, it may not be necessary for me to go there at all on the subject of the Separate School Bill. . . .

LONDON, Ontario, 27th of May, 1862.   E. RYERSON.

11. *Letter from Dr. Ryerson to Mr. Alexander Morris, M.P.:*

As you referred to me, in your remarks on the second reading of Mr. Scott's Separate School Bill, as approving of the general provisions of that Bill, I beg to say that I never saw the Bill until the day before the second reading of it was moved, [*i.e.*, on the 28th of April, 1862,] Mr. Scott's note, enclosing a copy of the Bill to me, [at Toronto,] being dated only three days before he moved the second reading of it, and more than two weeks after he had introduced it.

I felt that the only alternative of duty left to me was to apprize the Members of the Legislature for Upper Canada of my views of the Bill,—it being a private, and not a Government, measure,—as I had done, in regard to a Bill introduced into the Legislature, in 1856, by Mr. John G. Bowes. From that time until last week, I have been unable, (from illness,) either to prepare a Memorandum, or to come to Quebec, on the subject of the Bill.

Since I came to Quebec, I find that several of the most objectionable Sections of the Bill have been rejected, or amended, by a Select Committee of the House of Assembly; and, after lengthened explanations and discussions between Mr. Scott and myself, other clauses of the Bill, which I thought objectionable and injurious, or impracticable, have been erased, or amended, so as to render the Bill harmonious, with what I believe to be the integrity and efficiency of our Common School System, while it remedied the defects in the Law, of which the supporters of Separate Schools have complained.

This day the Representatives of the Roman Catholic Church have accepted the Bill, as thus amended, and have, in connection with Mr. Scott and myself, apprized the Head of the Administration of our agreement in the provisions of the Bill; and as the present, as well as the late, Government, have assented that Mr. Scott should proceed with his Bill, (as thus amended, and agreed upon,) I can have no wish but that the measure should be passed, if approved by a majority of the Representatives of Upper Canada, as best for the interests of our Public School System, and for the convenience of the supporters of Separate Schools.

I herewith enclose you a copy of the Bill, as agreed to, and amended, so that you may use it, as well as this Letter, in such a way as you may think proper, in your place in the House.

QUEBEC, 1st of June, 1862.   E. RYERSON.

12. *Letter from Dr. Ryerson, (Quebec,) to J. George Hodgins:*

Yesterday morning the (Rev. Angus Macdonell) Vicar-General of Kingston,—acting on behalf of the Roman Catholic Bishops of Toronto and Kingston,—and the Rev. Mr. Cazeau, Secretary of the Archbishop of Quebec, as Representatives of the Authorities of the Roman Catholic Church, accepted the Separate School Bill, as proposed to be amended by me, and agreed to by Mr. R. W. Scott; and afterwards us four waited upon the Premier, (Hon. J. S. Macdonald,) and informed him of the result of our consultation, and the desire of the Authorities of the Roman Catholic Church that the Government would affirm and facilitate Mr. Scott's proceeding with the Bill. The Attorney-General, J. S. Macdonald, was much pleased, and afterwards complimented me, as having done wonders by coming down from Toronto; and he said that he would assent to whatever I had agreed to. . . . The Attorney-General is much pleased and amused that the Separate School question thus falls to his Government to settle with so little trouble, or action, on their part, and that it is left to him to recommend the appointment of the Roman Catholic Bishop of Toronto as a Member of the Council of Public Instruction, (page 130). He says he will inquire about it immediately, and have the appointment made and *Gazetted.*. It is by procrastination and neglect in such matters that the late Administration have lost immensely even among their warmest supporters. . . . If anything important occurs, I will write to-morrow night.

QUEBEC, 2nd of June, 1862.   E. RYERSON.

13. *Letter from J. George Hodgins to Dr. Ryerson, Quebec:—*

I received a copy of Mr. Scott's amended Separate School Bill to-day. . . . I can scarcely believe it is the one which, by telegraph, Mr. Scott says that you had agreed to.

The word "adjoining," in the eighteenth line of Section three, will give rise to disputes. I fear that it conflicts with the like restriction in the Common School Act. When those Separate Schools can be thus united, the residence of the Trustees should be within such united Separate School Section.

Section four does not provide for the notification to this Office of the establishment of a Separate School.

I fear that the word "contiguous," in lines three and six, in Section five, is too indefinite. . . .

I think that Sections eleven and fourteen cover too much ground, and will have the affect of exempting too many persons as mere "supporters" of the Separate School. The words: "other School Sections," in line eight of Section eleven, are also quite too indefinite. The words: "Municipality and Municipalities," in Section fourteen, are also too wide in their application to the case of Separate Schools. . . .

The principle of Section twenty-three is a sound one; but it is questionable whether the Council of Public Instruction should have the power of appointing Examiners.

Section eighteen unwisely reverses the present arrangement, and will be too onerous on those who wish to support the Public Schools. . . .

Section nineteen conflicts with Section three, and will lead to disputes. The second part of that Section is good in itself; but it will also lead to disputes in determining the "three miles."

Section twenty will have the effect of drying up the Clergy Reserve Fund, which is now applied to the Common Schools. . . . The Municipalities may object to the Fund being claimed under this Section by Separate School Trustees.

Sections twenty-six, twenty-seven and twenty-eight are, to my mind, very objectionable.

There is no provision in the Act for the inspection of Separate Schools.

TORONTO, 4th of June, 1862. J. GEORGE HODGINS.

14. *Letter from J. George Hodgins to Dr. Ryerson, Quebec:—*

It is well that you got down to Quebec in time to modify Mr. Scott's Separate School Bill. I see by the telegram from Quebec, that he has withdrawn it, chiefly owing to Mr. T. R. Ferguson's opposition. . . .

TORONTO, 6th of June, 1862. J. GEORGE HODGINS.

15. *Letter from Dr. Ryerson to J. George Hodgins:—*

I left Quebec last night by steamer. . . . You have seen that Scott's Bill is thrown out. A strong feeling was excited against him in the House on account of his statement that I had approved of his Bill, and then his attack upon me, and his statement that he had enclosed it to me from Ottawa during the recess. I showed him from his own Letter to me at Toronto, that it was dated at Quebec on the 26th, only three days before he moved the second reading of his Bill, on the 29th. . . . He was deeply mortified, and admitted that he was wrong. . . .

MONTREAL, 7th of June, 1862. E. RYERSON.

DR. RYERSON'S DETAILED PROCEEDINGS IN REGARD TO THE SCOTT SEPARATE SCHOOL BILL OF 1862.

In addition to these Private and Confidential Letters, Dr. Ryerson, in July, 1862, wrote several others to the Editor of *The Leader*, in reply to the attacks which were made upon him, for having, (as asserted in *The Globe* newspaper at the time,) become an—.

Arch-traitor to destroy the work which he had employed nearly eighteen years to establish and mature,—namely, the Common School System of the country.

After dealing with other matters in his Letters to *The Leader*, he thus referred to the third abortive Roman Catholic Separate School Act of Mr. Scott, of 1862:—

When Mr. R. W. Scott, of Ottawa, introduced, during the late Session of our Legislature, his Separate School Bill, incorporating several extreme provisions in it, at the suggestion of the Ultramontane party in Toronto, that prompted Bishop de Charbonnel in his extravagant pretensions and wicked crusade against our School System, I rose from a sick bed to publicly entreat the Members from Upper Canada to reject so objectionable a Bill,—the author having sent me a copy of it only three days before he moved its second reading; but as he had impressed the House with the belief that I approved of the Bill, a majority voted for its second reading, with a view to refer it to a Select Committee, which pruned the Bill of some of its extreme provisions, and reported it, as amended, for the adoption of the House.

Now, were there one particle of truth in the statement, that I was conspiring with the Roman Catholic Bishops, and their agents, to subvert our School System, I would, of course, not have objected to Mr. Scott's Bill, as introduced by him; much less would I have objected to it as amended by a Committee of Upper Canada Members of the Legislative Assembly. But proceeding to Quebec as soon as I was able to travel, . . . I saw a copy of Mr. Scott's Bill, as amended by a Select Committee, which, it seems, was induced to consider the Bill before I could get to Quebec, and reported upon it the day previous to my arrival there.

I at once objected to any legislation at all on the subject, except under the auspices of the Government, who, I maintained, were responsible for the protection of the School System, as well as for the judicial and financial system, and for any and all measures necessary to correct the evils or remedy the defects of the one as well as of the other. Two Members of the present Administration, to whom I stated my objections and views, admitted their validity. I also objected to several provisions of the Bill as amended by the Committee; but it being understood that the Government would assent to Mr. Scott's proceeding with the Bill, provided it were amended so as to meet my views, he consented to the erasure of the clauses to which I objected, and to the insertion of the further amendments which I proposed. And what were those clauses and amendments ? . . .

The Select Committee had purged Mr. Scott's Bill of several of its Ultramontane provisions, such as that of making the Priests *ex-officio* School Trustees, with power of taxation,—a provision not admitted in Catholic

France, or Belgium, or even in Austria. But the Bill, as reported by the Committee, permitted Trustees of Separate School Sections to form Union Sections to any extent they might please. To this I objected, and insisted that the ratepaying parents should be the judges as to forming Union Sections for Separate Schools, as well as for Common Schools; and, of course, they would not agree to any Union Section so large as to prevent their children from attending the School, and especially as the Bill provided, (as amended by the Committee,) that no one should be recognized as a supporter of a Separate School who should reside more than three miles from it. My amendment was admitted.

Again, the Bill, as originally introduced, exempted the supporters of Separate Schools from paying Public School Rates, in whatever part of the Province their property might be situated. The Committee limited the exemption to the Municipality of the Separate School supporters. I insisted that the exemption should be limited to the School Section, as all property in each School Section should be liable for the education of the youth of the Section—as it was by the joint labours of such youths and their parents that the value of property in such Section was created or maintained. My amendment was admitted.

By the Bill, as reported by the Committee, it was also provided, that the Council of Public Instruction should appoint a Board of Examiners in each County for examining Separate School Teachers and giving them Certificates of Qualifications. I was aware that under the present Separate School law,—Trustees of each Separate School give the Certificates of Qualifications to their Teachers; such Teachers have no public standing in comparison of the Teachers of the Common Schools; that many of the Teachers of Separate Schools in the Townships and Villages are so poorly qualified that the most intelligent Roman Catholics in such places send their children to the Public Schools; that it was, therefore, desired to have some form of examination that would raise the position of Separate School Teachers. But I wholly objected to the creation of two distinct County Boards of Examiners of School Teachers; to the Council of Public Instruction, being made the instrument of selecting a Roman Catholic Board of Examiners in each County,—thus actually giving Separate Common School Teachers an apparent superiority over Public Common School Teachers, and creating the natural precursor of a Separate Provincial Normal School. I delared my intention, should such a provision become law, to recommend to the Council of Public Instruction to appoint the present County Boards of Public Instruction as Examiners of Separate School Teachers, as they are of Public School Teachers, and to prescribe the same programme of subjects and classification as are prescribed for Public School Teachers. This was formerly the practice, and no objection was ever made to it until the Charbonnel agitation. The result was the proposed dangerous innovation was abandoned, and the law left as it is. Finally, the Committee consented to retain the following extraordinary clauses in the Bill, as reported by them :

"26. The Holidays and Vacations prescribed by the Council of Public Instruction for the observance of Common Schools, shall not be binding on Roman Catholic Separate Schools ; but the Trustees of every such School may prescribe the observance of such other holidays and vacations as they may see fit; provided, always, that the number of school days in any Roman Catholic Separate School shall not exceed one hundred and twenty-nine days in the first half of every year, nor one hundred and sixteen days in the second half of the year." [The *minimum* of time each half year that the Public Schools are required to be kept open.]

"27. In all Roman Catholic Separate Schools, no rules shall be enforced for the government and management of such Schools, and no books shall be introduced or prohibited without the approbation of the Trustees of such Roman Catholic Separate Schools."

To these Ultramontane clauses I objected *in toto*, as unsanctioned by the example of Lower Canada in regard to the Dissentient Schools, and as unparalleled in any country in respect to Schools to which legislative aid is given. I wished that the Separate Schools in Upper Canada should be subject to public authority and oversight, the same as are Dissentient Schools in Lower Canada. The result was the erasure from the Bill of these two clauses, and the substitution of the following in their place :—

"25. The Roman Catholic Separate Schools, (with their Registers,) shall be subject to such inspection as may be directed, from time to time, by the Chief Superintendent of Education ; and shall be subject also to such regulations as may be imposed, from time to time, by the Council of Public Instruction for Upper Canada."

Such are some of the essential modifications which I got made in Mr. Scott's Bill, even after it had been amended and recommended by a Select Committee of the Legislative Assembly,—so much so that a Member, well acquainted with the nature and administration of the School Law, . . . said, on reading the Bill, as thus modified, "it is better than the present Separate School law, I wish it would pass the Legislature." . . .

Nor did I stop with these essential changes in the provisions of this Bill, though now rendered unobjectionable. I stated that I would resist its further progress in the Legislature, except on two conditions :—First, that the Bill thus modified should be accepted as a settlement of the question by the authorities of the Roman Catholic Church. Secondly, that the Government should assent to Mr. Scott's proceeding with it. To secure the former of these objects, Mr. Scott got the Vicar-General Macdonell, (who had gone from Upper Canada to Quebec in behalf of the authorities of the Church to watch legislation on school matters,) and the Reverend Secretary of the Roman Catholic Archbishop of Quebec, (the Head of the Roman Catholic Church in Canada,) to meet me in the

Parliamentary Library, where we discussed the provisions of the Bill, and where they accepted it on the part of the authorities of the Roman Catholic Church as finally amended in its present form; after which two copies of the Bill, as thus agreed upon and accepted, were made,—the one for Mr. Scott, and the other for myself; and the parties concerned waited upon the head of the Administration, and informed him that they accepted the Bill as thus modified, and requested the assent of the Government to Mr. Scott's proceeding with the Bill. . . .

Every one who examines this third and expurgated edition of the Bill, will see that it brings back the School system in respect to Separate Schools, as near as possible, to what it was before the passing of the Roman Catholic Separate School Bill of 1855. . . .

This is an object I have been most anxious to accomplish. It was with this view that, before the late Session of Parliament, I conferred with Roman Catholic Bishops in Upper Canada, within whose dioceses most of the Separate Schools are established,—resolved that if they, abandoning the extreme pretensions of Bishop de Charbonnel, desired nothing more than that the amendment of the Separate School Law of 1855, so as to restore to the supporters of Separate Schools what that law deprived them, I would recommend a measure to that effect. (Page 130.) I felt no disposition to renew the causeless, and, to Roman Catholics, injurious Separate School agitation of Bishop de Charbonnel, but the simple removal of evils caused by the Separate School Bill of 1855, which was one of the fruits of the Charbonnel agitation. I accordingly prepared a draft of Bill of former claims which was accepted, entitled, "An Act to restore to parties therein named certain rights which they heretofore enjoyed, and of which they have been deprived by the Separate School Act of 1855." . . (See page 128.)

It is a fact, known to the country, that from the commencement of the Ultramontane Separate School agitation, under Bishop de Charbonnel, down to the Ultramontane Separate School Bill introduced into the Legislature at its late session, by Mr. Scott of Ottawa, I have both publicly and privately resisted every measure or clause that would, in the slightest degree, weaken our Common School System.

TORONTO, 10th of July, 1862.   E. RYERSON.

CHAPTER XXIV.

SEPARATE SCHOOL DISCUSSION IN THE ANGLICAN SYNOD IN 1862.

During several years preceding 1862, the Anglican Church, through its Toronto Synod, invariably petitioned the Legislature annually on behalf of Church of England Separate Schools. It took no part, however, in the current discussions of the day on the subject of Roman Catholic Separate Schools, except to base its argument for Church of England Separate Schools on the existence of those for Roman Catholics, under the authority of the Legislature. It claimed equal rights,—that was all.

Being a Lay Representative in the Synod of June, 1862, from the Cathedral Church of St. James, Toronto, I naturally took part in the discussion on Church of England Separate Schools, when the yearly question on the subject came up. I took occasion to refer to the proposal which Dr. Ryerson had then made to the Government, in the preceding March, to provide a way by which "the most needy and neglected" children in Cities and Towns might be reached and educated. In this matter, I said, that he had consulted the Bishop and other experienced men on the subject. For this *The Globe* censured him.

When the Report of a Committee of the Synod, in favour of Church of England Separate Schools, came up for adoption, I objected to a statement in it to the effect, that, in Dr. Ryerson's Bill, he had "conceded the just claims of the Church of England." The following report of my remarks in the Synod is taken from *The Globe* newspaper of the time.* I said:—

---

* Several Members of the Synod took part in the debate, but I only insert the remarks which I made, with a view to explain the nature of the Special School Bill then proposed, in regard to "needy and neglected children," and also to point out what had been done, up to that time, on the general subject of School Legislation.

In that Bill, the words: "Church of England," did not occur at all. Even the words: "Separate Schools," had no place in it. But it was simply proposed, in that Bill, to meet a want, and to supply a deficiency which was felt in all the Cities and Towns. He had no doubt his Lordship, the Bishop, from his long experience in those matters, and his long acquaintance with the Chief Superintendent of Education, must have arrived at this conclusion, that all his amendments to the System of Public Instruction in this country had been of a directly practical character. The measure which Dr. Ryerson prepared last winter, and submitted to his Lordship, and, he believed, to the other Prelates of the Church in this country, and which, he believed, received their sanction, was of this nature:

We were aware that, in the Cities and Towns of Upper Canada, there was a large proportion of the juvenile population which never attend any School whatever, Separate, Common, or even Sunday Schools. We were also aware that the agitation against the continuance of the Common School System in the Cities and Towns, on account of its great expense, had been repeatedly urged. A learned gentleman on the Bench (Mr. Justice Hagarty) had frequently, in his Charges, called attention to this growing evil in our midst. We all admitted the existence of the evil; but parties were divided as to how it should be remedied. He believed he might separate those who entertained different views on the subject into three classes. *First*, there were those who contended that the Common School System was unjust, that it taxed the people heavily to support the Public Schools, but that it failed in bringing within their influence those very portions of the population for whose benefit they were intended. They said, therefore, that the great expense to which the Cities and Towns were put on account of the Common Schools, was comparatively lost. . . .

There was another part of the community, whose views the Chief Superintendent had endeavoured to meet, and which, after all their talk on Separate Schools, had probably the deepest hold on the hearts of every one present. The Chief Superintendent's object was to meet the religious feelings and sentiments of the country, not exclusively of the Church of England, but of every Protestant Denomination in Upper Canada. His object was not to change, but to supplement the Common School System, and to bring within the doors of some School-house the children now wandering about our streets, and being educated in the School of theft and vice.

Dr. Ryerson had for years revolved it over and over again in his mind, how he could meet this difficulty, whether by adopting the views he had just referred to, or the view of the very small minority, the third party, those who were anxious to have a law passed, called in other Countries a Truancy law, to compel all children, if Schools were provided for them, to attend those Schools, or else to give a good account of themselves.

One party, then, consisted of those who objected to the Common School

System, on account of its great expense, and sought, by means of Separate Schools, to meet the difficulty, and to lessen the expense.

Mr. J. G. Hodgins gave notice that he would move, as an amendment to the Resolution to be moved by Dr. Bovell, and seconded by Rev. W. S. Darling, the following :—

That, as members of the United Church of England and Ireland in this Diocese, we do not desire to seek any interference with the Common School System, as established by law, or to demand exclusive privileges not at present shared in equally by other Protestant Denominations in Upper Canada.

Dr. Bovell moved the following Resolution :—

That a respectful Memorial be again presented to the Legislature, setting forth the continued desire of the Church of England and Ireland in Canada, to have Separate Schools in Cities and Towns;

And, further, to respectfully remind the Government that they seek not any improper interference with the Common School System, as established by law, but claim to be entitled to the same privileges, and to have a similar measure of justice meted out to them as Members of the said Church, as have been accorded to their Roman Catholic fellow-countrymen.

Mr. J. G. Hodgins asked that he might be permitted to give a brief historical retrospect of this question, since the first provision for Separate Schools was introduced, twenty-one years ago, applying both to Upper and Lower Canada, but chiefly designed to apply to the latter. The words used were: "Dissentient Schools," and the foundation of the Separate School provision of our law was designed primarily for the protection of the Protestant minority of Lower Canada. The first law on this subject, applicable to both sections of the Province, was not found to work satisfactorily, and, in 1843, the Hon. F. Hincks introduced a law, in which was continued the provision for Separate Schools in Upper Canada. In 1847, Boards of Trustees in Cities and Towns were empowered to determine the number and description of Schools, and to decide "whether they should be Denominational, or Mixed." In 1850, the law was revised, and provision was made for the establishment of Separate Roman Catholic and Coloured Schools. In 1855, the Taché Act was passed, applying exclusively to the Roman Catholics, but not with the entire concurrence of the Chief Superintendent. He agreed that our System of Public Instruction should be based on Christianity. Provision was made for the Schools being opened with prayer and the reading of the Scriptures. In 2,500 of the 4,000 Common Schools, the daily work was opened and closed with prayer; in 2,800 the Scriptures were read daily. But the Church of England claimed further, that religious instruction should be given according to her standards. Provision also had been made for this, by the regulations issued two or three years ago, allowing Clergymen to come to the Schools and give religious instruction to the children of their own persuasion for one hour a week, after School hours.

Dr. Bovell had referred to the disobedience of children in this country. Was this the fault of the Common Schools? He asked gentlemen to look at that card over the door of this Room, emanating from the Department of Public Instruction, the first thing which children saw when they entered school was, as shown on this card: "Honour thy Father and thy Mother." When they turned round, they saw that other precept: "Fear God and Honour the King." Of the Common School Teachers, 800 were Members of the Church of England; 1,250 were Presbyterians; 1,250 Methodists; 230 Baptists; and 85 Congregationalists. All Clergymen, too, were Visitors of the Common Schools.

Mr. Hodgins then referred to the argument that, because Roman Catholics had Separate Schools, the Church of England should have them also. Was the principle of Separate Schools in itself a sound one? The laity of this country did not think it was, and, if it was wrong for the Roman Catholics, it was wrong for the Church of England, and two wrongs could not make a right. The Roman Catholic standards, however, differed *in toto* from the standards of every Protestant Denomination, and that distinction was recognized by the School Law. But to demand Separate Schools simply because the Church of Rome had them, was beneath the dignity of the Church of England. He had looked over the Resolutions passed on this subject from year to year. They appear to have passed with very little dissent, but he was satisfied that they did not represent the religious convictions of the laity of the Church of England in Upper Canada. And he would ask, if Separate Schools for the Church of England were established, what guarantee had they for the religious instruction that would be communicated in them? (A Voice—"The Catechism would be taught.") What guarantee, he would ask, was there that the children, by the instruction given them, would not be influenced in a direction in which many Protestant Churchmen could not concur? . . .

The Bishop, before putting the question to the vote, wished to make a few remarks. Last year, on this question, he said they had a right to Separate Schools, and that they ought not to appear before the Legislature as mere suppliants. If 50,000 persons were required to petition the Legislature for the rights of the Church of England, they could be got, and they ought to continue to demand them until they were granted. He could not, therefore, agree to the Amendment, although he admitted it had been introduced by Mr. Hodgins with great moderation and great talent.

Mr. Hodgins' Amendment was then put, and negatived. Yeas—Clergy, 9; parishes, 12; total, 21. Nays—Clergy, 45; parishes, 29; total, 74.

SCHOOL BILL RELATING TO NEEDY AND NEGLECTED CHILDREN.

The Bill which Dr. Ryerson proposed to meet the special case of "needy and neglected children," was as follows:

1. Whereas, there are large numbers of children of School age not attending any School in the Cities and Towns of Upper Canada, notwithstanding the Schools in several of said Cities and Towns are free ; and, whereas, it is the duty of the Legislature to employ all practicable means to prevent such children from growing up in ignorance and vice, by imparting to them the advantages of a sound Christian education ; and, whereas, it is desirable to exhaust all the agencies and influences of voluntary exertion and religious benevolence, before resorting to measures of coercion, in order to promote the education of the most needy and neglected, as well as of other classes of the population, of such Cities and Towns.

2. Be it enacted, etc., that it shall be lawful for any Benevolent Association, Society, or Congregation, of any Religious Persuasion, or any two, or more, such Congregations may write, in any City, or Town, to establish one or more Schools in such City, or Town, in Upper Canada ; and any premises and houses acquired by such Association, Society, Congregation, or Congregations, for the purposes of this Act, shall be held in the same manner as are premises and places for the ordinary purposes of such Association, or Society, or as are premises and places for public worship acquired and held by such Congregation, or Congregations.

3. Every such Association, Society, Congregation, or two or more Congregations united, establishing a School, or Schools, shall notify the same to the Chief Superintendent of Education, and to the Clerk of their Municipality, on or before the first day of January, or the first day of July, next after their establishment, and shall, according to their usual mode of appointing their Association, Society, or Church officers, appoint, annually, three persons for the management of each such School.

4. The Managers of each School established under the provisions of this Act, shall, on or before the thirtieth day of June, and the thirty-first day of December, of each year, transmit to the Chief Superintendent of Education for Upper Canada, according to a form prepared by him, a correct statement of the number of pupils attending such School, together with their average attendance during the six next preceding months, or during the number of months which may have elapsed since the establishment thereof, and the number of months it shall have been so kept open ; and the Chief Superintendent shall thereupon determine the proportion which the Managers of such School shall be entitled to receive of the School moneys aforesaid, and shall pay over the amount apportioned from the Legislative School Grant to the Managers of such School, and shall notify the Chamberlain, or Treasurer, of the City, or Town, in which such School is situated of the proportion payable to it from School moneys provided by local assessment ; whereupon such Chamberlain, or Treasurer, shall, upon receiving such notification, pay said proportion to the Managers of such School, or Schools, established under the provisions of this Act.

5. Every such School established under the provisions of this Act, shall

be entitled to assistance towards its support from the Common School moneys of the City, or Town, in which it is established, (not including School fees or moneys provided for the purchase of Public School sites, or the erection of Public School buildings, and their appurtenances,) according to the average attendance of pupils during each half year, as compared with the half-yearly average attendance of pupils at the Common Schools of such City, or Town.

6. The Managers and Teachers of every School established under the provisions of this Act, shall be subject to all the regulations and obligations which apply to Trustees and Teachers of Common Schools in Cities and Towns, shall keep a School Register, and make half-yearly returns and annual reports in the form and manner and at the times prescribed in regard to Common Schools; and shall be subject to the same penalties, to be collected in the same way, in case of false returns, as are imposed by law upon Trustees and Teachers of Common Schools.

7. Any moneys which may be paid out of the Legislative School Grant under the provisions of this Act, shall be expended in the payment of the salaries of Teachers, and for no other purpose, and the Schools, with their Registers, established by the authority of this Act, shall be subject to such inspection as may be directed, from time to time, by the Department of Public Instruction for Upper Canada.

DR. RYERSON'S EXPLANATION OF HIS BILL RELATING TO NEEDY AND NEGLECTED CHILDREN IN CITIES AND TOWNS.

The reference to Dr. Ryerson's Bill, relating to "needy and neglected" children in the Anglican Synod, led to an animated discussion in *The Globe* of Toronto at the time. In reply to the Editor's criticism on his proceedings in the matter, Dr. Ryerson said :—

There is one class, and unfortunately an increasing class, of the population of Cities and Towns, which is without the sphere of any influence, secular or religious, which has yet been exercised for the education of their children. These are the children, (and not the children of Common Schools,) that swell the calendars of juvenile crime in Cities and Towns. The problem is, What means can be employed to dry up this fountain of idleness and crime, and make these now poor and neglected youth useful members of Society? The influence of even our excellent Common Free Schools has not reached them. Nay, in the presence of these noble Schools the number of unschooled vagrant children increase,—at least in the City of Toronto. In 1860, during an official tour of Upper Canada, I submitted the question in various counties for public consideration, as to whether the municipalities should not be invested with power to make regulations for educational purposes in regard to vagrant children, between the ages of 7 and 14 years, not attending any School, and not engaged in any lawful employment. . . .

It is admitted on all sides, that some agency is necessary, in addition to that now employed, to meet the case of vagrant children in Cities and Towns. I have proposed to supplement and combine with our Common School agency the additional agency of voluntary religious and benevolent effort,—an agency which has reached the cases of more degraded classes of parents in London and Edinburgh, than any which exist in the Cities and Towns of Upper Canada. . . .

In the measure which I proposed and submitted to the consideration of Government on this subject, I adopted the course which I had invariably pursued in regard to every measure I ever submitted to Government for the improvement of our School System. I prepared the first draft of it without consultation with any one; and then consulted all parties acquainted and interested in the subject as far as I had opportunity. . . .

In the present case, the first person with whom I conferred was a distinguished minister of the then United Presbyterian Church—a man of large experience in our School System, and deeply interested in the amelioration of the neglected classes of youth in Cities and Towns. Afterwards, when I conferred with the venerable Bishop of Toronto, (as I had done in regard to every School Bill I ever proposed,) and such of the Clergy of the Church of England, (as well as of other Churches,) who happened to call upon me, I was gratified to find that they were willing to accept of my proposed measure for supplementing the Common Schools of the Cities and Towns in order to reach, if possible, the cases of the neglected and vicious poor, in place of what some of them had advocated in regard to Separate Schools. This I regarded as so much gained to the unity of our Common School System. Some of these gentlemen, afterwards, (in Synod of the Church of England of Toronto,) made an unauthorized and unwarrantable use of my name, and ascribed to me objects and views with which I had no sympathy. Mr. Hodgins, (Deputy Superintendent of Education, and acquainted with my views and proceedings from the beginning,) who was a member of the Synod, corrected the representations which were there made of my views. In the memorandum which I had prepared on this Bill, I said :—

The giant evil of youthful demoralization is confessedly increasing in our Cities and Towns; and the importance of arresting it, as far as possible, cannot be over-estimated in regard either to these centres of population themselves, or in respect to the country at large. In comparatively new Cities and Towns, and a young country, the foundation of society should be deeply and broadly laid in religion, virtue and knowledge, and for that purpose every possible religious influence and benevolent effort should be developed and associated with the instruction of the masses in rearing the structure of society.

The chief and almost only remedy which has been proposed for the evils of youthful ignorance and crime in our Cities and Towns, is coercion,— compulsory attendance at School. Every member of society has undoubtedly a right to such an education as will fit him for his duties as a Christian citizen, as much as he has a right to food and clothes; and society has a right, and it is in duty bound to see that each of its members is fitted for his duties, and not trained to be a public pest and burden. I have frequently urged this view of the subject, and have suggested and prepared measures to give it practical effect as an element of our Public School System, especially in Cities and Towns. But I have found an utter unwillingness on the part of public men of different parties, to do what seemed to intrench upon individual and parental rights. . . . To compel any class of children to attend the Public Schools, has proved impracticable; and, as it has been truly urged, could that be done? Secular instruction alone would not reach the seat of the moral evils to be corrected, of the moral and religious feelings, on the influence and culture of which depend chiefly and essentially the results desired.

Under these circumstances, I propose to develop and encourage the exercise of a voluntary, religious and moral agency which has hitherto remained almost dormant in this country, which is practically discouraged by our free Public School System; but which has accomplished, and is accomplishing, immense good in behalf of the neglected and vicious poor in many Towns in England and Scotland. . . .

But I am far from proposing the establishment of ragged, or of any description of Pauper Schools in Upper Canada. Our whole School System is founded on the opposite principle,—that of the mutual rights and obligations of the citizen and the State,—not of the pauper and the donor. But I propose that our School System, which has not the vital power of religious zeal and benevolence to bring into the Schools large numbers of the most needy and dangerous classes in Cities and Towns, shall be supplemented by developing and encouraging that religious spirit of benevolence and zeal which, under great disadvantages, has wrought out such beneficial results elsewhere. . . .

CHAPTER XXV.

PASSAGE OF THE SCOTT SEPARATE SCHOOL BILL, OF 1863.

AFTER the failure of the Scott Roman Catholic Separate School Bill, of 1862, to receive the assent of the Legislature at its Session of that year, renewed efforts were made to have it again introduced into the Legislature at its next Session, in 1863. Of this the Hon. John Sandfield Macdonald, who was Premier at the time, had cognizance. He, therefore, on the 2nd of February of that year, wrote to Dr. Ryerson urging him to be down in Quebec about the middle of the month, when the opening of the Legislature would take place. The following are copies of the private and confidential correspondence which took place in connection with the final passage of the Scott Separate School Bill, of 1863:—

1. *From the Hon. John Sandfield Macdonald, Attorney-General, to Dr. Ryerson, Chief Superintendent of Education:*

I think you should be down here about the time of the opening, as I am clear that explanations, in regard to the School Bill,* which you alone can satisfactorily give, will be required, and it may happen that, without your presence, our explanations would not be acceptable to some.

QUEBEC, 3rd of February, 1863. J. S. MACDONALD.

2. *From Dr. Ryerson, at Quebec, to J. George Hodgins:—*

I saw Mr. Sandfield Macdonald a few minutes yesterday morning. The Draft of Grammar School Bill, and Memorandum, is being printed in slips for the use of Members of the Government. I have not yet seen any Members of the Government but the Attorney-General. He wants me to stay and help them through the difficulties of the Separate School Bill, which he is inclined to make a Government measure,—also the Grammar School Bill. He is very friendly.

QUEBEC, February 24th, 1863. E. RYERSON.

3. *From J. George Hodgins to Dr. Ryerson, at Quebec:—*

I enclose a Letter in reference to the School Bills, which may be of use to the Premier. . . . I called on the Right Rev. Dr. Lynch, Roman Catholic Bishop of Toronto, and the Rev. Dr. Cahill, from Ireland, yesterday, and had a friendly interview with them of about two hours. The Bishop was cordial in his praises of our Public School System, and of the tolerance to the claims of his Church. In conversation with the Rev. Dr. Cahill, he spoke in the highest terms of the state of affairs in Canada, as compared with other places, and of his utter dislike to the course of the Montreal *True Witness*, and other kindred papers, in regard to you and the School System. The Bishop promised to bring up Dr. Cahill to see

---

* *i.e.*, The Grammar School Bill,—a draft of which Dr. Ryerson had transmitted to the Government,—and the Separate School Bill introduced by Mr. R. W. Scott.

our establishment. In the course of conversation, the Bishop stated that he had forbidden any of his Clergy to write in the newspapers without his knowledge, and the revision, either by himself, or by some other Dignitary, of their articles. I think that if simple justice and fair-minded treatment were accorded to the Roman Catholics, he (Bishop Lynch) and others would be made fast friends.

TORONTO, March 26th, 1863.   J. GEORGE HODGINS.

4. *Letter from Dr. Ryerson, Quebec, to J. George Hodgins:—*

I had an interview with two Ministers,—the Attorney-General, (J. S. Macdonald,) and Mr. William McDougall,—yesterday, respecting the Grammar and Separate School Bills. The Attorney-General seemed rather alarmed about what some one had said to him about giving Grammar School Trustees, etc., more power; but Mr. McDougall said that he had read the Bill, with the Memorandum on it, and thought it a good Bill; that he had given it to Mr. Reesor, an old County Warden, and well acquainted with School matters, and that Mr. Reesor thought it was the very thing that was wanted. This quite changed the aspect of the question in the mind of the Attorney-General. I am to see the Upper Canada Members of the Cabinet on the subject, as soon as they can meet me. . . . Then came up the Separate School question. I read to them your account of your interview with the Roman Catholic Bishop of Toronto, (Dr. Lynch,) with which they were much pleased. Mr. McDougall thought it best to introduce my little amendment Bill, [to Restore Certain Rights] of 1862, but the Attorney-General thought it best to introduce the Bill that the Authorities of the Roman Catholic Church had agreed to, which was less objectionable than the one agreed to by a Select Committee of the House, in 1862, and which was, in substance, the same as mine; that, if my amendments were introduced, the clauses would have to be given, to show how they would read.

Both agreed that the Government should take the matter in hand. I intend to propose to-day their introduction of the Bill, (with one alteration,) as agreed upon by me in 1862, (after conference with the Representatives of the Roman Catholic Church,) and with the Title of my amended Bill. . . .

QUEBEC, March the 3rd, 1863.   E. RYERSON.

5. *From Dr. Ryerson, Quebec, to J. George Hodgins:—*

The Ministry were to decide yesterday upon their course of proceeding in regard to the Grammar School Amendment Bill and the Separate School Bill. . . . It is a sort of Bedlam to me to stay here; but the Attorney-General says that I must remain until they get over these School difficulties. . . .

QUEBEC, 5th of March, 1863.   E. RYERSON.

6. *Letter from J. George Hodgins to Dr. Ryerson, Quebec :—*

I have just seen a copy of the Scott Roman Catholic Separate School Bill. . . . I do not see that it provides for an annual report from the Separate School Trustees,—which it ought to do. . . . I notice that you and the Local School Superintendents are Visitors of these Schools ; but why are you classed with these Officers ? as your functions, in regard to these Schools, are so entirely different ; and it is only through them that you would care to exercise any of your power, or authority, over them. . . .

TORONTO, 7th of March, 1863.   J. GEORGE HODGINS.

7. *From Dr. Ryerson, Quebec, to J. George Hodgins :—*

I met the Attorney-General, J. S. Macdonald, at dinner, and had a good deal of conversation with him. I expressed an earnest desire to return to Toronto, . . . but he said I "must not leave," . . . that my "hints and suggestions to him on the School Bill, and on several other matters, had already been of great assistance to him ;—that he did not think he could spare me before Easter," etc. (This is entirely confidential.) . . . I think that both School Bills, (Grammar and Separate Schools,) before the House will pass. . . .

QUEBEC, 9th of March, 1863.   E. RYERSON.

8. *From Dr. Ryerson, Quebec, to J. George Hodgins :—*

Mr. R. W. Scott's Bill passed through Committee, and was ordered to a third reading to-day. I will try and get the addition you suggest inserted at the third reading of the Bill. . . .

QUEBEC, 12th of March, 1863.   E. RYERSON.

9. *From J. George Hodgins to Dr. Ryerson, Quebec :—*

I see by the news telegram from Quebec to-day, that the Scott Separate School Bill had a majority of ten Upper Canada Members against it. . . . I have just seen a copy of the Bill, as amended in Committee. I would never have agreed to Section six, in its form, in that copy. The words " Separate School Section," (though commonly used,) is unwarranted by the Bill itself. That Bill does not provide for the establishment of a " Separate School Section " as such, but for the establishment of a Separate School in a " Common School Section," (quite a different thing.) . . . Under the Bill, Separate Schools may be established in adjoining Municipalities,—that is, in adjoining Counties, as well as in adjoining Townships, —and, in that case, be designated " Separate School Sections." . . .

From the result of last night's vote, I feel convinced that the Roman Catholic promoters of the Bill should have been contented with your original Draft of Bill. That would have been comparatively harmless; but, as *The Globe* shows to-day, the animus of the Bill is shown in Sections six and fourteen. The appeal, authorized in Section twenty-seven, is in the nature of an unnecessary threat. It was not required to be inserted in the Bill, as all of your decisions are, as a matter of course, subject to appeal. . . . It is another evidence of the animus of the Bill.*

TORONTO, 13th of March, 1863.   J. GEORGE HODGINS.

10. *From Dr. Ryerson, Quebec, to J. George Hodgins:*—

The Scott Separate School Bill, as amended, passed the House of Assembly last night, though a majority of ten Members from Upper Canada present voted against it. What course the Government will pursue, in regard to it now, I know not, as I have not seen any Member of the Government this morning.

In consequence of the whole of yesterday having been occupied with the discussion of the Separate School Bill, the Grammar School Amendment Bill has been laid over until next Government day. This, I am afraid, will detain me here another week. . . . The Government is weak. John Sandfield Macdonald has a poor opinion of many of his supporters, and I am not surprised at it. . . . John A. is conducting himself with great propriety. His speech last night, showing how he and his party had their revenge on those of their opponents who had hounded them through all Upper Canada as "supporters of Separate Schools," and as "slaves to the Priests,"—but who had now to support this Bill,—was very amusing, and very effective.

QUEBEC, 14th of March, 1863.   E. RYERSON.

11. *Letter from Dr. Ryerson, Quebec, to J. George Hodgins:*—

There is a sort of crisis in the ministerial ranks here, on account of the vote on the Separate School Bill. The Attorney General, (J. S. Macdonald,) told me this morning that, if his "Clear Grit" supporters did not come to his terms, he would deal with them in a way that they little anticipated. (This is *entre nous.*) The plan now is, I believe, for some slight amendment to be made to the Bill in the Legislative Council, so as to bring it back to the House of Assembly, so as to make the ministerial supporters vote for it out and out. . . . The Attorney General is unwilling for me to leave, until the School Bills are disposed of. . . .

QUEBEC, 16th of March, 1863.   E. RYERSON.

12. *Letter from J. George Hodgins to Dr. Ryerson, Quebec:*—

To an outsider like myself, the ministerial proceedings at Quebec are interesting. . . . As in war, so in politics, a clear-headed, prompt and determined man, decisive in action, is the man to be relied on in a crisis, as he thus makes himself the hero of the public. It may not occur to

---

* The reason for the insertion of this "appeal" section was given by Mr. Scott, in his speech in the Senate in 1894. (See page 166, *post.*)

politicians in action at Quebec, that their proceedings there are daily reviewed here with a calmness and a penetration, as to apparent motives and results, that those on the spot cannot do. It is in this light, and from this standpoint, that the action of the Attorney-General is viewed, and he is judged accordingly. He has clearly shown a degree of firmness on the Separate School question, (if he can maintain it), which recalls the days of Hincks. . . .

In regard to the Separate School Bill: I think that Section six, in its present shape, is decidedly objectionable; but Section twenty is very much more so. This latter Section provides that the Roman Catholic Separate Schools shall share in all Municipal School Rates, and all Municipal Grants for Common School purposes, whether the Separate School supporters have contributed to these Rates and Grants, or not.

I, of course, do not refer to the Rates required to be raised by the County Council, as an equivalent to the Legislative School Grant, but I refer to Grants which may be made by Township, Town, or City, and County Councils, under the authority of the Municipal, (not School,) Act. The Section, if passed, will have the effect of drying up, (or diverting entirely from Common School purposes,) the Grants from the Municipal Clergy Reserves Fund; and thus the Separate School Act will come rudely into collision with the policy and traditionary instincts of Upper Canada, in preventing this Fund from being applied, (as has been so long and so often advocated,) to Common School education. . . .

The twenty-second Section should provide for the Separate School Returns being made according to a form provided by the Education Department for that purpose, as in the case of the Common Schools.

There is one omission in the Separate School Act,—if the design was to restore the provisions of the former Acts of 1850-53; and that is, that the supporters of Separate Schools are not required to pay to the Separate School a rate, or subscription, equal to what they would have had to pay to the Common School, had they not been separated from it. As it is, any supporter in one County of a Separate School in an adjoining County, (to the extent of even a few cents), can escape all County, Township, or School Section, rates altogether! We well know what a premium this will be on pure selfishness.

TORONTO, 18th of March, 1863.   J. GEORGE HODGINS

13. *From Dr. Ryerson, Quebec, to J. George Hodgins:*—

Mr. McGee made a very good speech last night about paying faithful and efficient public servants good salaries. I will try and turn it to your account. . . . I am to take a family dinner with the Attorney-General, (J. S. Macdonald), this evening, as I have not been able to accept the two previous invitations. . . . I think that the trouble in the Government, on account of the Separate School Bill, is not yet over. I think I mentioned to you before, that I believe that the patched-up difficulty is to be settled by getting some friend of the Government to introduce some unimportant amendment, or amendments, to the Separate School Bill in the Legislative Council, so as to have it brought again before the House of Assembly, when each supporter of the Government there, or a majority of them from Upper Canada, was to support the Bill. But I understand that the Opposition in the Council are on the alert, and Col. Taché, Messieurs Ross, Shaw and others are going to support the Separate School Bill there intact, and they will probably have a majority, while the professed supporters of the Government will be in the odd position of striving to amend a Government Bill, and the Opposition supporting it without amendment! If the Attorney-General does not, in some way, have the vote of a majority of the House from Upper Canada in favour of that Bill, I do not think he will have it to become law. He is determined that his professed supporters of the Government will support it on its declared policy in regard to settling the Separate School and the Representation question, or he will leave them to their fate.

QUEBEC, 17th of March, 1863. E. RYERSON.

14. *Telegram from Dr. Ryerson, Quebec, to J. George Hodgins:*

Get five thousand copies of the present and proposed Separate School Act, as compared, printed, folded and sent in parcels of one hundred each to Mr. Spink, (Parliamentary Distribution Officer,) by express, without a moment's delay. Send them daily, as printed.

QUEBEC, 13th of April, 1863. E. RYERSON.

15. *Letter from Dr. Ryerson, Quebec, to J. George Hodgins:*—

The Members of the Government, and of all parties, have thanked me most heartily for the analysis and comparative view of the Separate School Law (of 1855) and Bill (of 1863).* Nothing that I have done, or written, since the de Charbonnel controversy seems to have been so popular. Mr. Skead, of Ottawa, (successor of the Hon. Mr. Vankoughnet,) wished me to get a thousand copies for him, to send among his constituents, and other Members expressed a desire to have large numbers for the same purpose. . . .

The Attorney-General called upon me yesterday and said many agreeable things. . . . It is very pleasant to be on such good terms with the leading men of both parties, without being suspected of either, and it being perfectly understood by both that I take no part in their party intrigues, nor ever betray them. . . .

QUEBEC, 13th of April, 1863. E. RYERSON.

---

* This "Analysis and Comparison" is appended to Dr. Ryerson's annual report for 1862, pages 160-170.

16. *Letter from J. George Hodgins to Dr. Ryerson, Quebec :—*

Your telegram was received, and I put the matter in hand at once. I sent a copy of the "Comparison" to *The Leader* some days ago, with a private note, requesting the Editor to give it prominence, so as to allay the agitation on the subject. He did so, and inserted the whole document, with an Editorial Note. He again refers to the matter to-day. *The Globe* gives no inkling of the contents of the same paper which I sent to it. . . . I see that *The Quebec Mercury* is quite jubilant over this "Comparison of Separate School Acts of 1855 and 1863." . . .

TORONTO, 14th of April, 1863.   J. GEORGE HODGINS.

17. *Letter from Dr. Ryerson, Quebec, to J. George Hodgins :—*

I telegraphed you a day or two ago, to get five thousand of my Comparison of the Separate School Bills of 1855 and 1863 printed and sent down, for the use of the Members. The Attorney-General wishes the expense to be charged to the Department, and has written me a note to that effect, as it is the diffusion of information on this Separate School Law and School System, without reference to party. Mr. G. Benjamin, M.P., told me that he was getting another edition printed here also.

QUEBEC, 15th of April, 1863.   E. RYERSON.

18. *Letter from Dr. Ryerson, Quebec, to J. George Hodgins :—*

The Separate School Bill passed the Committee of the Whole in the Legislative Council yesterday. The amendments are to be moved at the third reading. There was a majority of two or three from Upper Canada against the second reading; but there is likely to be a majority from Upper Canada in favour of the third reading to-day. I do not think that any amendments will be admitted. . . .

QUEBEC, 17th of April, 1863.   E. RYERSON.

19. *Letter from J. George Hodgins to Dr. Ryerson, Quebec :—*

I see by the news telegram from Quebec that the Separate School Bill has passed the Legislative Council without any amendment! This, I am sorry for; as it needed at the very least, the amendments which I suggested. Of course, for the defects in the Bill, the Department will have to bear all the blame. . . . I hope that, as a set-off to the Separate School Bill, you will be able to get the proposed financial additions made to the Grammar School Bill. They will aid the Department greatly by its Library Scheme, to spread truth and knowledge in Upper Canada, as well as promote the public good.

TORONTO, 18th of April, 1863.   J. GEORGE HODGINS.

20. *Letter from J. George Hodgins to Dr. Ryerson, Quebec : —*

The Rev. Mr. Ryan, Roman Catholic Priest at Oakville, called this evening to express his personal gratitude to you for your exertions in getting the Separate School Bill passed. He says that this feeling is general among Roman Catholics, for the signal service which you have rendered them, after all the battles of "lang syne." Mr. Ryan was formerly, and for six years, Roman Catholic Priest at Brantford; and he says that he will make it his business to wait upon your Brother William to thank him for his generous speech in the House, and for his manly vote. . . . Mr. Ryan is a warm-hearted Irishman, and feels very grateful to you. Thus, the lights and shades of the picture are presented to us. I am sorry to say that the shades prevail; but I trust that they will not overshadow us.

TORONTO, 23rd of April, 1863. J. GEORGE HODGINS.

21. *Letter of the Rev. M. Stafford to Dr. Ryerson:*—

Before leaving Toronto, I wish to return you my most sincere thanks for the kind courtesy with which you gave me so much of your time and attention this morning. I will be happy, on my return to Kingston, to be able to tell my Bishop, and the old Vicar-General, (Macdonell,) of your great kindness to me. . . .

TORONTO, 20th of January, 1863. M. STAFFORD, Pt.

CHAPTER XXVI.

DR. RYERSON'S NARRATIVE OF THE PASSING OF THE ROMAN CATHOLIC SEPARATE SCHOOL ACT OF 1863.

IN 1865, in consequence of a renewed agitation for further legislation in regard to Roman Catholic Separate Schools, Dr. Ryerson issued a pamphlet on the subject, entitled: "Remarks on the New Separate School Agitation. By the Chief Superintendent of Education for Upper Canada." In it, he mentions the result of his Conference with Roman Catholic Representatives of Upper and Lower Canada, and then the final passage of the Scott Bill of 1863:—

Mr Scott, a Roman Catholic lawyer, and, at the time, Member of the Legislative Assembly for the City of Ottawa, introduced a Separate School Bill during three successive sessions of 1860, 1861, and 1862, but failed to get it passed. After further consultation with the Members and Authorities of his Church, he introduced his Bill again, (with sundry alterations and additions,) in the Session of 1863. I believe he claimed the tacit assent of the Government for his introduction of this Bill.

In the discussion on its second reading and reference to a Special Committee, Mr. Scott made a personal attack upon me.* I remembered, as I still do, Lord MACAULAY's advice, given as early as January, 1827, in the *Edinburgh Review*, in respect to replying to attacks. He says:—

"No misrepresentations should be suffered to pass unrefuted. When a silly letter makes its appearance in the corner of a provincial newspaper, it will not do to say, 'What stuff!' We must remember that such statements constantly reiterated, and seldom answered, will assuredly be believed."

I therefore answered Mr. Scott's attacks, in a Letter addressed to him, through the public press. In that Letter, I also took occasion to point out the anomalies in his School Bill, and to show that, under the pretext of affording relief to Roman Catholics, it contained provisions which invaded the private rights of citizens, the legal rights of Common School Corporations, and of County and Township Municipalities. I also objected, as I had done in private Letters to Members of the Government, against any unofficial Member of the Legislature being allowed to introduce a Bill affecting our Public School System, which had been established by the Government, and which should be protected by it, and only legislated upon by bills introduced by, and on the responsibility of, the Government itself.

At this juncture, a change of administration took place: the Hon. J. Sandfield Macdonald formed a new administration, and an adjournment of the Legislature, for several weeks, was agreed upon. On the re-assembling of Parliament, Mr. Scott's Special Committee reported his Bill with certain amendments, which were printed; but very general and strong opposition in Upper Canada was entertained, and was manifesting itself more and more to the Bill.

At this time I had proceeded, officially, to Quebec; and when asked my opinion, I objected scarcely less strongly to the amended Bill, than I had done to the Bill as first introduced. The opposition to it among Upper Canada Members was very strong; and the Government did not appear to countenance it. At length Mr. Scott called upon me, to explain some personal matters, and to know my specific objections to his Bill. I replied, that I objected to the very principle of a private Member of Parliament doing what the Government alone should do, namely, bringing in measures to amend, (when deemed necessary,) a System of Public Instruction for the country; but Mr. Scott wished to know what objections I had to the Bill itself. I then showed, and, at his request, lent him a copy of the amended Bill, with my erasure of objectionable clauses, and notes on others requiring modifications to assimilate them to the Common School law.

---

* In regard to a former gratuitous attack, in 1862, founded on Mr. R. W. Scott's own mistake, see page 132, *ante*.

Then follows in this narrative, an account of the stipulation which Dr. Ryerson made with Mr. Scott that his assent to the Bill in any form depended on its acceptance "by the Authorities of his Church as a final settlement of the question." This matter will be treated in a separate chapter, under the heading of : " Was the Separate School Act of 1863 a Finality ? "

In the same publication, Dr. Ryerson instituted a comparison between the provisions of the Separate School Act of 1863 and those in force in regard to the Public Schools. He says :—

I am prepared to show, before any Committee, or tribunal, that the Separate School Act of 1863 contains all the provisions in behalf of Trustees and supporters of Separate Schools, that the Common School Act does in behalf of the Trustees and supporters of Common Schools, (and several additional ones, as shown above,) with two exceptions :—

1. The supporters of Common Schools have to provide by assessment a sum equal to the Legislative School Grant, in order to be entitled to it. The law formerly required the same condition on the part of the supporters of Separate Schools, in order to their sharing in the Legislative School Grant ; but they complained of it as a grievance, and the Separate School Acts of both 1855 and 1863 relieved them of that condition.

2. The Trustees of Common Schools, as also Trustees of Separate Schools, can levy and collect rates of their supporters for all school purposes ; but, in addition, the former can call upon the Municipal Councils to levy rates on their supporters for them, while the latter cannot require the Municipal Council to levy and collect rates of their supporters, though they could at all times levy and collect such rates themselves.

Dr. Ryerson thus points out the reason why the law is restrictive in this matter :—

The reason of this difference is, first, the School Law of Lower Canada took away in 1857, from Municipal Councils there, the power of levying and collecting rates in behalf of Dissentient, or Protestant, Schools ; and, of course, the Upper Canada School Act of 1863 contained a corresponding provision in respect to Separate Schools. This, however, is of trifling importance on either side, as Trustees can quite as well, through their own Collector, collect their School Rates, as to collect them by the agency of the Municipal Council. But the primary reason is, that on the principle of the declared " separation of Church and State," the Municipalities, any more than the Legislature, cannot impose and collect taxes for Church Schools, any more than they can impose and collect taxes for Church Buildings, or Church Ministers, of any kind.

It is, then, impossible to extend the provisions of the Separate School law, without including one or both of two things; and both of these things were included in the first drafts, or copies, of the Separate School Bills of 1855 and 1863. The first of these provisions prohibited either Municipalities, or Trustees of Common Schools, from levying and collecting any rate for either the building of a School House, or paying a Teacher, without levying and collecting rates for the supporters of a Separate School, in proportion to their population, as compared with that of the rest of the School Section, or Municipality,—thus actually proposing to make Municipalities and Protestant School Trustees tax-gatherers for Roman Catholic Schools,—a practical illustration of the doctrine, that "the State shall be subject to the Church," as well as that Protestants should not only support the Public Schools, but collect rates to support the Roman Catholic Schools, or have no schools themselves! The second provision is, that the Roman Catholics, as a body, shall be defined as supporters of Separate Schools, and thus by law be excluded from the Common Schools. This was in the first project of the Bills referred to,—thus depriving every Roman Catholic of the right or liberty of choice, as to whether he would support a Common, or Separate, School; and every Roman Catholic parent of the right or liberty of choice as to whether he would send his children to the Common or Separate School.

A recent Encyclical Letter from Rome condemns this individual right of judgment or choice; . . . yet is it the very soul of our civil and religious liberties, and as dear to the hearts of Roman Catholics as to the hearts of Protestants, though the former may not be able, equally with the latter, to maintain by speech, writing and action, this birthright of our common humanity.

Now, I assume that our Parliament never will legislate away the rights of citizens and of men, by adopting either of these provisions; without doing which it cannot extend, as required, the provisions of the Separate School Law. . . .

Separate Schools cannot be claimed upon any ground of right, as I have often shown in discussing the subject in former years. All that any citizen can claim as a right on this subject is equal and impartial protection with any other citizen. All that can be claimed, or granted, beyond this, must be upon the ground of compact, or of expediency, or indulgence. . . .

This feature of the subject,—as it affects the future of the youths educated in Schools isolated from those of the General System of the Province,—will be discussed in the concluding Chapter of this Volume. In that Chapter, the views of the Roman Catholic Archbishop Ireland, on the subject of "State Schools," will be given.

CHAPTER XXVII.

INCIDENTS OF THE PASSING OF THE SEPARATE SCHOOL ACT OF 1863.

Mr. R. W. Scott introduced his Roman Catholic Separate School Bill, for the fourth time, on the 27th of February, 1863. On the 5th of March, a motion was made for the second reading of the Bill.

It was then moved in amendment, by Mr. Leonidas Burwell, seconded by Mr. Alexander Mackenzie, that the Bill be read that day six months.

For this motion the Upper Canada vote was 21 yeas, and 34 nays. The total vote was, however, 22 yeas, and 80 nays. The Bill was then referred to a Special Committee, consisting of Messieurs R. W. Scott, John S. Macdonald, John A. Macdonald, William Clarke, and H. W. McCann.*

When the Bill, as amended, came back from this Committee, it was moved by Mr. Donald A. Macdonald, (afterwards Lieutenant-Governor of Ontario,) seconded by Mr. James Lyons Biggar, that the following words be added to the Second Section :—

Provided always, that no such Separate School shall be established in any Township, unless the Roman Catholic residents therein constitute the minority of the inhabitants of such School Section.

The vote on this motion by the Upper Canada Members, was 33 yeas, (and 3 Lower Canada votes,) 36; the nays, 24, (and 54 Lower Canada votes); total, 36 yeas, and 78 nays.

---

* On page 17, I have called attention to the fact that the first Government Common School Bill of 1841, which provided for the establishment of Separate Schools, was referred to a Special Committee, in violation of the principles of "responsible Government." This Bill, however, of 1863, was a private one, and in private hands, until it was assumed by the Government, after it had received Dr. Ryerson's approval.

Incidents of the Passing of the Act of 1863. 165

It was then moved by the Hon. John Hillyard Cameron, seconded by Mr. W. Anderson :—

That the word : "Authorities" be left out of the twentieth Clause, and that the following be inserted : Provided always, that the amount of the Legislative Grant to any Separate School, in any one year, shall not exceed the aggregate amount contributed by rates, fees, or otherwise, by the supporters of such Separate School in said year.

The vote of the Upper Canada Members on this motion was, 34 yeas, (and 2 Lower Canada yeas), 36 : the nays were 13, (and 52 Lower Canada nays). Total : 36 yeas ; and 65 nays.

On the motion for the third reading of the Bill, the Upper Canada yeas were : Messieurs Anderson, Bell, (Russell,) Benjamin, Buchanan, Carling, Clarke, Crawford, Foley, John A. Macdonald, John S. Macdonald, McCann, McDougall, McLachlan, Patrick, Ryerson, Rykert, Scott, Sherwood, Simpson, Walsh, and Wilson : 21. Lower Canada yeas, 55. The Upper Canada nays were : Messieurs Ault, Biggar, Brown, Burwell, J. H. Cameron, Cockburn, Cowan, Daly, Dickson, Ferguson, Harcourt, Haultain, Hooper, Jackson, Jones, Mackenzie, McKellar, Morris, Morrison, Mowat, Munro, Notman, Powell, J. S. Ross, Rymal, Scatchard, Scoble, Smith, Stirton, White and Wright : 31. There were no Lower Canada nays.

Thus, 21 Upper Canada Members voted for the Roman Catholic Separate School Act of 1863, and 31 against it; majority of Upper Canada votes against the Act, 10. The Lower Canada yeas made the vote to stand thus : Yeas, 76 ; Nays, 31.

In the Legislative Council, on the motion that the Bill do now pass, it was moved by the Hon. David Christie, seconded by the Hon. J. C. Aikens,
That the Bill be amended as follows :—
In Section 30, leave out the words : And shall be entitled also to a share in all other public grants, investments, and allotments, for Common School purposes, now made, or hereafter to be made, by the Province, or the Municipal authorities.
At the end of Section 30, add the words : Provided, that a School shall have been kept by a qualified Teacher, for at least six months during the year. Contents, 12 ; non-contents, 44.
It was moved by the Hon. G. W. Allan, seconded by the Hon. James Gordon :—
Provided always, that no such Separate School shall be entitled to any such grant, investments, or allotments, except under such circumstances, and subject to the same restriction as such grants, investments, or allotments, are made to Common Schools in Upper Canada. Contents, 13 ; non-contents, 43.

On a motion that the Bill do now pass, the vote stood thus: Contents, 44; non-contents, 13.

The names of the Upper Canada Members who voted yea, were the Hon. Messieurs A. J. Ferguson-Blair, Malcolm Cameron, George Crawford, William H. Dickson, George J. Goodhue, James Gordon, John Hamilton, E. Leonard, Donald Macdonald, W. McCrea, Roderick Matheson, Samuel Mills, Ebenezer Perry, Robert Read, John Ross and James Shaw, 16, and 28 Lower Canada yeas); total, 44. Those who voted nay, were the Hon. James C. Aikens, George Alexander, George W. Allan, Thomas Bennett, Oliver Blake, George S. Boulton, Andrew Jeffrey, William McMaster, John McMurrich, John Simpson, James Skead and Harmanus Smith, 13. There were no Lower Canada nays.

The Upper Canada yeas were 16; the nays, 13.

CHAPTER XXVIII.

SEPARATE SCHOOL ACT OF 1863—MR. SCOTT'S STATEMENT.

In the Senate, on the 4th of April, 1894, Mr. R. W. Scott made the following statement, in regard to the passing of his Upper Canada Roman Catholic Separate School Act of 1863:—

In the British North America Act there is an appeal to the [Dominion] Privy Council from any Act affecting the rights of the Catholic and Protestant minorities. . . . In the Manitoba Act . . . the appeal shall be to the Governor-General-in-Council from any Act, or decision of the Legislature of the Province. . . . These words are peculiar to the Manitoba Act alone,* proving most conclusively that there was a jealous resolve on the part of the framers of the Act at the time, that there should be a direct appeal to the Governor-General-in-Council from any hostile decisions,—that they were not to be forced into the Courts,—that the remedy was to be short and quick.†

---

* This is not so. The words relating to "appeal" is the same in both Acts.

† The subject of an appeal "from any Act, or decision, of the Legislature" of this Province was brought up in the Ontario House of Assembly on the 16th of March, 1895, by Dr. George Sterling Ryerson, M.P.P., nephew of the Reverend Doctor Ryerson. *The Globe* newspaper thus reports the circumstances:—

In the House of Assembly, the question was asked by Dr. G. S. Ryerson as to the application of the recent decision of the Imperial Privy Council to the Separate School Laws of Ontario. The Premier replied that that decision did not apply to this Province.

MR. RYERSON asked whether, under the recent decision of the Judicial Committee of the Imperial Privy Council, the amendments to, and changes in, the Separate Schools Act in Ontario passed since Confederation can be repealed

These words are very peculiar. How did they occur? I think I know something of the history of them, inasmuch as the original words were introduced in an Act that I drafted in the year 1862, or 1863. I hold in my hand the original Act of 1863. . . . The conferences I had in drawing up the Separate School Act in Old Canada in 1861, 1862 and 1863, were chiefly with Dr. Ryerson. There was not on any occasion any clerical interference. . . . The conferences were held with Dr. Ryerson in the Library, and it is due to his memory to say, that I always found him ready to meet the wishes of the minority;—that he exhibited no prejudice or bigotry. . . . There was only one occasion when a clerical gentleman was present, the Rev. Mr. Macdonell of Kingston, Vicar-General,—and he was the only clerical gentleman who was present on any occasion at the framing of these clauses.* I had circulars sent out to the [Roman Catholic Separate School] Trustees all over Ontario, asking for suggestions and advice, with a view to making the Law more workable.

Dr. Ryerson offered no impediment; but there was a strong feeling prevailing with [Roman] Catholics that he was hostile to the Act. People believed that he was always decidedly against Separate Schools. I am not aware that, after this [Roman Catholic Separate School] Act [of 1863] was passed, there was a single appeal under it. . . . I drew up the clause [which is now the Twenty-Seventh Section of the Roman Catholic School Act of 1863†]. . . . There is where the idea was taken for an appeal, as provided in the British North America Act. It was only to be found in this particular Act; and it was simply based upon that idea that the Chief Superintendent, (Dr Ryerson,) was not friendly to the Separate School System, which was a mistake, because he was sincerely anxious to do what was really fair to make the Law workable. That is where the appeal comes by this Legislature. And whether, in the event of the repeal of any such amendments, an appeal will lie to the Governor-General-in-Council, under the Ninety-Third, or other, Section of the British North America Act?

SIR OLIVER MOWAT—Under the decisions of the Judicial Committee of the Imperial Privy Council, the enactments of the Legislature of Ontario in regard to Separate Schools since Confederation can be repealed by this Legislature. The effect of such a repeal is authoritatively declared by the late Judgment of the Judicial Committee of the Imperial Privy Council, and I can add nothing to what appears from their Judgment as to whether, in the event of such repeal, an appeal would lie to the Governor-General-in-Council, under the Ninety-Third, or other, Section of the British North America Act.

* There is a singular discrepancy here. The two Vicars-General were present at both of the conferences held with Dr. Ryerson in 1862 and 1863. See pages 139, 154 and 162.

† Dr. Ryerson's note appended to this Section of the Separate School Act of 1863, in his "Roman Catholic Separate Schools Act of 1850 and 1863 Compared," is as follows: "This is . . . a new legal provision. The latter part of this Section is needless, and is not contained in the Grammar, or Common Schools, Act, as all decisions of the Chief Superintendent may be appealed from to the Governor-in-Council. His decisions have been appealed from on several instances, but have, in every instance, been sustained."—(Chief Superintendent's Annual Report for 1863, page 170.)

in. It does not exist anywhere else. I intended the appeal, [in the Act of 1863,] to be prompt and direct. It was thought that the Governor-in-Council would be the fairest tribunal, and they would dispose of it at once. . . . In our Public Schools in Ontario, as they were originally established, Religion was intended to be taught. . . . D. Ryerson was sent abroad to examine the [School] Systems in England, Germany and the United States. . . . He was a man of very large observation, and one whom I always found free from prejudices, and possessed of a fair and just mind. He says:—"In France religion formed no part of the elementary education for many years, and, in some parts of the United States, the example of France has been followed." . . . I should like to point out some evidences that Dr. Ryerson's prophecies have been, to a considerable extent, fulfilled in the Eastern States, where this system of separating God from the Schools was first introduced. . . . (*Hansard Senate Debates, 4th of April, 1894.*)

CHAPTER XXIX.

SIR JOHN MACDONALD AND HON. ALEXANDER MACKENZIE ON THE SEPARATE SCHOOL ACT OF 1863.

MR. JOSEPH POPE, in his "Memoirs of Sir John Macdonald," thus refers to the Roman Catholic Separate School Act of 1863:

Mr. Macdonald's brief respite from the cares of office had done wonders for him; and he took his seat at the opening of the Session of Parliament on the 12th of February, 1863, ready for the fray. . . .

His experience told him that the (J. S.) Macdonald-Sicotte Government, pledged to the impossible scheme of the "double majority," could not hope to weather the Session, in the face of the opposition rising against them,—not only among the Conservatives, but also in the ranks of the Reform party. A new ground of dissatisfaction against them was speedily afforded by the Separate School measure of Mr. R. W. Scott, which the Ministry supported. This action of Messieurs Foley, McDougall and Wilson was reprobated by *The Globe* newspaper, which unsparingly denounced them for their political recreancy in thus yielding up another principle of Liberalism.

"Representation by population and no Sectarian Schools" had long been watchwords of the Reform party; yet here was a so-called Liberal Ministry "basely sacrificing their principles to the exigencies of party. That Mr. John A. Macdonald should aid in riveting the fetters of Rome upon a free people was to be expected ;"—such a course was in conformity with his whole record ; but that such men as Foley, Howland, Wilson, and . . McDougall . . . should, for the sake of office, league themselves with the foes of religious liberty, was enough to cause one to despair of humanity. Mr. Macdonald warmly supported the Scott Bill, which had been before the House during his term of office, when it was bitterly opposed by those very Members now forming the Upper Canadian section of Sandfield Macdonald's Cabinet. The spectacle presented by these men, now speaking and voting in favour of the Bill, was, in the judgment of Mr. Macdonald, "a splendid vindication" of the policy of the late Government, and of the principle which he had long advocated with respect to the School System of Upper Canada.

The appeal of *The Globe* . . . was not made in vain, for, while Mr. Scott's Bill passed, it was carried by the votes of Lower Canada, and of Mr. John A. Macdonald and his personal friends. A large number of the Upper Canadian supporters of the Government, greatly to the wrath of Mr. J. S. Macdonald, voted against it, thereby placing the Ministry in a minority of ten votes, as regarded Upper Canada.

Having formally announced their resolve to abide by the "double-majority" principle, the Ministry, by this vote, were placed in an embarrassing position. The question was put direct to the Premier, whether he proposed, in the face of a declared opposition of the majority of its representatives, to force the Separate School Act upon Upper Canada. To this pertinent question, Mr. Sandfield Macdonald made an evasive reply, but the "double-majority" principle was then heard of for the last time. . . .

In an argumentative and temperate speech, Mr. John A. Macdonald proceeded to explain the reasons upon which his motion of non-confidence was based. . . . He asked : Did the Prime Minister, (J. S. Macdonald,) in his efforts to maintain himself in office, reflect that, in forcing the Separate School measure upon Upper Canada, against the will of a majority of its Representatives, he was doing violence to the convictions of his whole political life ? (Vol. I., pages 244-246.)

. . . There remains but one question of practical politics in relation to which I propose to outline Sir John Macdonald's attitude. I refer to those issues of race and religion, which periodically threaten the peace of Canada. . . .

In 1855, he introduced, and carried, a Bill in the interest of the Separate Schools of Upper Canada, against the bitter opposition of George Brown.

In 1863, he supported, by speech and vote, Mr. R. W. (now Senator) Scott's Act, establishing a System of Separate Schools.

In 1867, he perpetuated this right to the Roman Catholics of Ontario. . . . (Vol. II., page 248.)

THE HON. ALEXANDER MACKENZIE AND THE SCOTT ROMAN CATHOLIC SEPARATE SCHOOL ACT OF 1863.

The following is taken from "The Life of the Hon. Alexander Mackenzie, by Mr. William Buckingham and the Hon. George W. Ross":—

The great measure of 1863 was Mr. R. W. Scott's Bill respecting Separate Schools in Upper Canada. Mr. Scott had introduced the Bill several times, and had advanced it so far in the previous Session as to reach a division on its second reading.

The principle of Separate Schools was first introduced into Canada under an Act of 1841, and was further enlarged by the Act of 1855. Mr. Scott proposed still further to extend the privileges of Roman Catholics with regard to Separate Schools.

The main features of Mr. Scott's Bill were :—Extending the facilities for establishing Separate Schools in rural districts; permitting Roman Catholics to give notice of their intention to become Separate School supporters once for all, instead of annually, as under the former Act; relieving Trustees from certifying the average attendance of pupils under oath; providing for the inspection of Separate Schools, and for their general administration [?] through the Council of Public Instruction.

In the session of 1862, the Bill passed its second reading; but, owing to the defeat of the Government, it stood over. The Bill passed very quickly through all its stages, and was approved by the House on the 13th of March; the yeas being 74, and the nays 30. When the second reading of the Bill was under consideration, Mr. Burwell moved, seconded by Mr. Mackenzie, what is commonly known as "the six months' hoist."

On that motion Mr. Mackenzie gave his views on the question of religious instruction. He opposed the Bill on three grounds : *Firstly*, he feared it would be injurious to the Common School System of the Province. *Secondly*, he feared it would lead to a demand for Separate Schools from other denominations. *Thirdly*, the establishment of Separate Schools in certain localities would divide the resources of the people, already very limited, and thus lower the standard of education. "He had no desire," he said, "to make this a religious question, as he was not disposed to vote against any Bill, which even Roman Catholics themselves deemed necessary to secure perfect freedom in the exercise of their religious faith; but, as our School System was undenominational, the Bill under consideration was therefore unnecessary."

The vote on this Bill was the first substantial decision of the House to which the principle of "double majority" would apply, as 31 members from Upper Canada voted against it, while its supporters from Upper Canada numbered only 21.

Mr. John A. Macdonald rallied the Upper Canadian Members of the Government—MacDougall, Foley, Wilson and Sandfield Macdonald—on their change of front on the question of Separate Schools, quoting from the Journals of the House how, in previous years, they had voted either against the principle of Separate Schools, or for the repeal of the existing Separate School Act; while now, they were practically responsible for a Bill extending the scope of Separate Schools. The Premier was also asked if the measure was to be forced on Upper Canada in the face of the opposition of a majority of its Representatives? To this Mr. Sandfield Macdonald made no reply.

The agitation which arose in Upper Canada, on account of the Separate School policy of the then Government, greatly weakened them in public estimation.

THE HON. GEORGE BROWN AND SEPARATE SCHOOLS.

For one who devoted so large a portion of his time and attention to the question of Denominational Education, it is surprising how little is said on the subject by his Friend and Biographer, the Hon. Alexander Mackenzie. Even what is said is both meagre in detail, and somewhat apologetic in spirit and tone. In referring to Mr. Brown's part in the Separate School controversy, Mr. Mackenzie, (in Chapter V. of his "Life and Speeches of the Hon. George Brown,") says:—

Like all religious, or semi-religious, controversies, this one developed hard words, and harder feelings. . . . Apart from the special controversy, . . . (in England, on the "Papal aggression,") there was much agitation in Canada West over the demands for Separate Schools for Roman Catholics. . . . It is not to be denied that deep offence was taken at many articles in *The Globe*, and other papers, by a large majority of the Roman Catholics who did not come into personal contact with Mr. Brown personally, and appreciate his kindly and honest nature. Looking back, it is impossible to deny that many harsh words were written, which had better not have been written. . . .

When Mr. Brown formed his Cabinet in 1858, it was upon an agreement that the Separate School question would be dealt with, after a full inquiry should be made into the School Systems in other Countries,—Catholic and Protestant;—and there is no reason to doubt, that had his Ministry been permitted to go on, means would have been found to harmonize the various views held by himself and his political Associates.

The Amended Separate School Act of 1863, and the immediately succeeding arrangement effected in the Confederation Act, removed this question from the field of controversy; but, even before then, nearly all irritation had ceased in Ontario. . . .—(*Pages 33–35.*)

CHAPTER XXX.

WAS THE ROMAN CATHOLIC SEPARATE SCHOOL ACT OF 1863 A FINALITY?*

ONE of the most unpleasant and harassing features of the Roman Catholic Separate School Question was the unsettled opinions and uncertain moods of its chief supporters.

The supposed settlement of the question in 1850, by the adoption of the then well-known "Nineteenth Section of the General School Act" of that year, was hailed by those then interested as embodying a very practical way of meeting the individual conscientious convictions of Members of the Roman Catholic Church. It was so regarded by them until after the Meeting of the Roman Catholic General Council at Baltimore in 1851. By the promoters of that Council, or by his Church, as he expressed it, Bishop de Charbonnel was, as he twice intimated, practically called to account; first, in his Letter to Dr. Ryerson, of the 1st of May, 1852, he stated that:—

All my previous intercourse with you, and the Council of Public Instruction, has been polite and Christian, and sometimes tolerant to an extent that I have been required to justify;—

And then, afterwards, when he made his meaning on this point more clear, in his Letter of the 26th of the same month, to the Hon. S. B. Harrison, Chairman of the Council of Public Instruction, he said:—

All my precedents with you, the Reverend Doctor, and the Council of Public Instruction, have been polite and Christian, and sometimes of a tolerance for which my Church has made me responsible.

---

* *i.e.* Finality as to assumed "rights," and as to such further demands for Separate Schools, as would affect the integrity and stability of our Public School System; but not, of course, finality in regard to details of administration, or as to which would be the better way to do things which the law allowed, or authorized, or prescribed;—no doubt, just such a finality as Mr. Scott meant, in his Letter to Dr. Ryerson of the 26th of April, 1862, when he said: "I want the Bill to be a *finality*."

The result of the controversy which followed these statements of Bishop de Charbonnel, in 1852, was the passage of the much discussed Taché Roman Catholic Separate School Act in 1855. That the passage of that Act was satisfactory to Bishop de Charbonnel at the time, is evident from the following extract of a Letter from Sir John Macdonald to Dr. Ryerson, dated the 8th of June, 1855, in which he said :—

Our Separate School Bill, which is, as you know, quite harmless, passed with the approbation of our Friend, Bishop de Charbonnel, who, before leaving here, formally thanked the Administration for "doing justice to his Church." He has, however, got a new light since his return to Toronto, and now says that the Bill won't do. . . .

It was such a "new light" as this, which so invariably broke in upon the promoters of Roman Catholic Separate Schools, after the passage of each successive Separate School Act, which caused so much trouble ; and which kept the Province in such a state of educational turmoil and unrest, that it made it all the more difficult for Dr. Ryerson to deal with each particular case, or with the many imaginary grievances which were, as often as real ones, the cause of the continued agitation.

It was this state of vacillation and uncertainty, on the part of the promoters of Separate Schools, which so continually embarrassed Dr. Ryerson in his administration of the Separate School Law, as it stood,—even giving it, as he did, the most liberal interpretation possible, or, as Mr. R. W. Scott, in his Senate speech of 1894, put it, when he said that—

Dr. Ryerson "was sincerely anxious to do what was really fair to make the Law workable."

In accounting to the Governor-General, (in his Confidential Report of 1868,) for the continual agitation of the Roman Catholic Separate School Question, Dr. Ryerson said :—

It is worthy of remark that, on the passing of each of the three Acts, (1850, 1853, and 1855,) amending the Law, in regard to Separate Schools, the Roman Catholic Bishop of Toronto and the Upper Canada Roman Catholic newspaper organs expressed their entire satisfaction with them, (at the time,) but afterwards complained of them, when it was found that they did not accomplish the object [desired]. . . .

COMPACT WITH THE REPRESENTATIVES OF THE ROMAN CATHOLIC
CHURCH IN 1862 AND 1863.

Before Dr. Ryerson went down to Quebec, late in May, 1862, he received a private Letter from the Hon. John A. Macdonald, dated the 3rd of that month, in regard to the Roman Catholic Separate School Bill which Mr. R. W. Scott sought to get passed by the Legislature. In that Letter, Mr. Macdonald said:—

. . . Scott . . . introduced the present Bill without showing it to me. . . . He has been looked up to as the exponent of Roman Catholic views on the subject; and the Bill, when "amended to suit me," will be carried through the House by him, and must be accepted by the Roman Catholics as their Bill.

After Dr. Ryerson reached Quebec late in May, he wrote me a private Letter, dated the 2nd of June, 1862, in which he said:

Yesterday morning the (Rev. Angus Macdonell) Vicar-General of Kingston,—acting on behalf of the Roman Catholic Bishops of Toronto and Kingston,—and the Rev. Mr. Cazeau, Secretary of the Archbishop of Quebec, as Representatives of the Authorities of the Roman Catholic Church, accepted the Separate School Bill, as proposed to be amended by me, and agreed to by Mr. R. W. Scott; and afterwards us four waited upon the new Premier, (Hon. John Sandfield Macdonald,)* and informed him of the result of our consultation, and the desire of the Authorities of the Roman Catholic Church that the Government would affirm and facilitate Mr. Scott's proceeding with the Bill.

In his Letter to *The Leader* newspaper of the 10th of July, 1862, Dr. Ryerson again referred to the conditions of his concurrence with the Roman Catholic Separate School Bill in the hands of Mr. Scott, and said:—

When at Quebec, . . . I stated that I would resist its further progress in the Legislature, except on two conditions:—

First. That the Bill thus modified should be accepted as a settlement of the question by the authorities of the Roman Catholic Church.

Secondly. That the Government should assent to Mr. Scott's proceeding with it. To secure the former of these objects, Mr. Scott got the Vicar-General Macdonell, (who had gone from Upper Canada to Quebec in behalf of the authorities of the Church to watch legislation on school matters,) and the Rev. the Secretary of the Roman Catholic Archbishop of

---

* The Hon. John Sandfield Macdonald succeeded the Hon. John A. Macdonald as Attorney-General and Premier, on the 24th of May, 1862.

Quebec, (the Head of the Roman Catholic Church in Canada,) to meet me in the Parliamentary Library, where we discussed the provisions of the Bill, and where they accepted it on the part of the Authorities of the Roman Catholic Church, as finally amended in its present form; after which, two copies of the Bill, as thus agreed upon and accepted, were made,—the one for Mr. Scott, and the other for myself; and the parties concerned waited upon the Head of the Administration, and informed him that they accepted the Bill as thus modified, and requested the assent of the Government to Mr. Scott's proceeding with the Bill. . . .

Practically, the same procedure was observed by Dr. Ryerson in 1863, when the Bill was finally passed, as the following extract from his narrative of the circumstances, which he published in 1865, will show. In that narrative, he states that he pointed out to Mr. R. W. Scott, the promoter of the Bill of 1863, what were his objections to it. . . . He then proceeds:—

In a day or two Mr. Scott called upon me again, stating that, having consulted his friends, he acceded to my objections, and would propose to amend the Bill accordingly. I replied that I still objected to any other party than the Government conducting a measure of that kind through the Legislature; but as he removed from the Bill what I considered objectionable, I would waive my objections on his proceeding with the Bill, and would aid him to get it passed,—on two conditions :—

First, that it should be assented to on the part of the Government, and therefore passed on their responsibility; and secondly, that it should be accepted by the Authorities of his Church as a final settlement of the question. On this latter point, I addressed Mr. Scott as nearly as I can recollect to the following effect :—

" You are only a private Member of Parliament ; you are not a Representative of the Roman Catholic Church ; you may assure the House, as well as myself, that this Bill is accepted as a final settlement of the Separate School question; so did Sir Etienne Taché, when he introduced the Separate School Bill of 1855, and even on its final passage its advocates assured the Legislature that it would put at rest the agitation of the Separate School question. Now it is said that they had no authority from the Heads of your Church to make such statements ; and so it may be said in regard to any assurance you may give as to this measure being accepted as a final settlement of the question by the Authorities of your Church ; and unless I am satisfied of that, I will do what I can to prevent the passage of your Bill, however modified, and will urge the standing upon the settlement of the question, as agreed to in 1855."

Mr. Scott called upon me again, I think, the following day, and told me that he had seen the Archbishop of Quebec, the Head of the Roman Catholic Church in Canada, and that the Archbishop had agreed to accept the Bill as I proposed ; and that, as the Archbishop was not able to go out himself, he proposed that his Secretary, the Very Rev. Vicar-General Cazeau, and the Very Rev. Vicar-General Macdonell,—who had been sent by the Bishops from Upper Canada to watch the legislation on educational matters.—should meet me on the subject.

I agreed to the meeting proposed, to be held the following day, in the Parliamentary Library. At that meeting, Mr. Scott pointed out the erasures, and read over the clauses amended, to each of which in succession, the Ecclesiastical Representatives of the Roman Catholic Hierarchy in Canada, nodded assent as explicitly as did any couple ever nod assent to the vows contained in the Marriage Service.*

Then Mr. Scott had two copies of the Bill, as thus agreed upon, made out and compared,—the one for himself and the other for me, and proposed that we should all wait upon the Premier, (Hon. J. Sandfield Macdonald,) and state to him the result. We proceeded to the Speaker's room, where, (not I, but,) Mr. Scott, informed him of the result of our conference, and the two venerable Ecclesiastics earnestly requested the Attorney-General to give the support of the Government to Mr. Scott's Bill, as a satisfactory and final settlement of the Separate School question.†

---

* It is possible that on this silent nodding "assent" that the two Vicars General base their denial of assent to the settlement of this Separate School question of 1863, as stated in their joint Letter of the 11th of March, 1865. Dr. Ryerson was naturally unsuspicious, and he must, therefore, have been too credulous in his belief that when the Vicars-General "nodded assent" to each clause of the Bill, as read over to them. they "merely," (as stated in their Letters,) "accepted it as an instalment of what they believed the (Roman) Catholics in Upper Canada were justly entitled to," . . . and consented reluctantly to have it introduced, with Dr. Ryerson's amendment to it. . . . Dr. Ryerson was clearly of opinion that no such qualified assent to the "compact" or "settlement" was given by the Vicars-General.

† In the "revised edition of Mr. Scott's speech in the Senate," on the 4th of April, 1894, he said : "The conferences I had in drawing up the Separate School Act of 1861, 1862 and 1863, were chiefly with Dr. Ryerson. There was not, on any occasion, any clerical interference. It has been recently stated that the Archbishop of Quebec interfered. I deny that. The conferences were held with Dr. Ryerson in the Library. . . . There was only one occasion when a clerical gentleman was present,—the Rev. Mr. Macdonald (sic), of Kingston, Vicar-General,—and he was the only clerical gentleman present on any occasion at the framing of the clauses." In his speech Mr. Scott makes no mention of the two conferences with Dr. Ryerson of the two clerical gentlemen and himself in the Library. In their Letter to the Editor of *The Globe*, of the 11th of March, 1865, they state that they were present at a conference in the Library—one of them was the Vicar-General of Quebec, and Secretary to its Archbishop. Mr. Scott, when he said that the Archbishop of Quebec did not "interfere" in the Separate School question of Upper Canada, was probably not aware of the Letters which were written on the subject by the Archbishop, and by his Vicar-General, which are given on pages 66, 73 and 80. These Letters of the Archbishop's Secretary could scarcely have been written, nor his conference twice with Dr. Ryerson in the Parliamentary Library, on the subject of the Upper Canada Separate School Bill, without the Archbishop's direction, or sanction.

It was with this understanding, and under these circumstances, that the Bill was supported by the Government, and passed through the Legislature. But even then, though I had, at the request of the Premier, prepared and published notes on the Bill, showing its harmony with the School System of Upper Canada, and recommending its adoption, and, though it was supported by the leaders of the then Conservative Opposition, as well as by the Government; yet such was the opposition in Upper Canada to any further legislation on the subject, that a majority of ten Upper Canada Members of the Legislative Assembly voted against it, and a majority of only two or three Upper Canada Members of the Legislative Council voted for it.

I affirm, therefore, that the passage of the Separate School Act of 1863, was an Honourable Compact between all parties concerned, for the final settlement of that question; and that the renewed agitation of it, in less than two years, is not only a violation of that Compact, but a warning to the people of Upper Canada, that if they are compelled again to legislate on the subject, their peace, and the safety of their institutions will require them to sweep the last vestiges of the Separate School law from their statute book, and place all Religious Persuasions in the same relation of equality to their Schools as exists in the New England States, and in the neighbouring State of New York. . . .

THE HON. GEORGE BROWN, T. D. McGEE AND BISHOP LYNCH ON THE SEPARATE SCHOOL SETTLEMENT OF 1863.

That two of our leading politicians and public men of the day held the same opinion of this question of the "finality,"—as I have defined it,—of the Roman Catholic Separate School Act of 1863, there can be no doubt. The Hon. Thomas D'Arcy McGee,—representing the Roman Catholics,—was one, and the Hon. George Brown,—representing the opponents of Separate Schools,—was the other. The Hon. George Brown, in his speech on the Resolutions relating to the Confederation of the Provinces on the 8th of February, 1865, and in reference to the Roman Catholic Separate School settlement of 1863, said :—

> Now, it is known to every honourable Member of this House that an Act was passed in 1863, as a final settlement of this sectarian controversy. I was not in Quebec at that time; but if I had been there I would have voted against that Bill, because it extended the facilities for establishing Separate Schools.
>
> It had, however, this good feature, that it was accepted by the Roman Catholic Authorities, and carried through Parliament, as a final compro-

)mise of the question in Upper Canada. When, therefore, it was proposed that a provision should be inserted in the Confederation Scheme to bind that compact of 1863, and declare it a final settlement, so that we should not be compelled, as we have been since 1849, to stand constantly to our arms, awaiting fresh attacks upon our Common School System, the proposition seemed to me one that was not rashly to be rejected. . . . But assuredly I, for one, have not the slightest hesitation in accepting it as a necessary condition of the scheme of union ; and doubly acceptable must it be in the eyes of honourable gentlemen opposite who were the authors of the Bill of 1863. . . .

The Hon. Mr. McGee, on behalf of the promoters of the Bill of 1863, referring to Mr. Brown's statement that the condition in the Confederation Scheme, affecting the Separate Schools of Upper Canada, would be "doubly acceptable" to the authors of that Bill, replied on the next day, as follows :—

I will merely add, in relation to an observation of my friend, (Hon. George Brown,) last night, on the subject of Catholic Separate Schools in Upper Canada, that I had accepted, for my own part, as a finality, the amended Act of 1863. I did so, for it granted all the petitioners asked, and I think they ought to be satisfied. I will be no party to the reopening of the question. . . . (*Parliamentary Debates on the subject of the Confederation of the British North American Provinces, pages 95 and 144, Quebec, 1865.*)

The *Globe* newspaper, having assumed that the *Canadian Freeman*, a Roman Catholic newspaper, was the organ of Bishop Lynch, in saying that the Separate School Bill of 1863 was "an insult to the Roman Catholics of Upper Canada," the Bishop caused his Secretary to write the following Letter to *The Globe* :—

His Lordship wishes it to be understood that he has no official organ. He wishes me also to state, that as far as he knows the sentiments of his Right Reverend brethren, the Catholic Bishops of Upper Canada, and of the Catholics generally, they are quite satisfied with Mr. Scott's Separate School Bill.*

TORONTO, 20th of March, 1863.   GEORGE NORTHGRAVES.

---

* On the 2nd of March, 1865, Bishop Lynch wrote as follows to *The Globe* :— When earnestly pressed to accept [the Separate School] Bill of 1863 as a finality, I studiously avoided the term. . . . I said I was content ["quite satisfied" were the words used, see above], with the Bill, as were also my Brethren in the Episcopacy, as far as I knew their sentiments. . . . I, therefore, rejoice that I did not use the word "finality," which even, had I used it, could certainly not be interpreted "final" under any and all circumstances, but final so long as the position of the two Provinces remained unchanged.

TORONTO, 2nd of March, 1865.   + JOHN JOSEPH LYNCH, *Bishop of Toronto.*

After the publication of Dr. Ryerson's Letter of the 18th of March, 1865, (in reply to that of Vicars-General Cazeau and Macdonell,) in which Dr. Ryerson quoted the Bishop's words, Bishop Lynch wrote a second Letter to *The Globe*, (on the 22nd of that month,) in which he said :—

In the first part [of the sentence quoted by Dr. Ryerson in his Letter of the 18th of March, 1865,] I deny that I used the word " final." In the second part, I defined the meaning which should attach itself to the term, had it been used by me.

What the Bishop did say in the "second part" was: "but final so long as the position of the Provinces remained unchanged." These were the exact words quoted by Dr. Ryerson. The Bishop's explanation does not seem to make his original statement any different from what it was in his Letter of 2nd of March, 1865, or any the clearer. Dr. Ryerson, in referring to this Letter, closed his narrative of 1865 on this subject as follows :—

I have become accustomed to respect the Right Rev. Dr. Lynch, like the late lamented Bishop Power, as a just and honourable man ; and I have hoped to be able in future years, as I have the last two years, to act cordially with him in all School matters. I have not yet heard that his Lordship, or any Roman Catholic Prelate in Upper Canada, has authorized this new agitation ; and I shall be much surprised and disappointed to learn that such has been the case in any instance.

DISCLAIMER OF THE VICARS-GENERAL THAT THEY WERE CONSENTING PARTIES TO THE SEPARATE SCHOOL SETTLEMENT OF 1863.

Soon after the publication of Dr. Ryerson's Statement, the two Vicars-General concerned, (to whom he had referred as being present at the conference of 1863, (and also at that of 1862,) with Mr. Scott, wrote a Letter to *The Globe* newspaper, in which they said :—

As the names of the undersigned have been very improperly made use of in a pamphlet written, it appears, by Dr. Ryerson, Chief Superintendent of Education for Upper Canada, in connection with a Memorial from the Catholics of Upper Canada, requesting that some amendments should be made to the present Separate School Bill, we deem it proper, in order to elucidate the truth, to make the following declarations :—

First.—It is not true that one of us had been deputed by the Archbishop, and that the other represented the Catholic Bishops of Upper Canada, with a view to come to an understanding with Dr. Ryerson in reference to the amendments to be made to the Separate School Bill. . . .

Second.—It is quite true that both of us, seeing that the Bill, as it was introduced by Mr. Scott, Member for Ottawa City, had no chance of being accepted by a majority of the House, owing to Dr. Ryerson's violent opposition to some of its measures, consented, reluctantly, to have it introduced with Dr. Ryerson's amendment to it, but upon their own responsibility, and without consulting either Bishop, or any other person ; and because we considered it as some improvement on the former Separate School Law.

Third.—It is also true that we both consented to call upon Hon. John S. Macdonald, then Prime Minister, in company with Mr. Scott and Dr. Ryerson, and requested him to get the Government to support the Bill in its amended state ; but it is not true, that they have ever considered the Bill as a final settlement of the Separate School question, or that we ever even thought of anything of the kind. We merely accepted it as an instalment of what they believed the Catholics of Upper Canada were justly entitled to, and, had we thought that a day would arrive when our conduct would receive a different construction, we would not have failed to protest against it.

QUEBEC, 11th of March, 1865.

ANGUS MACDONELL, *V.-G.*
C. F. CAZEAU, *V.-G.*

DR. RYERSON REITERATES HIS STATEMENTS THAT THE SEPARATE SCHOOL ACT OF 1863 WAS A FINALITY.

On seeing this Letter in *The Globe* newspaper, Dr. Ryerson wrote in reply to it as follows :—

. . The following facts are not disputed :—

1. That I was opposed to Mr. Scott's Bill, as introduced by him on the ground, [formerly stated, viz., that I objected to any unofficial Member of the Legislature being allowed to introduce a Bill affecting our Public School System,. which had been established by the Government, and which should be protected by it, and only legislated upon by Bills introduced by, and on the responsibility of, the Government itself].

2. That Mr. Scott removed my opposition to the Bill itself by removing what I objected to.

3. That he took steps to remove my two-fold objection to his proceeding with his Bill, by getting the assurance of the Authorities of his Church that the Bill would be accepted as an end of the Separate School agitation ; and the assent of the Government to the passing of the Bill.

These facts are not disputed. The question then arises, What object could have been proposed by Mr. Scott's asking me to meet Vicars-General Cazeau and Macdonell in the Parliamentary Library ? It could not have been for me to meet them as individuals ; for it was not a fig's importance or interest to me whether they, as individuals, accepted the Bill or not.

Nor could I have consented for a moment to meet any Lower Canada

Priest, (however reputable, and whatever his position,) as an individual on the subject; for I privately and openly denied the right of any individuals of Lower Canada to interfere with such a question in Upper Canada. Besides, I knew nothing of Mr. Cazeau, or of his relations to the Archbishop of Quebec. I had never seen him; I only met him in the capacity in which he was named to me by Mr. Scott, as the Archbishop of Quebec's Secretary, and Representative, as Vicar-General Macdonell was mentioned as the Representative of the Roman Catholic Bishops of Upper Canada.

The very proposal for me to meet them in any other capacity would have been absurd. Whether Mr. Scott defined their position and relations accurately, or not, in his request to me to meet them, I have no means of knowing. But I have no doubt of it; and in no other than in their official capacity could I have met them on such a subject.

The next question is, What object could there have been in the interview at all, except to satisfy me, and, through me, others, that the Bill would be accepted by the Authorities of the Roman Catholic Church as a final settlement of the Separate School agitation?

My objection to legislating at all on the subject was, that it would only be the starting point and pretext of another Separate School agitation, as there was no more assurance of the Bill being accepted by the Authorities of the Roman Catholic Church, as a final settlement of the question than of the (Taché) Act of 1855.

It was to furnish that very assurance that Mr. Scott desired me to meet Messrs. Cazeau and Macdonell. That was the sole object and reason for the interview, as it was not to discuss any clause of the Bill; nor was there any discussion of them. And whatever terms were employed, and whatever understanding was come to must have been employed, and understood, in harmony with the sole object and reason of the interview.

As to the terms of the statements made by Messrs. Cazeau and Macdonell, you [the Editor] have so thoroughly analyzed them, that I need not say anything more on the subject. I will only add two remarks:—

The first is, that if Messrs. Cazeau and Macdonell had caused it to be understood (at the time) that the passing of the Bill was not to finally settle the question of Separate School agitation, but was,—as they [now] state in their Letter—

Merely accepted as an instalment of what they believed the [Roman] Catholics of Upper Canada were justly entitled to—

I venture to say, without fear of contradiction, that not only would I not have been a consenting party to it, but that neither the Government, nor five Upper Canada Members of the Legislature, would have entertained it for a moment.

My next remark is, that not only did the Hon. T. D. McGee accept it as a final measure, and the Members of the Legislature so consider it; but the Roman Catholic Bishop of Toronto (Dr. Lynch) has, in his Letter in *The Globe* of the 6th instant, [dated the 2nd instant,] declared that it was so accepted,—thus furnishing a complete refutation of all statements to the contrary, and conclusive evidence of the accuracy of what I have stated. His Lordship says that it was accepted as—

Final, so long as the position of the two Provinces remained unchanged.
TORONTO, 18th of March, 1865. E. RYERSON.

FURTHER TESTIMONY AS TO THE FINALITY OF THE SEPARATE SCHOOL SETTLEMENT OF 1863.

So far as I have been enabled to ascertain, no reply was made to this conclusive Letter of Dr. Ryerson. In the following year, (1866,) Dr. Ryerson, in his Letter to the Provincial Secretary, of the 4th of August, 1866, again referred to the binding character of these conferences with the two Vicars-General and Mr. R. W. Scott, as follows:—

1. I refused even to consult with Mr. Scott in regard to his Separate School Bill of 1863, much less to be a party to its passing into an Act, except on two conditions :—

First. That what we agreed upon should be accepted by the Authorities of his Church, as a final settlement of the Separate School question in Upper Canada.

Secondly. That it should have the sanction and responsibility of the Government for its passing.

The manner in which the authorized Representatives of the Roman Catholic Church met Mr. Scott and me in the Parliamentary Library, at Quebec, and in which a duplicate copy of the Bill agreed upon was made out,—one for each party,—and in which both parties waited upon the Head of the Ministry, and represented the Bill, as thus agreed upon, to settle the question in Upper Canada, is well known, and was shortly afterwards published.

Nothing can be more dishonourable and truthless, than for either party now to deny that settlement of the question, and seek to subvert it.

TORONTO, 4th of August, 1866. E. RYERSON.

In the "Appellant's Factum," submitted to the Supreme Court of Canada, in 1891, by Mr. John S. Ewart, Counsel for the Appellant, he says:—

4. Some years prior to 1867, when "The British North America Act" was passed, the Parliament of the late Province of Canada had passed a Separate School Law for Upper Canada, which was understood to be a final settlement of a long-standing subject of contention. . . .

FRUITLESS APPEAL TO MR. R. W. SCOTT FOR INFORMATION ON THIS SUBJECT.

As it was desirable that light should be thrown upon the conflicting statements of Dr. Ryerson and the Vicars-General, in regard to the compact entered into between Mr. Scott and them in regard to the Separate School Act of 1863, I wrote to him the following Letter on the subject:—

About a month ago, I wrote to you a Letter, asking if you could furnish me with any information, (not already published,) regarding the passing of the Roman Catholic Separate School Act of 1863,—of which you were the principal promoter. I also enclosed to you a copy of the Publisher's Prospectus of the work on the subject which I was about to issue, so that you might be aware of the character of the Book, for which I had asked you for information.

Up to this time, I have neither received any acknowledgment of the receipt of that Letter, nor any reply to it. I wrote to you a few years ago on the same subject, and with a like result.

In the Pamphlet on Roman Catholic Separate Schools, which Dr. Ryerson published in 1865, he said, (speaking of that Act):—

The passage of the Separate School Act of 1863 was an honourable compact between all parties concerned for the final settlement of the question.

Shortly after the publication of that Pamphlet, the Very Rev. Vicars-General Cazeau, of Quebec, and Macdonell, of Kingston,—whom you had introduced to Dr. Ryerson as authorized Representatives of the Roman Catholic Church in this matter,—wrote a Letter to the Editor of *The Globe*, dated the 11th of March, 1865, in which they repudiated the statement of Dr. Ryerson, in regard to their action in the matter.

Dr. Ryerson replied on the 18th of that month, (March, 1865,) and reiterated his previous statements, and referred to you in connection with the matter. No doubt, you saw both Letters at the time, or subsequently.

Please let me know if, at that time, or afterwards, you corroborated the statements of the Vicars-General, or those of Dr. Ryerson, or dissented from the statements of either party?

I have seen nothing from you on the subject, and, therefore, I should be obliged if you would now be kind enough to give me the desired information on the subject.

TORONTO, 20th of February, 1897.   J. GEORGE HODGINS.

Up to 20th of March, 1897, not even the simple courtesy of an acknowledgment of this, (or any of my previous Letters to Mr. R. W. Scott,) has been received by me.

CHAPTER XXXI.

BRITISH NORTH AMERICA ACT RELATING TO EDUCATION.

AMONG the Resolutions adopted by the House of Assembly, on the 13th of March, 1865, was the following:—

43. *Resolved*, That the Local Legislature of each Province shall have power to make Laws respecting . . .

6. Education ; saving the rights and privileges which the Protestant, or Catholic, minority in both Canadas may possess, as to their Denominational Schools, at the time when the Union goes into effect.

It was upon this Resolution that the following provisions of the Imperial British North America Act : 30th and 31st Victoria, Chapter 3, Section 93, (1867,) were founded :—

In and for each Province, the Legislature may exclusively make laws in relation to education, subject and according to the following provisions :—

1. Nothing in any such law shall prejudicially affect any right or privilege with respect to Denominational Schools which any class of persons have by law in the Province at the Union.

2. All the powers, privileges, and duties at the Union, by law conferred and imposed in Upper Canada, on the Separate Schools and School Trustees of the Queen's Roman Catholic subjects, shall be, and the same are hereby, extended to the Dissentient Schools of the Queen's Protestant, and Roman Catholic, subjects in Quebec.

3. Where in any Province a system of Separate, or Dissentient, Schools exists by law at the Union, or is thereafter established by the Legislature of the Province, an appeal shall lie to the Governor-General-in-Council from any Act or decision of any Provincial Authority affecting any right, or privilege, of the Protestant, or Roman Catholic, minority of the Queen's Subjects, in relation to education.

4. In case any such Provincial Law, as, from time to time, seems to the Governor-General-in-Council requisite for the due execution of the provision of this Section is not made, or, in case any decision of the Governor-General-in-Council, on any appeal under this Section is not duly executed by the proper Provincial Authority in that behalf, then, and, in every such case, and as far only as the circumstances of each case require,

the Parliament of Canada may make Remedial Laws for the due execution of the provisions of this Section, and of any decision of the Governor-General-in-Council, under this Section.

LEGAL OPINION ON THE FOREGOING 93rd SECTION OF THE BRITISH NORTH AMERICA ACT.

The following is the joint opinion of Messrs. Stephen Richards, Adam Crooks and Edward Blake, on the legal effect of Provincial Legislation under the authority of the 93rd Section of the British North America Act of 1867, obtained in that year by *The Globe* Publishing Company of Toronto:—

The effect of the 93rd Section taken by itself is to confer upon the Provincial Legislatures exclusively the power to make laws in relation to Education, subject to certain restrictions, or provisions; but, at the same time, to authorize the Parliament of Canada, in certain cases, and only so far, in those cases, as the circumstance of each case require, to pass remedial laws on the same subject. The restrictions, or provisions, to which the Provincial Legislatures are subject are as follows :—

1st. The first sub-section provides that no law of the Provincial Legislature shall prejudicially affect any right, or privilege, with respect to Denominational Schools which any class of persons has established by law in the Province at the time of the Union.

2nd. The second sub-section provides that all the powers, privileges and duties, which, at the time of the Union, are by law conferred and imposed in Upper Canada on the Separate Schools and School Trustees of Roman Catholic subjects, shall be, and they are, by this sub-section, extended to the Dissentient Schools of Protestant and Roman Catholic subjects in the Province of Quebec. We think the Schools referred to are those established under the School Law of Lower Canada.

3rd. The first sub-section, it will be seen, restrains the Local Legislature from prejudicially affecting any existing right, or privilege. The second sub-section requires the extension of, and does extend to, Dissentient Schools in Lower Canada certain powers, privileges and duties, but there is no obligation to introduce a system of Separate, or Denominational, Schools into any Province where no such system now exists. If, however, the Legislature of such Province should hereafter establish a Separate, or Denominational, School System, then the right to the continuance of the system is so far secured by the third sub-section, that an appeal would lie, under that sub-section, to the Governor-in-Council, from any Act, or decision, of any Provincial authority affecting any right, or privilege, of the Protestant, or Roman Catholic, minority in relation to education. The right of appeal given by this sub-section applies also to Lower Canada and to any Province, where a system of Separate Schools prevails at the time of the Union. The effect of an appeal, under sub-section three, is considered below.

The above embraces all the restrictions, or obligations, by this Section imposed on the Local Legislatures; and subject thereto, any law which a Provincial Legsilature may enact on the subject of Education will have effect, but the Parliament of Canada may, in the causes, to which the fourth sub-section applies, but only to the extent authorized thereby, modify, or render inoperative, the local enactment.

4. Under the 4th sub-section there are two cases, or classes of cases, on which the Parliament of Canada may pass certain remedial laws on the subject of Education:—

First,—Where such law is not made by the Local Legislature as to the Governor-General-in-Council seems requisite for the due execution of the provisions of this 93rd Section, the Parliament of Canada may, so far only as the circumstances of the case require, make remedial laws for the due execution of the provisions of the Section. The Governor-in-Council, we take it, should make known to Parliament, by Order in Council, Message or other Official Act, what law he considers necessary.

Second,—Where an Appeal is made to the Governor-in-Council under the 3rd sub-section, and his decision thereupon is not duly executed by the proper Provincial authority, the Parliament of Canada may, so far only as the circumstances of the case require, make Remedial Laws for the due execution of such decision.

It is only in the above cases, and to the extent mentioned, that the Parliament of Canada have authority to legislate under this Section, and, in each case, the preliminary action of the Governor-in-Council, referred to in the preceding paragraphs, is necessary to give jurisdiction.

Among the "provisions" to be executed, contemplated in the first case, are those of the 2nd sub-section; for, though that sub-section seems at once to extend to the Province of Quebec all privileges, powers, and duties therein mentioned, yet legislation may be required to arrange the machinery and details for practically carrying out the provisions referred to.

Possibly cases may arise affecting the provisions of the 1st and 3rd sub-sections, in which the Governor-in-Council might act without any Appeal being had to him.

The Appeal provided by the 3rd sub-section is, from "any Act, or decision, of any Provincial authority affecting any right, or privilege, of the Protestant, or Roman Catholic, minority, in relation to education," in any Province in which a system of Separate, or Dissentient, Schools exists by law at the time of the Union, or is thereafter established by the Legislature of the Province. This gives the right of appeal from any Act, or enactment, of the Local Legislature affecting the right, or privilege, mentioned. Also, from decisions affecting such right, or privilege, by the Department of Education, or any similar authority, having charge of the administration of the law on the subject of Education, on matters which a jurisdiction, or discretionary action, is, by law, given to such Department, or authority, so that, in case the Legislature in a Province, where a system of Separate, or Dissentient, Schools is established, enact a law affecting an existing privilege, of the Protestant, or Roman Catholic, minority, in relation to Education, an Appeal will lie to the Governor-in-Council; and, if his decision upon such Appeal is not executed, or carried out, by the Local Legislature passing the necessary law for the purpose, the Parliament of Canada may make a Remedial Law necessary for the execution of such decision; but, to warrant the Appeal referred to, there must be an existing right, or privilege, to be affected by the local enactment appealed from. So, also, in case of an Appeal from the decision of the Department of Education, or other similar authority, if the decision of the Governor-in-Council is not duly executed by the Department, or other authority referred to, the Parliament of Canada may pass the law requisite for enforcing the decision.

But the decision to be appealed from must be one affecting an existing right, or privilege, of the minority. No new rights, or privileges, are to be acquired by means of an Appeal under the 3rd and 4th sub-sections.

STEPHEN RICHARDS.
ADAM CROOKS.

TORONTO, March 9th, 1867.   EDWARD BLAKE.

We also incline to the opinion that an Appeal would lie to the Governor-in-Council from any decision of a Provincial Court affecting any existing right, or privilege, of a minority, and that the Governor-in-Council may declare it necessary to pass a law providing the requisite machinery for the enforcement of his decisions, and that Parliament may, upon such declaration, and, at the failure of the Local Legislature to act, pass such law.

ADAM CROOKS.
EDWARD BLAKE.

CHAPTER XXXII.

INSPECTION OF ROMAN CATHOLIC SEPARATE SCHOOLS.

ALTHOUGH the Roman Catholic Separate School Act specifically provided for the inspection of Separate Schools, yet the right to do, under that Act, was resisted in Kingston and Toronto, as the following statement will show:—

The Separate School Law having authorized the Chief

Superintendent of Education to provide for this inspection of Separate Schools, and also the Registers of those Schools, the Inspectors of Grammar Schools were authorized to inspect such of these Schools as were within the limits of that part of Upper Canada assigned to them for inspection purposes.

In October, 1865, the Inspector appointed to the eastern part of Upper Canada was refused permission to inspect the Register of pupils' names, and the record of their attendance, at the Roman Catholic Separate School in Kingston. This refusal having been reported to the Chief Superintendent, he wrote to the Chairman of the Roman Catholic Separate School Board in Kingston on the subject. In his Letter he said :—

As the Law requires me to make and pay the apportionment of the Legislative Grant to Separate Schools, it is my duty and right to see whether the data on which I make and pay such apportionment are properly prepared and are reliable. This can only be done by having the Registers of Separate Schools examined by a duly appointed Officer.

The 26th Section of the Separate School Act of 1863 expressly provides that "The Roman Catholic Separate Schools, with their Registers shall be subject to such inspection as may be directed, from time to time, by the Chief Superintendent of Education." . . .

The same objection was made by Archbishop Lynch in Toronto late in 1871, and he addressed the following Letter on the subject to the Chief Superintendent of Education :—

To our great amazement we find that our Separate Schools are visited by the Inspectors of the Common Schools. We take this occasion to protest against this intrusion, as it is contrary to the spirit of the Law establishing Separate Schools ; and we will be obliged to give notice to the Trustees not to receive those visits ; not that we are afraid of them, but we do not want their interference.

In his reply to the Archbishop, Dr. Ryerson said :—

I beg to observe that the protest you make, and the intention you avow, are in direct opposition to the Separate School Act, the twenty-sixth Section of which expressly provides [for such inspection.] (See this Section quoted above.)

I have construed the Separate School Act, to authorize Trustees of Separate Schools in Cities, Towns and Incorporated Villages, to appoint . . . the Local Superintendent of their Schools ; but that does not preclude this Department from directing an inspection of the Register and condition of any Separate School. . . .

Dr. Ryerson then referred to the General Regulations under which the Grammar School Inspectors were directed to inspect Separate Schools in the neighbourhood of Grammar Schools. He then said:—

I believe these visits were very acceptable to the Managers and Teachers of the Separate Schools, and the Inspector's report respecting them was most favourable. . . . But in one (Kingston) he was refused admittance . . . by the head Teacher of the principal Separate School. . . .

A few days after I had written [to Kingston on the subject], I received a Letter from the Roman Catholic Bishop of Kingston, (Dr. Horan,) apologizing for the conduct of the head Teacher of the Separate School, who had mistaken his duty, and assuring me that the Inspector would be courteously received at any time he might think proper to visit the School. . . .

I can adduce indubitable proof that I have sought to administer the Law, as much for the benefit of Separate Schools, as of Public Schools, and have given the Separate Schools the advantage of every doubt, and of any discretionary power I might have, to assist them. . . .

But while I have thus sought to aid Separate Schools to the utmost extent of my power, and to give the most liberal construction of the School Law in their behalf, I must say that I think your Grace's protest and intimated course of proceedings, are directly contrary to the express provisions of the Separate School Act—the inspection of which class of Schools, under the authority of this Department, is not, as a matter of suffrage, at the discretion of the Trustees of Separate Schools, but a matter of right, provided for by law, and which every Government ought to possess, and exercise to inspect, at its discretion, the doings of every School, or Institution, aided out of the public revenues of the Country.

TORONTO, 5th of December, 1871.   E. RYERSON.

No further difficulty was experienced in this matter.

CHAPTER XXXIII.

SCHOOLS IN FRENCH AND GERMAN SETTLEMENTS, 1851-1875.

THERE was one class of Separate Schools which gave the Chief Superintendent very little trouble. These were the French and German Schools,—chiefly Roman Catholic,—which were scattered here and there throughout Upper Canada. All that had to be done in their case was to give them such teaching facilities, as enabled them to go into operation under Teachers who could speak the language of the ratepayers concerned, and that language only.

Happily that facility could be given under the general,—not the Separate,—School Law, and that with the sanction of the Chief Superintendent.

There were two principles which Dr. Ryerson laid down at an early period in his administration of the Education Department.

The first was,—that whenever he could meet special cases by a liberal, and often, (with the sanction of the Government,) a generous interpretation of his powers under the School Acts, and in terms of his Commission as Chief Superintendent of Education, it was his duty to give that interpretation, in cases not specifically provided for,—except by analogy,—in the School Law.

The second principle which Dr. Ryerson laid down, and, which he generally adhered to, was not to propose too frequent legislation, with a view to meet special cases; but only to seek such legislation at intervals of from five to ten years.

Fortunately I was familiar with Dr. Ryerson's views, as expressed in the first of the foregoing principles, which he had laid down for his guidance, when the first application was made in 1851 to grant a Certificate of Qualification to a French Teacher in the County of Essex,—which had been largely settled by French-Canadians. At the time that this application reached me from the Board of Public Instruction for the County of Essex, Dr. Ryerson was absent in England, and I had charge of the Department, as Acting Chief Superintendent. I, therefore, submitted the application, which had been received, to the Council of Public Instruction for Upper Canada, with the recommendation that it be granted. This was concurred in by the Council of Public Instruction; and I was, therefore, enabled to inform the Essex County Board that:—

> The Council of Public Instruction for Upper Canada has sanctioned a liberal construction of the programme to which you refer, making the term "English" convertible into the term "French," where it occurs, and when applied to French candidates for examination before the County

Board of Public Instruction. The certificate should, of course, be expressly limited to teaching in the French language.

A copy of this intimation was also sent to the then Local Superintendent of Education at Sandwich, with the following addition:—

The School Act expressly authorizes Trustees to employ any qualified Teacher they please; should, therefore, the one to whom you refer, obtain a certificate from the County Board, the Trustees can engage his services, and no Board, or School Officer, can prevent them, as has been assumed in a Memorial transmitted to me by the Secretary of the County Board of Public Instruction, from certain inhabitants of School Section No. 6, Sandwich.

In 1858, a partial extension of the principle here laid down, was applied to German Teachers; and, to meet the case, a knowledge of the German Grammar was, by the Council of Public Instruction, substituted in the programme of examination, for a knowledge of the English Grammar.

In 1871, a further difficulty arose, owing to a delay of the Council of Public Instruction to provide fully for the examination and licensing of German Teachers in the German settlements of Upper Canada. To meet a special case, which occurred in the County of Waterloo, I told the Local Superintendent, who had called upon me, in Dr. Ryerson's absence:

To grant six months' certificates to such German candidates as would present themselves for examination in July; and I said that, by giving the Department early notice of the real requirements in the case, attention would be given to the matter by the Council of Public Instruction, and every provision made for the examination of such candidates, at all future examinations.

This was confirmed by Dr. Ryerson; and he informed the Local Superintendent of the County, that examination papers in German Reading, Spelling, Etymology and Grammar might be prepared by Members of the County Board, and that the other ordinary examination papers could be used in the case of the Teachers who could read English.

Similar applications, made in 1872 and 1875, were dealt with in the same spirit; and, in this way, every facility was given by the Education Department for the successful operation of

French and German Public and Separate Schools in the French and German settlements of Upper Canada.

WHY PERPETUATE NATIONALITIES IN ELEMENTARY SCHOOLS?

While a movement has been inaugurated in this Dominion to discourage the use of a dual language, in certain parts of it, a corresponding movement to discourage its use in the elementary Schools, in parts of the United States, received the strong commendation of Cardinal Satolli, during his visit to that country. Thus, in an article in *The Forum*, New York, for February, 1897, the Rev. Dr. McGlynn says:—

With regard to the question that has caused some disturbance,—of the desire of (Roman) Catholic immigrants of other speech than the English, to maintain in their Churches, and Church Schools, for an indefinite time, a foreign speech, and, in some measure, a foreign nationality, Archbishop Satolli saw clearly, at an early day, how detrimental this must be to the general interests of the Church; . . . therefore, he not only compelled a German pastor to restore a Church, (of which his Bishop had permitted him to take possession,) to the use of the English-speaking people, who had built it; but he also advised him to preach, even in his own Church, in the "normal" language of the country. . . . In the same spirit he wrote, in April, 1895, to certain French Canadians in Connecticut, as follows:—

Your attachment to your religion is most consoling, and that to your native language most natural and praiseworthy. But, at the same time, you must remember that you have left the country in which the use of that language is common, and have voluntarily come to another in which a different tongue is spoken.

You must not, then, expect that here the same provision can be made with the same perfection for the propagation and continued use of your own language.

Cardinal Satolli can now, Dr. McGlynn says, make:—

. . . Clear to the Pope, and his eminent advisers in Rome, that any attempt to perpetuate here *quasi* colonies of nationalities of foreign speech, can, in the long run, but be ruinous to the religious interests of the next, and succeeding, generations, who, by an inevitable attraction, will perforce be Americans, and will glory in the name. . . .

I have quoted these passages from the article in *The Forum*, by the Rev. Dr. McGlynn, and also the remarks of Archbishop Ireland, in the concluding chapter, with a view to show what the opinion of distinguished and enlightened Roman Catholics in the United States are, on questions which have a practical bearing upon our own future, and on the "evolution,"—so to speak,—of the various nationalities among us into a homogeneous Canadian nationality,—loyal, brave, and true,—of which we, as a people, might well be proud.

CHAPTER XXXIV.

DR. RYERSON'S FINAL UTTERANCES ON SEPARATE SCHOOL AGITATIONS.

EARLY in the year 1865, a renewed agitation was commenced in Upper Canada by the promoters of Roman Catholic Separate Schools. In consequence of this new movement, Dr. Ryerson issued a pamphlet to counteract its effects, under the title of "Remarks on the New Separate School Agitation." In his "Prefatory Notice," he said:—

Each successive Separate School Law agitation, during the fifteen years from 1850 to 1865, has been commenced by attacks upon the Education Department, and the Separate School Law for the time being. . . .

I have felt it due to the supporters of our Public School System, to furnish them with materials for refuting the statements put forth for showing the unreasonableness of the demands made. . . . This I deem to be the more necessary now, as a formal agitation for the extension of the Roman Catholic Separate School System has been inaugurated in various parts of Upper Canada. Already influential meetings of Roman Catholics, to promote this oject, have been held in Toronto, Kingston, Ottawa, Perth, and other important towns, and resolutions of a more sweeping character than usual passed unanimously.

The cause of this renewed agitation, Dr. Ryerson very properly ascribed to the movements then in progress, of a—

"Certain number of Protestants in Montreal, . . . prompted by the *Montreal Witness*," . . . who make pretentions, and claims to a separate every-thing,—from the Chief Superintendent of Education down to the humble Teacher, . . . involving the principle of subjection of the State to the Church, . . . incompatible with the universal education of any people—embodying views subversive of the School System, and of Municipal rights in Upper Canada, and which have been, again and again, all but unanimously condemned by its Representatives and Electors. Such pretentions, on the part of *The Witness* and others in Montreal, could never have really prompted, any more than it can justify, this new Separate School agitation in Upper Canada, though it may be the pretext for it.

There are, indeed, certain anomalies in the School Law of Lower Canada, which by no means afford to Protestants these facilities for Protestant Schools, equal to those possessed by Roman Catholics for Separate Schools in Upper Canada ; but, I believe no one has been more ready to correct those anomalies than the Hon. P. J. O. Chauveau, Chief Superintendent of Education there, who has more than once officially recommended the amendment of the Law for that purpose. . . .

Mr. Hodgins, Deputy Superintendent of Education for Upper Canada, when in Montreal in October last, having been applied to on the subject, endeavoured to impress some of the parties concerned with the error of their course—so at variance with the views of the people of Upper Canada, and so impracticable and unpatriotic.

I have ever objected to Lower Canada interference in Upper Canada School matters ; and I do not think Upper Canada will interfere with Lower Canada School matters.* . . .

Dr. Ryerson then takes a rapid survey of the successive Roman Catholic Separate School agitations,—those of 1851, '52, 1857, '58, 1860-63. In regard to the latter year, he says :—

The present Separate School Law was passed, and accepted on the part of the Authorities of the Roman Catholic Church " as a final settlement of the question." But, in less than two years, in 1864, '5, the old agitation is recommenced, and the old terms of denunciation against the Separate School Law, and against the Chief Superintendent, are again . . . [indulged in] and put to work in the service of a fresh agitation, as pointed out.

Dr. Ryerson then very properly puts this question :—

Now, can it be that acute Ecclesiastics and learned Lawyers, and able Statesmen of the Roman Catholic Church, have been deceived thus, time

---

* While in Montreal, in October, 1864, I wrote the following Letter to Dr. Ryerson in regard to the matter to which he here refers. I said :—

I have seen Mr. William Lunn several times, and have sought to modify and soften the ill-feeling which exists between the Protestant School Committee and the Hon. P. J. O. Chauveau, Chief Superintendent of Education for Lower Canada. They feel very strongly against him ; and although I do not think his policy and mode of dealing with the difficulty is either wise, or judicious, in all respects, I have told both him and them that I could do, or say, nothing which would either compromise our position in Upper Canada, or our friendly relations with Mr. Chauveau.

MONTREAL, 8th of October, 1864.   J. GEORGE HODGINS.

after time, as to the import and character of Laws which they themselves have framed and advocated [or have agreed to]? . . . I can truly say, beyond the power of successful contradiction, that I have sought to the utmost, to give the most liberal application, and the fullest affect to these successive Separate School Acts. . . .

Speaking of the drafts of Bills, proposed by the supporters of Separate Schools in 1855 and 1863, Dr. Ryerson said:—

The first draft of Separate School Bill, that of 1885, prohibited either Municipalites, or Trustees of Common Schools, from levying and collecting any rate for either the building of a School House, or paying a Teacher, without also levying and collecting rates for the supporters of Separate Schools, in proportion to their population ! . . . thus actually proposing to make Municipalities and Protestant Trustees tax-gatherers for Roman Catholic Schools ! . . .

The second provision was, that the Roman Catholics, as a Body, should be defined as supporters of Separate Schools, and thus by law, be excluded from the Common Schools. This was in the first "project" of the Bills referred to, thus depriving every Roman Catholic of the right, or liberty of choice, as to whether he would support a Common, or a Separate, School. . . .

THE SEPARATE SCHOOL BILL OF 1866 THE RESULT OF THIS LAST AGITATION.

The result of this combined and simultaneous movement in Upper Canada, to re-open the "final settlement" of the Separate School question of 1863, was the introduction, without notice, or warning, of a specious, and, as it happily proved, an abortive measure affecting the integrity of the Public School System of Upper Canada. The title of this Bill was as follows:—

A Bill to extend to the Roman Catholic minority in Upper Canada similar and equal privileges with those granted by the Legislature to the Protestant minority in Lower Canada.*

---

* A Letter from Mr. Lunn to Dr. Ryerson, written in November, 1866, throws some light on this subject. He said:—
We have recently had a meeting of leading gentlemen in Montreal, on the Education question, at which a number of Resolutions were passed, appointing a Committee of six, with plenary powers. Dr. J. W.—[afterwards Sir William] —Dawson and I are on that Committee. We met Mr.—[afterwards Sir Alexander]—Galt in town last week by appointment, who gave us a history of his recent communications with Lord Monck and the Ministry. The result was, a Minute of Council, approved by the Governor-General, guaranteeing to the Protestants of Lower Canada the same rights possessed by the Roman Catholics

As soon as Dr. Ryerson heard of this new effort to tamper with the Separate School Law Settlement of 1863, then he wrote a strong and effective Letter to the Provincial Secretary on the subject, pointing out to him the disingenuous character of the Bill itself, and remonstrating with the Government for permitting private Members of the House thus continually to deal with a question involving Provincial and vital interests, which the Government itself was especially bound to protect and promote.

This Letter is the more interesting and important, from the fact that it was the last of the kind which Dr. Ryerson ever wrote on these ever recurring and pernicious agitations,—which no compact, or understanding, seemed to be sacred enough to which to bind the parties, or to prevent them from making these periodical attacks upon the integrity of that Public School System, which he had been at such labour and pains to place upon, what he regarded as, a firm, sound and practical foundation. Dr. Ryerson said:—

I observe that a discussion took place last night in the House of Assembly on Mr. R. Bell's introduction of a new Separate School Bill for Upper Canada; and I have, this morning, read the provisions of that Bill, the most disingenuous, partial and insidious that can be conceived.

When I went lately to Ottawa on Departmental business, I had no idea that the Separate School Question of Upper Canada would be even mooted in the House of Assembly; but during the two days that I was there, I heard that several Ecclesiastics were there from Upper Canada, though I did not meet with any of them; and I was told that, in settling the Lower Canada School question, it was intended by the advocates of Roman Catholic Separate Schools to get further provisions on the subject in Upper Canada. I need not repeat what I said to you and to Mr. Alexander Mackenzie, and other Members of the Legislature on the subject; but I beg to offer the following remarks:—

1. I refused even to consult with Mr. R. W. Scott, in regard to his

---

of Upper Canada by the Separate School Act; and giving them, also, the right of appeal to the General Legislature for amendments to the School Law, and to the Legislature the right to legislate on that question.

This information is given to us with the understanding that it is not to be published in the newspapers, but may be communicated to any of our confidential friends. I, therefore, give it to you.

MONTREAL, 7th of November, 1866.   WILLIAM LUNN.

Separate School Bill of 1863, much less to be a party to its passing into an Act, except on two conditions:

First.—That what we agreed upon should be accepted by the Roman Catholic Authorities of his Church as a final settlement of the Separate School question in Upper Canada.

Second.—That it should have the sanction and responsibility of the Government for its passing.

The manner in which the authorized Representatives of the Roman Catholic Church met Mr. Scott and me, in the Parliamentary Library at Quebec, and in which a duplicate copy of the Bill agreed upon, was made out, one for each party, and in which both parties waited upon the Head of the Ministry, and represented the Bill as thus agreed upon to settle the question in Upper Canada, is well known, and was shortly afterwards published. And nothing can be more dishonourable and truthless than for either party now to deny that settlement of the question and seek to subvert it.

2. The question of the Separate School Law was thus settled for Upper Canada, without any reference to what had been done, or might be done, in Lower Canada.

3. The School question between Roman Catholics and Protestants in Lower Canada, is peculiar to Lower Canada,—having nothing analogous in Upper Canada, except that there are Roman Catholics and Protestants here, as well as there. The Roman Catholics in Lower Canada, being in the majority, have resolved that the Schools of the majority there should be Roman Catholic Schools, as much so as are the Convents themselves,— except that they are Day, and not Boarding, Schools. The Protestants in Upper Canada, being in the majority, have resolved that by Law, and in fact, the Schools of the majority here should not be denominational,—not Roman Catholic, or Protestant, but National,—equally common and acceptable to Protestants and Roman Catholics. In confirmation of this fact, I refer, not merely to the provisions of the Law, and the General Regulations, but to two facts in connection with the operations of our School System.

(1). Of the 544 Roman Catholic Teachers of Common Schools employed in Upper Canada, according to my last printed report, 190 of them are employed in the Separate Schools, and 354 in the Public, or National, Schools.*

(2). Of the sixty odd thousand (60,000) Roman Catholic children taught in the Common Schools in Upper Canada, all but seventeen thousand, (17,000),—or about 43,000,—of them are taught in the Public, or National, Schools. Thus a majority of nearly three-fourths of the Teachers, and pupils of the Roman Catholic Church are connected with the Schools of the

---

* During the last full year (1875) that Dr. Ryerson was Chief Superintendent of Education, the number of Roman Catholic Teachers employed was 726,—516 in the Public Schools, and 210 in the Separate Schools.

majority,—they preferring those Schools to Separate Schools, notwithstanding the ecclesiastical influence employed to sever them from the Public, and connect them with the Separate Schools, and, notwithstanding, the facility afforded by Law for the establishment and support of Separate Schools. I have conversed with a sufficient number of Roman Catholics, or rather, a sufficient number of them have come and conversed with me, to satisfy me that a majority of the Roman Catholic laity do really regard the Separate School Law as an injury, rather than a benefit, to themselves and families. I have given the most liberal interpretation and application of the Separate School Law, as I am sure every Roman Catholic Priest and Layman, who has had to do with my Department, will testify.

4. I will not discuss the provisions of Mr. Bell's outrageous Bill. I may remark that the very first provision proposes to make Municipal Councils tax-collectors for the Schools of the Roman Catholic Church, one of the most degrading features of "Church and State" connection, so formally renounced by our Legislature; while, at the same time, by the Lower Canada School Act of 1857, the supporters of Dissentient Schools alone are authorized to levy and collect rates for the support of their Schools. The 55th Section of Chapter 15, of the Consolidated Statutes of Lower Canada declares that :—

The Trustees of Dissentient Schools shall alone have the right of fixing and collecting assessments to be levied on the inhabitants so dissentient.

5. I will not advert to the provision relative to Colleges and higher Seminaries, except to observe that the wedge is there apparent, which it has been long sought to get inserted in our system of Public Instruction, to separate the Roman Catholics "as a Body" from the rest of the population in School matters, and thus to accomplish a favourable Ultramontane object.

6. Nor will I notice the provision for a separate Superintendent, Council of Public Instruction, etc., except to remark that it is at variance with all English, as well as American precedent. In Ireland, Separate Schools may be established; but there is one National Board of Education. In England, though the system of Elementary Schools is denominational, [and was wholly so until the Forster Act of 1870], there is but one Governmental Department of Education.

7. If the two parties in Lower Canada agree upon a peculiar and double-headed system, it is, of course, their own affair. I am persuaded that the minority will "gain a loss" by it in many ways they now little anticipate. But, I have not interfered with the Lower Canada System; and I have advised all Upper Canada Members of the Legislature to leave the Lower Canada School questions to be settled by parties connected with that Province; and then, not suffer them to interfere in our School affairs, any more than that they should attempt to impose upon Upper Canada two Houses of the Legislature, because they wish for them in Lower Canada.

8. Although the Government cannot prevent a private Member from

insulting Upper Canada by the introduction of such a Bill as Mr. Bell's, yet I think the people of Upper Canada, as well as Lower Canada, have a right to look to Government for the protection, as well as the improvement of their School System, and to give the decision and influence of the Government against any Bill, or measure, which would subvert, or weaken that System established under its auspicies, and maintained by its authority, as well by the all but unanimous voice of the people of Upper Canada.

E. RYERSON.

TORONTO, 4th of August, 1866.

CHAPTER XXXV.

END OF DR. RYERSON'S DIFFICULTIES IN SEPARATE SCHOOL MATTERS.

EXCEPT in the duty of settling purely local differences, in regard to Separate Schools,—receiving their reports and apportioning to them the Legislative grant, Dr. Ryerson's relations with the managers of these Schools after Confederation, in 1867, were pleasant and agreeable. Nothing particular occurred during the years 1872-1876, in regard to Separate Schools, to mar that harmony. His difficulties in the administration of the Education Department, during these years, were of a very different kind, and chiefly arose with parties who had no connection whatever with Separate Schools.

Dr. Ryerson shared the fate of many a man before him. He was a man of large and long experience, and one who had mastered principles, and was familiar with various schemes of education. He had personally to deal with, and combat, educational and administrative theories, which he knew to be thoroughly unsound, as they were impracticable;—theories which were the result of superficial observation of such work as his, and of experience gained in very different fields from that in which he had laboured during the whole of his later life. He often sought to get relief from what he felt to be unnecessary burthens and new duties,—many of which were made distasteful to him.

At length, on the 21st of February, 1876, he finally retired from the Headship of the Education Department, after having, for thirty-two years, done noble service for his native country, in founding its System of Public Schools, and in raising to a high degree of efficiency its Grammar Schools, and, in the form of Collegiate Institutes, founding a number of local Colleges in the various Counties of the Province.

I have already referred,—in a "Sketch" of his career as President of Victoria College,—to Dr. Ryerson's reticence in regard to the Department, after he had left it, and to his dislike to having the subject mentioned to him. In this connection, I may say that, after he had retired from the Department, many things done were spoken of, as though he had personal knowledge of them, and approved of them,—but, of which, as a matter of fact, he personally knew nothing. To me he confided his inmost thoughts and feelings; but, in regard to one thing, he was very firm. He would not let me mention, or discuss, any Departmental matter. He said that he had "done with all of that now;—that things were in the hands of others, for which they alone must enjoy the praise, or bear the blame." So I ceased entirely to speak of our old work altogether; and, in the course of the year of his retirement, he went to England, where he remained for over a year. Within five years after his return, he peacefully passed away, and was laid to rest in the Mount Pleasant Cemetery in February, 1882,—just six years, (and in the month,) in which he had ceased to be the Chief Superintendent of Education for the Province of Ontario.

CONCLUDING CHAPTER.

EXPEDIENCY OF SEPARATE EDUCATION CONSIDERED BY DR. RYERSON AND ARCHBISHOP IRELAND.

APART from the purely local aspect of Separate School Education, the question often forces itself upon the more thoughtful among us,—whether the system of separate and isolated education for a portion of the future merchants, professional men, and ordinary citizens of a Country, is one which a wise, far-seeing statesman should endorse and promote.

Any one who will read the later utterances of Dr. Ryerson on this subject, and the brave, practical, and outspoken words of a distinguished Prelate of the American Roman Catholic Church,—Archbishop Ireland,—will be led to ask himself whether, after all, there is not "a more excellent way" to solve this question than by persistently following an educational *noli me tangere* system, which is fraught with so many disadvantages.

Archbishop Ireland practically puts the question in this form: Whether an efficient system of State Schools, with a satisfactory provision for religious instruction, would not be best for all parties. After discussing the general question of "State Schools," the Archbishop proposes two plans by which the subject of popular education might be successfully dealt with. His views on this question will be given further on in this Chapter.

Dr. Ryerson, in his remarks, deals chiefly with the question from a national standpoint, and in its practical aspect, as to how the separate and isolated system of education fits the children of its adherents and promoters for the after "battle of life."

The discussion of this vexed question of Roman Catholic Separate Schools in Upper Canada has been marked by so much bad feeling and bitter personal controversy, that it is refreshing to be able to contemplate it in the absence of both of these exasperating adjuncts to its discussion heretofore.

In his general remarks Dr. Ryerson says:—

> Separate Schools cannot be claimed as a right. . . . All that any citizen can claim as a right . . . is equal and impartial protection, with every other citizen. . . .
>
> I think that no one will maintain that Separate Schools are expedient for the interests of the State. Nay, those interests are more or less injured by every act of class legislation; and its strength is weakened by every sectional division, which its citizens have created by law. . . It was

a source of individual pride, and of strength to the State, in ancient days, for a man to say "*Romanus Sum.*" . . . So would we be so now, under a legislation of "Equal Rights" and privileges,—without distinction, in regard to sect or party, for a man to say: "*Canadensis Sum*," . . . standing in all respects upon the equal ground of right and privilege with every other man (in Canada) in relation to the State and to the Law. . . .

The youth, who grows up to manhood in a School of separation, commences "the battle of life," not only with inferior mental and social preparation, but comes forth into the arena of competition and enterprise estranged from, and a stranger to, the habits, views and associations of those with whom his pursuits and fortunes are linked. . . . There may, now and then, be an exception, . . . but such an example is a rare exception to the general rule, which dooms the victim of isolation to inferiority, failure and obscurity. . . .

The fact is, that the tendency of the public mind and of the institutions of Upper Canada is to confederation, and not to isolation,—to united effort, and not to divisions and hostile effort,—in what all have a common interest. The efforts to establish and extend Separate Schools, . . . are a struggle against the instincts of Canadian Society, against the necessities of a sparsely populated country, against the social and political present and future interest of the parents and youth thus separated [by these Schools] from their fellow-citizens. . . .

These remarks of Dr. Ryerson present, in striking language, the matured and thoughtful utterances of a Canadian statesman. They also embody the views entertained on the system of isolated and Separate School education, which are shared in by thousands of practical men, and by such thoughtful Roman Catholics as the late Hon. Donald A. Macdonald, formerly Lieutenant-Governor of Upper Canada, and his noted brother, Hon. John Sandfield Macdonald, a former Premier of the late Province of Canada, and afterwards of Upper Canada.

Among other distinguished Roman Catholics who deprecated isolated denominational education was the Right Hon. Thomas Wyse, long an influential Member of the Imperial Parliament and Educationist, and afterwards Her Majesty's Minister at the Court of Greece, wrote largely on the universal education of the Irish People, and in favour of mixed Schools, as essential to its attainment. In his well-known work on "Education Reform," he thus speaks of a system of Separate, or Denominational, Schools, and of the kind of instruction given in them:—

We grow Protestants and we grow Catholics, . . . and degrade Seminaries for the universal mind of the country into rival garrisons of faction.

In a somewhat extended Report which I prepared, in the autumn of 1896, at the request of the Minister of Education for Ontario, I quoted at some length the eloquent and outspoken words of the Most Rev. Archbishop Ireland, of St. Paul, in answering the question, proposed by himself, at the Meeting of the American National Education Association, held at St. Paul in 1890. The question which the Archbishop proposed to discuss at that Meeting was: *State Schools and Parish Schools: Is union between them impossible?*

Coming from so high and enlightened a Dignitary of the Roman Catholic Church, as the Archbishop of St. Paul, Minnesota, his utterance on this important subject will be read with much interest and attention. They are like a ray of sunshine on a darkened subject, and have the sound of a pleasant voice amid jarring strife.

In answer to this question, (in part) Archbishop Ireland said:—

I am the friend and advocate of the State School. I uphold the Parish School. I sincerely wish that the need of it did not exist. I would have all Schools for the children of the people State Schools.

The right of the State School to exist, I consider, is a matter beyond the stage of discussion. I fully concede it. To the child must be imparted instruction in no mean degree. The imparting of this is primarily the function of the child's parent. The family is prior to the State. The State intervenes, whenever the family can not, or will not, do the work that is needed. The place of the State, in the function of instruction is *loco parentis*. As things are, tens of thousands of children will not be instructed, if parents remain solely in charge of this duty. The State must come forward as an agent of instruction; else ignorance will prevail. Indeed, in the absence of State action, there never was that universal instruction which we have so nearly attained, and which we deem necessary. In the absence of State action, I believe universal instruction would never in any country have been possible.

State action in favour of instruction implies free Schools. . . . In no other manner can we bring instruction within the reach of all children. . . . Blest, indeed, is that nation, whose vales and hill sides the [free

School] adorns, and blest the generations upon whose souls are poured their treasures. . . .

It were idle for me to praise the work of the State School of America in the imparting of secular instruction. . . . It is our pride and glory. The Republic of the United States has solemnly affirmed its resolve that within its borders no clouds of ignorance shall settle upon the minds of the children of its people. To reach this result its generosity knows no limit. The Free School of America! Withered be the hand raised in sign of its destruction! . . .

The American people are naturally reverent and religious. Their Laws and Public Observances breathe forth the perfume of religion. The American School, as it first reared its log walls amid the Villages of New England, was religious through and through.

I would solve the difficulty by submitting it to the calm judgment of the Country :—

I would permeate the regular State School with the religion of the majority of the children of the land, be it Protestant as Protestantism can be ; and I would, as they do in England, pay for the secular instruction given in Denominational Schools according to results ; that is, each pupil passing the examination before the State Officials, and in full accordance with the State programme, would secure to his School the cost of the tuition of a pupil in the State School.

There is also another plan :—

I would do as the Protestants and Catholics have done [for over twenty years] in Poughkeepsie and other places in our Country have agreed to do, to the greatest satisfaction of all citizens and the great advancement of educational interests.*

Do not tell me of the difficulties of detail in working out either of my schemes. . . . Other schemes more perfect in conception and easier of application will, perhaps, be presented in time ; meanwhile, let us do the best that we can and do know."

It is delightful to turn from a contemplation of the narrowness of the Canadian isolation system, so strenuously advocated by the promoters of our Separate Schools, to the enjoyment of

---

* Having written to Archbishop Ireland for some information in regard to the Poughkeepsie plan, which is otherwise known as "the Faribault scheme" of education, he referred me to the Rev. James Nilan, Parish Priest at Poughkeepsie, for definite information on the subject. He said, however, that "The 'Faribault Plan' is nothing else than the 'Irish School Plan,' which has been in working order throughout Ireland for the last fifty years. It was first applied in this Country in Poughkeepsie, New York." . . .

In the Report, to which I have referred, the particulars of this Poughkeepsie scheme are given in detail.

the large-hearted schemes and manly utterances of the Archbishop of St. Paul, Minnesota.

There is, in these utterances, a statesmanlike grasp of the question, as it touches our social condition as a people, and as it reaches forward and embraces the vast educational future yet before us. For, after all, we are only in the early stage of our intellectual growth, and have barely done more than lay the foundation, of our three-fold educational system. The men who were most noted for their far-seeing prescience in laying these foundations, have only just passed away. They were men who encountered endless difficulties, and opposition, in accomplishing even what they did in this noble work.

No doubt the time will come, in this young and vigorously growing country,—"this Canada of ours,"—when the comprehensive views of Archbishop Ireland will prevail amongst those who, at present, only see a prospect of the decay of their faith in the hearts and minds of such of the Roman Catholic children who would frequent the "State Schools" of this Province,—where, it is well known, proselytism is never attempted, and where there is no such thing as tampering with the religious belief of any of the pupils.

When that eventful, and long-wished for, day comes, the wonder will be that there did not, long ago, arise a wise Separate School Counsellor in Canada, in the matter of public education in the "State Schools," such as the large-hearted and far-seeing ecclesiastical statesman,—the Archbishop of St. Paul.

APPENDIX No. I.

THE ROMAN CATHOLIC SEPARATE SCHOOL ACT OF 1863.

Compared with the Taché Act of 1855 on Pages 95-99.

The following copy of the Roman Catholic Act of 1863, compared by Dr. Ryerson, with that of 1855, contains also his annotations in its most important Sections. (See his Letter on the subject on pages 158, 159.)

26 Victoria, Chapter 5,—"An Act to restore to Roman Catholics in Upper Canada certain Rights in respect to Separate Schools." Received the Royal Assent on the 5th of May, 1863.

Whereas it is just and proper to restore to Roman Catholics in Upper Canada certain rights which they formerly enjoyed in respect to Separate Schools, and to bring the provisions of the Law respecting Separate Schools more in harmony with the provisions of the Law respecting Common Schools : Therefore, Her Majesty, by and with the advice and consent of the Legislative Council and Assembly of Canada, enacts as follows :—

1. Sections eighteen to thirty-six, both inclusive, of Chapter sixty-five of the Consolidated Statutes for Upper Canada, intituled, "An Act respecting Separate Schools," are hereby repealed, and the following shall be substituted in lieu thereof, and be deemed to form part of the said Act.

II. Any number of persons, not less than five, being heads of families, and freeholders or householders, resident within any School Section of any Township, Incorporated Village, or Town, or within any Ward of any City, or Town, and being Roman Catholics, may convene a public meeting of persons desiring to establish a Separate School for Roman Catholics, in such School Section, or Ward, for the election of Trustees for the management of the same.

III. A majority of the persons present, being freeholders, or householders, and being Roman Catholics, and not candidates for election as Trustees, may, at any such meeting, elect three persons resident within such Section, or an adjoining Section, to act as Trustees for the management of such Separate School, and any person, being a British subject, not less than twenty-one years of age, may be elected as a Trustee, whether he be a freeholder, or householder, or not.

(NOTE.—In Common School Sections, any number present, however few, at a lawful Meeting for the election of Trustees, can elect them. There is no reason for a different provision in regard to the number present for the election of Separate School Trustees.)

IV. Notice in writing that such meeting has been held, and of such election of Trustees, shall be given by the parties present at such meeting to the Reeve, or head, of the Municipality, or to the Chairman of the Board of Common School Trustees, in the Township, Incorporated Village, Town, or City, in which such School is about to be established, designating by their names, professions and residences, the persons elected in the manner aforesaid, as Trustees for the management thereof; and every such notice shall be delivered to the proper officer by one of the Trustees so elected, and it shall be the duty of the officer receiving the same to endorse thereon the date of the receipt thereof, and to deliver a copy of the same so endorsed, and duly certified by him, to such Trustee, and from the day of the delivery and receipt of every such notice, or in the event of the neglect or refusal of such officer to deliver a copy so endorsed and certified, then, from the day of the delivery of such notice, the Trustees therein named shall be a body corporate, under the name of "The Trustees of the Roman Catholic Separate School for the Section number   , in the Township of   , or for the Ward of   , in the City, or Town, (as the case may be,) or for the Village of   , in the County of   ." (a)

(a) These Sections embrace the eighteenth to twenty-second Sections, inclusive, of the existing Separate School Act of 1855, and are the same in substance as they; as are the second and third Sections substantially the same as the eighteenth and nineteenth Sections of the present Separate School Act.

V. The Trustees of Separate Schools heretofore elected, or hereafter to be elected, according to the provisions of this Act, in the several Wards of any City, or Town, shall form one body Corporate, under the title of "The Board of Trustees of the Roman Catholic Separate Schools for the City (or Town) of   ." (b)

(b) This Section is the substitute for the twenty-third Section of the present Separate School Act, (of 1855,) and assimilates the provision of the law in regard to Separate Schools and their supporters, to that of the Common School Act.

VI. It shall be lawful for the majority of the ratepaying supporters of the Separate School, in each Separate School Section, whether the Sections be in the same or adjoining Municipalities, at a public meeting duly called by the Separate School Trustees of each such Section, to form such Sections into a Separate School Union Section, of which union of Sections the Trustees shall give notice within fifteen days to the Clerk, or Clerks, of the Municipality, or Municipalities, and to the Chief Superintendent of Education; and each such Separate School Union Section thus formed, shall be deemed one School Section for all Roman Catholic Separate School purposes, and shall every year thereafter be represented by three Trustees, to be elected as in Common School Sections.

2. And the said Trustees shall form a body corporate, under the title of "The Board of Trustees of the Roman Catholic United Separate Schools for the United Sections, Nos.   , (as the case may be,) in the   , (as the case may be.)" (*c*.)

(*c*) This clause, or Section, is designed to provide that the supporters of Separate Schools may form Union Sections, the same as they may now do in the Cities, and Towns, and which supporters of Common Schools may also do, as provided in the forty-first, forty-second, forty-third and forty-fourth Sections of the Consolidated Common School Act. Previous to 1855, the Township Councils prescribed the boundaries of Separate, as well as of Common, School Sections; but as the names of all the petitioners for a Separate School had to be included in the Separate School Section to be formed, they virtually formed their own Section. By the Roman Catholic Separate School Act of 1855, the boundaries of a Separate School Section were made identical with those of the Common School Section, but no provision was made for the union of Separate Schools in adjoining Sections, as had been made for the union of Common School Sections. This clause supplies the omission of the Roman Catholic Separate School Act of 1855.

VII. The Trustees of Separate Schools, forming a body corporate under this Act, shall have the power to impose, levy, and collect, School rates, or subscriptions, upon and from persons sending children to, or subscribing towards the support of such Schools, and shall have all the powers in respect of Separate Schools, that the Trustees of Common Schools have and possess under the provisions of the Act relating to Common Schools. (*d*)

(*d*) This Section is the same as the twenty-fourth Section of the present Roman Catholic Separate School Act.

VIII. The clerk, or other officer, of a Municipality within, or adjoining, which a Separate School is established, having possession of the Assessor's, or Collector's, roll of the said Municipality, shall allow any one of the said Trustees, or their authorized collector, to make a copy of such roll in so far as it relates to the persons supporting the Separate School under their charge. (*e*.)

(*e*) There is no provision in the present Roman Catholic Separate School Act of 1855, by which the Trustees, or their Collector, can have access to the Assessor, or Collector's, roll, as is provided by law, in regard to the Trustees of a Common School and their Collector. This Section supplies the omission.

IX. The Trustees of Separate Schools shall take and subscribe the following declaration before any Justice of the Peace, Reeve, or Chairman of the Board of Common Schools:—" I,   , will truly and faithfully, to the best of my judgment and ability, discharge the duties of the office of School Trustee, to which I have been elected:"—and they shall perform the same duties, and be subject to the same penalties as Trustees of Common Schools: and teachers of Separate Schools shall be liable to the same obligations and penalties as teachers of Common Schools. (*f*.)

(*f*) This Declaration of Office is required of Common School Trustees by the Common School Amendment Act of 1860; and the duties and penalties here imposed upon Separate School Trustees and Teachers are the same as those imposed by the twenty-fifth Section of the Roman Catholic Separate School Act of 1855.

X. The Trustees of Separate Schools shall remain respectively in office for the same periods of time that the Trustees for Common Schools do, and as is provided by the thirteenth Section and its sub-sections, for the Common School Act of the Consolidated Statutes for Upper Canada ; but no Trustee shall be re-elected without his consent, unless after the expiration of four years from the time he went out of office ; Provided always, that whenever in any City, or Town, divided into Wards, a united Board now exists, or shall be hereafter established, there shall be for every Ward two Trustees, each of whom, after the first election of Trustees, shall continue in office two years and until his successor has been elected, and one of such Trustees shall retire on the second Wednesday in January, yearly in rotation ; and provided, also, that at the first meeting of the Trustees after the election on the second Wednesday in January next, it shall be determined by lot, which of the said Trustees, in each Ward, shall retire from office at the time appointed for the then next annual election, and the other shall continue in office for one year longer. (*g*.)

(*g*) This Section is a substitute for the twenty-sixth Section of the Roman Catholic Separate School Act of 1855, and assimilates the Separate to the Common School Law, in respect to the election of Trustees, and their continuance in office, in both Sections, and Cities, and Towns.

XI. After the establishment of any Separate School, the Trustees thereof shall hold office for the same period and be elected at the same time in each year that the Trustees of Common Schools are, and all the provisions of the Common School Act relating to the mode and time of election, appointments and duties of Chairman and Secretary at the annual meetings, term of office and manner of filling up vacancies, shall be deemed and held to apply to this Act. (*h*.)

(*h*) This Section contains a general provision for assimilating the provisions of the Separate and Common School Acts.

XII. The Trustees of Separate Schools may allow children from other School Sections, whose parents, or lawful guardians, are Roman Catholics, to be received into any Separate School under their management, at the request of such parents, or guardians ; and no children attending such School shall be included in the Return, hereafter required to be made to the Chief Superintendent of Education, unless they are Roman Catholics.(*i*)

(*i*) This Section corresponds precisely with the twenty-seventh Section of the Roman Catholic Separate School Act of 1855.

XIII. The Teachers of Separate Schools, under this Act, shall be subject to the same examinations, and receive their Certificates of qualification in the same manner as Common School Teachers generally ; provided that persons qualified by law as Teachers, either in Upper or Lower Canada, shall be considered qualified Teachers for the purposes of this Act.(*j*)

(*j*) This Section is a substitute for the twenty-eighth Section of the Separate School Act of 1855; and is, all must admit, a very great improvement upon it.

XIV. Every person paying rates, whether as proprietor or tenant, who, by himself, or his agent, on, or before, the first day of March in any year, gives, or who, on, or before, the first day of March, of the present year, has given to the Clerk of the Municipality, notice, in writing, that he is a Roman Catholic, and a supporter of a Separate School situated in the said Municipality, or in a Municipality contiguous thereto, shall be exempted from the payment of all rates imposed for the support of Common Schools, and of Common School Libraries, or for the purchase of land, or erection of buildings, for Common School purposes, within the City, Town, Incorporated Village, or Section, in which he resides, for the then current year, and every subsequent year thereafter, while he continues a supporter of a Separate School.—And such notice shall not be required to be renewed annually; and it shall be the duty of the Trustees of every Separate School to transmit to the Clerk of the Municipality, or Clerks of Municipalities, (as the case may be,) on or before the first day of June in each year, a correct list of the names and residences of all persons supporting the Separate Schools under their management; and every ratepayer whose name shall not appear on such list shall be rated for the support of Common Schools.(*k*)

(*k*) This Section is a substitute for the twenty-ninth Section of the Separate School Act of 1855. It substitutes the first day of March for the first day of February,—which can cause inconvenience, or disadvantage, to nobody, as municipal rates for School purposes are never levied till long after March. The proprietor, or tenant, by himself, or his agent, gives notice; and it has already been legally decided that a notice by the agent of a proprietor, or tenant, is as valid, according to the Separate School Act of 1855, as a notice by himself in person, and is so accepted and acted upon. It is unjust, therefore, to omit expressing what is already held to be the law, merely to afford an opportunity and pretext for vexing and annoying individuals in certain localities. Another provision in this Section is, that the notice shall not be repeated by the individual annually, but shall be repeated, with his address, by the Trustees, as his agent. This is the practice which has already been pursued in some municipalities In Lower Canada, the supporter of the Dissentient, or Separate, School never repeats, or renews, his first notice as a supporter of such School; and why should the Roman Catholic be required to do that in Upper Canada which the Protestants are not required to do in Lower Canada, unless to inconvenience and annoy him as much as possible? This Section requires each Roman Catholic, proprietor, or tenant, to give notice to the Clerk of the Municipality when he desires to become a supporter of a Separate School; and the eighteenth requires him to give notice to the same Clerk when he desires to cease being a supporter of such School; and, in the interval, the Trustees are required annually to give to the same Clerk, (for the information of the Municipal Council, in levying School rates,) the name and residence of each supporter of a Separate School; and they are subject to a severe penalty in case they make an incorrect return.

XV. Every Clerk of a Municipality, upon receiving any such notice, shall deliver a certificate to the person giving such notice, to the effect that the same has been given, and showing the date of such notice.

XVI. Any person who fraudulently gives any such notice, or wilfully makes any false statement therein, shall not thereby secure any exemption from rates, and shall be liable to a penalty of forty dollars, recoverable, with costs, before any Justice of the Peace, at the suit of the Municipality interested.

XVII. Nothing in the last three preceding Sections contained, shall exempt any person from paying any rate for the support of Common Schools, or Common School Libraries, or for the erection of a School-house, or School-houses, imposed before the establishment of such Separate School.

XVIII. Any Roman Catholic who may desire to withdraw his support from a Separate School, shall give notice in writing to the Clerk of the Municipality before the second Wednesday in January in any year, otherwise he shall be deemed a supporter of such School : Provided always, that any person who shall have withdrawn his support from any Roman Catholic Separate School, shall not be exempted from paying any rate for the support of Separate Schools, or Separate School Libraries, or for the erection of a Separate School-house, imposed before the time of his withdrawing such support from the Separate School.

XIX. No person shall be deemed a supporter of any Separate School unless he resides within three miles (in a direct line) of the site of the School-house. (*l.*)

(*l*) No explanatory remarks are required ; and no one will object respecting the directions given, and the restrictions and penalties imposed by the fifteenth, sixteenth, seventeenth, eighteenth and nineteenth Sections of the Bill.

XX. Every Separate School shall be entitled to a share in the fund annually granted by the Legislature of this Province for the support of Common Schools, and shall be entitled also to a share in all other public grants, investments and allotments for Common School purposes now made, or hereafter to be made, by the Province, or the Municipal authorities, according to the average number of pupils attending such School during the twelve next preceding months, or during the number of months which may have elapsed from the establishment of a new Separate School, as compared with the whole average number of pupils attending School in the same City, Town, Village, or Township. (*m.*)

(*m*) This Section is a substitute for the first part of the thirty-third Section of the Separate School Act of 1855. The point of difference is, that this Section gives Separate Schools the right of sharing in other " Public Grants, investments, and allotments, for Common School purposes than the Parliamentary School Grant. The only public grant, or investment, that can come within this provision, is the Clergy Reserve Fund, when applied by Municipalities to Common School purposes. This fund is distributed by law among the several

Municipalities, according to the number of ratepayers in each,—Roman Catholic ratepayers, of course, as well as Protestant. This fund forms no part of the Common School Fund, and is not subject to Common School Regulations. When a Municipal Council chooses to apply the portion of the Clergy Reserves Fund apportioned to its Municipality to Common School purposes, it ought to do so in the equal interest of all the ratepayers, and not in a way to exclude any portion. If the Common School Law allows portions of those ratepayers, (both Protestant and Roman Catholic,) to have Common Separate Schools, they are acting under law in availing themselves of this permission, as much as those who avail themselves of the permission, to establish Common Schools. For a Municipal Council to apply the share of the Clergy Reserves Fund placed under its control, to aid one class of these Schools and not the other, is as clearly to exclude one class of ratepayers from their rightful share of that fund as if they were proscribed by name. Some Municipal Councils have acted very justly and fairly in regard to both classes of Common Schools; and if any other Councils have done, or should do, otherwise, the Legislature should surely protect rights of the minority against any such proscription.

XXI. Nothing herein contained shall entitle any such Separate School, within any City, Town, Incorporated Village, or Township, to any part, or portion, of School moneys arising, or accruing, from local assessment for Common School purposes within the City, Town, Village or Township, or the County, or Union of Counties, within which the City, Town, Village, or Township is situate. (*n*.)

(*n*) This Section corresponds with the second proviso of the thirty-third Section of the Separate School Act of 1855, and effectually protects all School moneys arising from local assessment against any claims in behalf of Separate Schools.

XXII. The Trustees of each Separate School shall, on or before the thirtieth day of June and the thirty-first day of December of every year, transmit to the Chief Superintendent of Education for Upper Canada, a correct return of the names of the children attending such School, together with the average attendance during the six next preceding months, or during the number of months which have elapsed since the establishment thereof, and the number of months it has been so kept open ; and the Chief Superintendent shall thereupon determine the proportion which the Trustees of such Separate School are entitled to receive out of the Legislative grant, and shall pay over the amount thereof to such Trustees. (*r*.)

(*r*) This Section is identical with the thirty-fourth Section of the Separate School Act of 1855, except that part which requires the returns to be made on oath,—a requirement never exacted of Common School Trustees, never required of Separate School Trustees before 1855,—not required of the Trustees of Protestant Separate Schools in Lower Canada since 1856,—and for which requirement no reason of justice, or necessity, exists, as the same penalties are imposed for making incorrect retuns to obtain additional aid, as if they were made on oath.

It may here be remarked, that the first proviso in the thirteenth Section of the Separate School Act of 1855, (which says, "that no Separate Schools shall be entitled to share in such fund, unless the average number of pupils attending the same be fifteen or more,") has been omitted. It was contained in the Bill as first introduced, but was struck out, at the suggestion of the Chief Superintendent, who stated it to be useless and inoperative,—not required in regard to Common Schools, the average half-yearly attendance in some of which fell below fifteen,—and although Separate Schools whose half-yearly attendance did not amount to fifteen, were not legally entitled to share in the Legislative School Grant, yet that any such School kept open by local liberality, according to law, by a legally qualified Teacher, was equitably entitled to aid according to its working, whether its pupils numbered more or less than fifteen.

There is also another point on which a remark may here be made. It has been erroneously alleged that this Bill relaxes the existing law in regard to the time of keeping open Schools each year. It will be seen, by referring to the first part of the thirty-third and the thirty-fourth Section of the Separate School Act of 1855, that a Separate School is entitled to receive aid from the Legislative School Grant, in proportion to the time, (in connection with average attendance,) it is kept open, whether more or less than six months; and the twenty-second Section of the Bill makes not the least change in that respect.

XXIII. All Judges, Members of the Legislature, the heads of the Municipal bodies, in their respective localities, the Chief Superintendent and Local Superintendent of Common Schools, and Clergymen of the Roman Catholic Church, shall be Visitors of Separate Schools. (*s.*)

(*s*) Hitherto none but Clergymen of the Roman Catholic Church have been admitted as Visitors of Separate Schools. This Section contains important and liberal provisions in the right direction.

XXIV. The election of Trustees for any Separate School shall become void, unless a Separate School be established under their management within three months from the election of such Trustees.

XXV. No person subscribing towards the support of a Separate School established as herein provided, or sending children thereto, shall be allowed to vote at the election of any Trustee for a Common School in the City, Town, Village, or Township, in which such Separate School is situate.

The provisions of the twenty-fourth and twenty-fifth Sections of the Bill need no remark, and will be objected to by none.

XXVI. The Roman Catholic Separate Schools, (with their Registers,) shall be subject to such inspection as may be directed, from time to time, by the Chief Superintendent of Education, and shall be subject, also, to such regulations as may be imposed, from time to time, by the Council of Public Instruction for Upper Canada. (*t.*)

(*t*) The provisions of this Section have not existed in any previous Act in respect to Separate Schools; they bring the Separate Schools as completely under the control of Public Regulations and inspection as the Common Schools.

XXVII. In the event of any disagreement between Trustees of Roman Catholic Separate Schools, and Local Superintendents of Common Schools, or other Municipal authorities, the case in dispute shall be referred to the equitable arbitrament of the Chief Superintendent of Education in Upper Canada; subject, nevertheless, to appeal to the Governor-in-Council, whose award shall be final in all cases. (*u.*)

(u) This is also a new legal provision. The latter part of this Section is needless, and is not contained in the Grammar, or Common, School Act, as all decisions of the Chief Superintendent may be appealed from to the Governor-in-Council. His decisions have been appealed from in several instances, but have, in every instance, been sustained.

XXVIII. This Act shall come into force, and take effect, from and after the thirty-first day of December next: But all contracts and engagements made, and rates imposed, and all corporations formed under the Separate School Law, hereby repealed, shall remain in force, as if made under the authority of this Act.

APPENDIX No. 2.

CANONS OF THE BALTIMORE GENERAL COUNCILS.

DECISIONS AND DIRECTIONS FOR THE SETTLING OF THE SCHOOL QUESTION AND THE GIVING OF RELIGIOUS EDUCATION, BY CARDINAL SATOLLI.

THE following "Decisions and Directions for the Settling of the School Question and the Giving of Religious Education," are practically an annotated edition of the Canons of the Baltimore General Councils, (quoted on page 37 of this Volume, by Bishop de Charbonnel,) by the Most Reverend Francis Satolli, Archbishop of Lepanto, Delegate of the Apostolic See to the United States of America,—in a Letter to the Archbishops of the Roman Catholic Church in the United States, assembled in New York in November, 1892:—

I. *What Roman Catholic Schools should be.*—All care must be taken to erect Catholic Schools, to enlarge and improve those already established, and to make them equal to the Public Schools in teaching and discipline.—*Concilia Plen. Balt. III., No. 197, page 101.*

II. *Public Schools the Alternative.*—When there is no Catholic School at all, or when the one that is available is little fitted for giving the children an education in keeping with their condition, then the Public Schools may be attended with a safe conscience, the danger of perversion being rendered remote by opportune remedial and precautionary measures; a matter that is to be left to the conscience and judgment of the Ordinaries.—*Ibid., No. 198, page 103.*

III. *Teachers Must be Qualified.*—We enact, and command, that no one shall be allowed to teach in a Parochial School who has proven his fitness for the position by previous examination. No Priest shall have the right to employ any teacher, male or female, in his School without a certificate of ability, or diploma from the Diocesan Board of Examiners.—*Ibid.*, *No. 203, page 108.*

IV. *Normal Schools a Necessity.*—Normal Schools, as they are called, are to be established where they are wanting and are evidently necessary. —*Ibid., No. 205, page 110.*

V. *Parents free to Choose Schools—No Penalty to be imposed on them.*— We strictly forbid anyone, whether Bishop or Priest, and this is the express prohibition of the Sovereign Pontiff, through the Sacred Congregation, either by act, or by threat, to exclude from the Sacraments as unworthy, Parents who choose to send their children to the Public Schools. As regards the children themselves, this enactment applies with still greater force.—*Ibid, No. 198, page 104, Conf. Tit. VI., Cap. I., II.; Tit. VII.*

VI. *Right of the Church to Teach.*—To the Catholic Church belongs the duty and the divine right of teaching all nations to believe the truth of the Gospel, and to observe whatsoever Christ commanded, (Matt. xxviii. 19); in her, likewise, is vested the divine right of instructing the young in so far as theirs is the Kingdom of Heaven, (Mark x. 14), (*Conf. Conc., Balt. Pl., III., No. 194*); that is to say, she holds for herself the right of teaching the truths of faith, and the law of morals, in order to bring up youth in the habits of a Christian life. Hence, absolutely and universally speaking, there is no repugnance in their learning the first elements, and the higher branches of the arts, and the natural sciences in Public Schools controlled by the State, whose office it is to provide, maintain, and protect everything by which its citizens are formed to moral goodness, while they live peaceably together, with a sufficiency of temporal goods, under laws promulgated by civil authority.

For the rest, the provisions of the Council of Baltimore are yet in force, and, in a general way, will remain so; to wit: "Not only out of our paternal love do we exhort Catholic Parents, but we command them by all the authority we possess, to procure a truly Christian and Catholic education for the beloved offspring given them of God, born again in baptism unto Christ, and destined for Heaven, to shield and secure them throughout childhood and youth from the dangers of a merely worldly education, and, therefore, to send them to Parochial, or other truly Catholic, Schools." United with this duty are the rights of Parents, which no civil law or authority can violate or weaken.

VII. *Co-operation with the Public Schools.*—The Catholic Church in general, and especially the Holy See, far from condemning, or treating with indifference the Public Schools, desires rather that, by the joint action of civil and ecclesiastical authorities, there should be Public Schools in every State, according as the circumstances of the people require, for the cultivation of the useful arts and natural sciences; but the Catholic Church shrinks from those features of Public Schools which are opposed to the truth of Christianity and to morality; and since, in the interest of society itself, these objectionable features are removable, therefore, not only the Bishops, but the citizens at large, should labor to remove them, in virtue of their own right, and in the cause of morality.

VIII. *Parish Schools less Necessary than Formerly.*—It is long since the Holy See, after consultation with the Bishops of the United States of America, decreed that Parish Schools and other institutions under the direction of the Bishops, each according to the conditions of its own diocese, were opportune and necessary for Catholic youth, from the fact that it was held for certain that the Public Schools bore within themselves a proximate danger to faith and morals, for various reasons (*Conc. Pl. Balt. III.*, No. 194, *seq.; App.*, *page 279*); viz.: because in the Public Schools a purely secular education is given,—inasmuch as it excludes all teaching of religion,—because Teachers are chosen indiscriminately from every sect, and no law prevents them from working the ruin of youth, so that they are at liberty to instil errors and germs of vice in tender minds. Likewise certain corruption seemed to impend from the fact that in these Schools, or at least in many of them, children of both sexes are brought together for their lessons in the same room.

Wherefore, if it be clear that in a given locality, owing to the wiser dispositions of public authorities or the watchful prudence of School Board, Teachers and Parents, the above-named dangers to faith and morals disappear, then it is lawful for Catholic Parents to send their children to these Schools, to acquire the elements of letters and arts, provided the Parents themselves do not neglect their most serious duty, and the pastors of souls put forth every effort to instruct the children and train them in all that pertains to Catholic worship and life.

IX. *Bishops' Discretion as to Parochial Schools.*—It is left to the judgment and the wisdom of the Ordinaries to decide whether, in a certain part of their respective dioceses, a Parochial School can be built and kept up in a fitting condition, not inferior to the Public Schools, taking into consideration the temporal condition of the parents, while graver needs for procuring their spiritual welfare and the decent support of the Church are pressing. It will be well, therefore, as was the wont of our forefathers, and as was done in the early days of the Church to establish weekly classes of Catechism, which all the children of the parish should attend; for the better success of this measure let the zeal of Pastors in fulfilling their duty and the love of Catholic Parents leave no effort unspared. (*Cf. Conc. Pl. Balt. III.*, No. 198)

X. *Right of Parents as to Choice of Schools.*—No reproach, either in public, or in private, shall be cast upon Catholic Parents who send their children to Private Schools or Academies where a better education is given under the direction of religious, or of approved and Catholic persons. If they make sufficient provision for the religious training of their children, let them be free to secure in other ways that education which the position of their family requires.

XI. *Arrangement with Public School Authorities Desirable.*—It is greatly to be desired, and will be a most happy arrangement, if the Bishop agree with the civil authorities, or with the Members of the School Board, to conduct the School with mutual attention and due consideration for their respective rights.

While there are Teachers of any description for the secular branches, who are legally inhibited from offending Catholic religion and morality, let the right and duty of the Church obtain of teaching the children Catechism, in order to remove danger to their faith and morals from any quarter whatsoever.

It seems well to quote here the words of our Holy Father Leo XIII. (See the Pope's Letter to the Archbishop of New York, and to the Bishops of the Province) :—

"We further desire you to strive earnestly, that the various local authorities, firmly convinced that nothing is more conducive to the welfare of the commonwealth than religion, should, by wise legislation, provide that the System of Education which is maintained at the public expense, and to which, therefore, Catholics also contribute their share, be in no way prejudicial to their conscience, or religion. For we are persuaded that, even our fellow-citizens who differ from us in belief, with their characteristic intelligence and prudence, will readily set aside all suspicions and all views unfavourable to the Catholic Church, and willingly acknowledge her merit, as the one that dispelled the darkness of paganism by the light of the Gospel, and created a new society, distinguished by the lustre of Christian virtues, and by the cultivation of all that refines. We do not think that anyone there, after looking into these things clearly, will let Catholic Parents be forced to erect and support Schools which they cannot use for the instruction of their children."

XII. *Religious Instruction should be Systematically Given.*—As for those Catholic children that, in great numbers, are educated in the Public Schools, where now, not without danger, they receive no religious instruction at all, strenuous efforts should be made not to leave them without sufficient and seasonable instruction in Catholic faith and practice. We know, by experience, that not all our Catholic children are found in our Catholic Schools. Statistics show that hundreds of thousands of Catholic children in the United States of America attend Schools which are under the control of State Boards, and, in which, for that reason, Teachers of every Denomination are engaged. Beyond all doubt, the one thing necessary, *i.e.*, religious and moral education according to Catholic principles, is not to be treated either lightly, or with delay ; but, on the contrary, with all earnestness and energy.

The adoption of one of three plans is recommended, the choice to be made according to local circumstances in the different States and various personal relations.

(1) The first consists in an agreement between the Bishop and the Members of the School Board, whereby they, in a spirit of fairness and good-will, allow the Catholic children to be assembled during free time and taught the Catechism ; it would also be of the greatest advantage if this plan were not confined to the Primary Schools, but were extended likewise to the High Schools and Colleges, in the form of a free lecture.

(2) The second to have a Catechism class outside the Public School Building, and also classes of higher Christian doctrine, where, at fixed times, the Catholic children would assemble with diligence and pleasure, induced thereto by the authority of their Parents, the persuasion of their Pastors, and the hope of praise and rewards.

(3) The third plan does not seem, at first sight, so suitable, but is bound up more intimately with the duty of both Parents and Pastors. Pastors should unceasingly urge upon Parents that most important duty, imposed both by natural and divine laws, of bringing up their children in sound morality and Catholic faith. Besides, the instruction of children appertains to the very essence of the pastoral charge ; let the Pastor of souls say to them, with the Apostle : "My little children, of whom I am in labour again until Christ be formed in you." (Gal. iv., 19.) Let him have classes of children in the Parish, such as have been established in Rome, and many other places, and even in Churches in this country, with very happy results.

Nor let him with little prudence show less love for the children that attend the Public Schools than for those that attend the Parochial ; on the contrary, stronger marks of loving solicitude are to be shown them ; the Sunday School and the hour for Catechism should be devoted to them in a special manner. And to cultivate this field let the Pastor call to his aid other Priests, Religious, and even suitable Members of the laity, in order that what is supremely necessary be wanting to no child.

XIII. *Certificated Teachers a Necessity.*—For the standing and growth of Catholic Schools, it seems that—

(1) Care should be taken that the Teachers prove themselves qualified, not only by previous examination before the Diocesan Board, and by a certificate, or diploma, from the School Board of the State, awarded after successful examination. This is urged, first, so as not to appear regardless, without reason, of what public authority requires for teaching.

(2) A better opinion of Catholic Schools will be created.

(3) Greater assurance will be given to Parents that in Catholic Schools there is no deficiency to render them inferior to Public Schools ; that, on

the contrary, everything is done to make Catholic Schools equal to Public Schools, or even superior.

(4) And lastly, we think that this plan would prepare the way for the State to see, along with the recognized and tested fitness of the Teachers, that the laws are observed in all matters pertaining to the arts and sciences, to method and pedagogics, and to whatever is ordinarily required to promote the stability and usefulness of the Schools.

XIV. *Reasons for Normal Schools Being Efficient.*—It is necessary that what are called Normal Schools should reach such efficiency in preparing Teachers of letters, arts and sciences, that their graduates shall not fail to obtain the Diploma of the State. For the sake of the Catholic cause, let there be among laymen a growing rivalry to take the Diploma and Doctorate, so that, possessed of the knowledge and qualifications requisite for teaching, they may compete for, and honorably obtain, positions in the public Gymnasia, Lyceums and Scientific Institutions.

The knowledge of truth of every kind, straightforward justice, united with charity, the effulgence and appreciation of the liberal arts,—these are the bulwarks of the Church.

NOTE.—All the above was read and considered at the Meeting of the Roman Catholic Archbishops of the United States,—the difficulties answered, and the requisite alterations made, on November the 17th, 1892.

In regard to this meeting of the American Archbishops, "*The Quarterly Register of Current History*," Volume II., of 1892, says:—

Cardinal Gibbons, who presided over the Conference, joined Archbishop Ireland in support of the views of Cardinal Satolli; and the Archbishops, who were pretty evenly divided on the question, finally passed Resolutions in substantial agreement with them. The most important step ever taken in this country towards liberalizing the Roman Catholic Church in its adjustment to American Institutions, has thus been made.—(*Page 427.*)

CONSECUTIVE INDEX OF SUBJECTS.

	PAGE
Early School Acts of Upper Canada	9
Education in Upper and Lower Canada, 1841	11
General Common School Act of 1841	14
The Bible as a Class-Book in the Schools	19
Upper Canada Common School Act of 1843	25
Irish National School System	32, 38, 112, 198
Controversy with Bishop de Charbonnel	37, 70, 75, 108
Separate School Legislation in 1850	49
Toronto Separate School Cases	53, 71, 73
Belleville Separate School Case	63
Dr. Ryerson's Letters to Hon. George Brown	45, 48, 49, 53, 70, 76, 78, 84, 111
Project of a Separate School Bill by three Bishops	85
The Taché Separate School Bill of 1855	92, 95, 100
Lower Canada and the de Charbonnel Controversy	108
The Bowes' Separate School Bill of 1856	110
The Bruyère-Pinsoneault-Dallas Controversy	113
Confidential Report to Sir Edmund Head, the Governor-General	118
Special Report on Separate Schools in Upper Canada	128
The Scott Separate School Bills	126, 127, 134, 140, 152, 160, 164, 166
Clergy Reserves Fund	140
The Anglican Synod and Separate Schools	145
Appeal in the Case of Ontario	167
Sir John A. Macdonald and Separate Schools	168
Hon. Alexander Mackenzie and Separate Schools	170
Hon. George Brown and Separate Schools	171, 177
Finality of the Separate School Act of 1863	172, 182
Hon. Thomas D. McGee and Separate Schools	178, 181
Compact with the Roman Catholic Representatives	174, 180
Repudiation of it by Vicars-General Macdonell and Cazeau	179
Fruitless Appeal on the Subject to R. W. Scott	183
British North America Act and Separate Schools	167, 182, 184
Legal Opinion on its Application	185
Separate School Inspection	187
French and German Schools	189
Renewed Separate School Agitation in 1865	193
Separate School Bill of 1866	195
End of Separate School Difficulties	199
Dr. Ryerson and Archbishop Ireland on the Expediency of Separate Schools	200
Appendices	205

PRINCIPAL PERSONAL REFERENCES IN THIS VOLUME.

Aikens, Hon. J. C., 95, 165, 166.
Allan, Hon. G. W., 126, 165, 166.
Anderson, William, 165.
Annand, William, 109.

Badgley, Hon. Judge, 122, 123.
Baldwin, Hon. R., 18, 47, 48, 49, 50, 53, 54, 61, 101.
Bell, R., 54, 165, 196, 198, 199.
Benjamin, George, 159, 165.
Bertelot, A., 18.
Bethune, Bishop, 21.
Biggar, J. L., 164, 165.
Blacquiere, Hon. P. B. de,—see De Blacquiere.
Blake, Hon. E., 38, 185, 187.
Bowes, J. G., 95, 110, 111, 112, 138.
Bovell, Dr. J., 147, 148.
Burns, Hon. Judge, 64.
Burwell, L., 164, 165.
Brown, Hon. G., 45, 48, 49, 65, 68, 69, 70, 76, 94, 100, 104, 106, 111, 170, 171, 177, 178.
Brown, Hon. James, 122.
Bruyère, Rev. J. M., 29, 113, 114, 115, 116.

Cahill, Rev. Dr., 153.
Cameron, Hon. J. H., 136, 165.
Cameron, Hon. Malcolm, 18, 46, 47, 48, 55.
Cameron, Hon. M. C., 133, 136.
Cartier, Hon. G. E., 110, 117.
Cartwright, Hon. J. S., 18.
Cayley, Hon. William, 94, 95, 122.
Cazeau, Vicar-General C. F., 73, 80, 139, 143, 167, 174, 176, 179, 180, 181, 182, 183.
Charbonnel, Bishop de, 35, 37, 39, 41, 42, 44, 54, 61, 63, 68, 71, 75, 77, 80, 81, 84, 87, 90, 104, 105, 108, 109, 112, 114, 115, 119, 120, 121, 124, 130, 144, 172, 173, 214.

Chauveau, Hon. P. J. O., 194.
Child, M., 18.
Chisholm, A., 33.
Christie, Hon. David, 69, 165.
Christie, Robert, 18.
Clarke, William, 164, 165.
Colborne, Sir John, 34.
Crooks, Hon. Adam, 94, 185, 187.
Crooks, Hon. James, 94.

Dallas, Angus, 83, 115, 116.
Daly, Hon. D., 18.
Darling, Rev. W. S., 147.
Dawson, Dr. J. W., 122, 195.
Day, Hon. C. D., 12, 14, 16, 18, 22, 23, 60.
De Blacquiere, Hon. P. B., 19, 20.
De Charbonnel, Bishop,—see Charbonnel, Bishop de.
Dollard, Rev. P., 113.
Drummond, Hon. L. H., 72, 92, 93, 131.
Dunn, Hon. J. H., 18.
Dunscombe, J. W., 18.

Elgin, Lord, 77.
Elmsley, Hon. John, 29, 71, 73, 74, 96, 117, 118, 126, 127.
Eugene, Bishop, 77, 81.
Ewart, J. S., 182.

Foley, Hon. H. M., 136, 165, 169, 171.
Forster, Right Hon. W. E., 198.
Foster, S. S., 18.

Galt, Hon. Sir A., 192.
Gamble, J. W., 69, 77, 93, 94, 95, 99.
Gaulin, Bishop, 21.
George, Rev. James, 22.
Gibbons, Cardinal, 219.
Goldsmith, O., 43.
Gordon, Hon. James, 165, 166.
Grasett, Rev. H. J., 30, 31, 47.
Gray, Hon. Judge J. H., 122.

Hagarty, Hon. Chief Justice, 146.
Harrison, Hon. S. B., 18, 30, 36, 40, 172.
Hartman, Joseph, 69, 94, 95, 111, 122.
Head, Sir Edmund, 118, 119, 121, 122.

Principal Personal References. 223

Hincks, Hon. Sir Francis, 16, 17, 18, 23, 25, 26, 27, 45, 46, 47, 48, 49, 50,
    54, 60, 61, 62, 63, 65, 69, 70, 72, 73, 77, 78, 80, 84, 93, 147, 157.
Holmes, Benjamin, 18.
Hopkins, Caleb, 55.
Horan, Bishop, 131, 133, 134, 189.
Hudon, Rev. H., 21.

Ireland, Archbishop, 163, 201, 203, 204, 205.

Lafontaine, Hon. L. H., 48, 50, 101.
Langton, John, 19, 77, 94, 95, 99, 104.
Leslie, Hon. James, 46.
Lunn, William, 194, 195, 196.
Lynch, Archbishop, 36, 66, 68, 72, 130, 131, 133, 139, 153, 154, 177, 178,
    179, 181, 188.

Macaulay, Lord, 161.
Macnab, Sir A. N., 77, 78, 80, 95.
McCann, H. W., 164, 165.
McDougall, Hon. William, 154, 165, 169, 171, 196.
McGauley, Rev. J. W., 38.
McGee, Hon., T. D., 159, 177, 178, 181.
McGlynn, Rev. Dr., 192.
Macdonell, Vicar-General Angus, 29, 33, 34, 35, 38, 54, 130, 133, 134, 139,
    160, 167, 174, 176, 179, 180, 181, 182, 183.
Macdonald, Sir John A., 30, 54, 59, 61, 77, 78, 80, 81, 84, 85, 87, 92, 93,
    94, 95, 100, 101, 102, 103, 104, 105, 107, 110, 111, 116, 117, 122,
    123, 132, 135, 136, 156, 164, 165, 169, 171, 173, 174.
Macdonald, Hon. J. Sandfield, 57, 61, 69, 139, 153, 154, 155, 156, 157,
    158, 161, 164, 165, 169, 171, 174, 176, 182, 202.
Macdonald, Hon. Donald A., 164, 202.
Mackenzie, Hon. A., 164, 165, 170, 171, 196.
Mackenzie, W. L., 33, 55, 68, 69, 94, 95, 106.
Manseau, Rev. A., 21.
Marling, Alexander, 126, 127.
Meilleur, Dr. J. B., 122, 123.
Merritt, Hon. W. H., 17, 18.
Moffat, Hon. George, 17, 18.
Monck, Lord, 192.
Morin, Hon. A. N., 18, 63, 72, 78, 81, 84.
Morris, Hon. A., 135, 138, 165.
Morris, Hon. W., 18, 23.
Morrison, Angus, 74.
Morrison, Hon. J. C., 30, 55.
Mowat, Sir Oliver, 165, 166, 167.
Murray, Archbishop, 38.

Neilson, Hon. John, 18.
Nilan, Rev. James, 204.
Northgraves, Rev. G., 178.

Ogden, Hon. C. R., 18.
O'Grady, Rev. Dr., 33, 34.
O'Sullivan, Dr. D. A., 33.

Parent, E., 18.
Parke, Thomas, 18.
Patrick, William P., 106, 165.
Patton, Hon. James, 136.
Penny, Hon. E. G., 108, 109.
Phelan, Bishop, 80, 81, 102, 103, 104, 112, 113, 134.
Pinsoneault, Bishop, 113, 115, 116.
Pius IX., Pope, 36, 37, 40, 163.
Pope, Joseph, 100, 101, 168.
Power, Bishop, 28, 29, 30, 31, 34, 35, 56, 57, 120, 179.
Prince, Col. John, 18, 54.

Quesnel, F. A., 18.

Reesor, Hon. David, 154.
Richards, Hon. Chief Justice, 66, 67, 68, 69, 72, 75.
Richards, Hon. Stephen, 185, 187.
Rintoul, John, 38.
Robertson, C., 18.
Robinson, Hon. Sir J. B., 38, 64.
Robinson, Hon. W. B., 99.
Roche, Rev. E. P-, 106.
Ross, Hon. John, 54, 157.
Ryan, Rev. J., 159, 160.
Ryerson, Dr. G. S., 166.
Ryerson, William, 135, 137, 160, 165.

Satolli, Cardinal, 38, 39, 192, 214, 219.
Saunders, Hon. J. S., 122.
Scobie, Hugh, 30.
Scobie, John, 165.
Scott, R. W., 60, 88, 104, 126, 127, 131-139, 140, 141, 143, 144, 153, 155, 156, 160-162, 164-166, 169. 170, 172-176, 179-183, 196, 197.
Sherwood, Hon. H., 54, 69.
Sidyme, Bishop of, 22.
Simpson, Hon. John, 18.
Skead, Hon. James, 158, 166.
Smith, James, 55, 69.

Smith, Henry, 113.
Spence, Hon. R., 95.
Spink, William, 158.
Stafford, Rev. M., 34, 160.
Stevenson, D. B., 55, 69, 95, 99.
Strachan, Rev. Dr., 27, 31, 148.
Sullivan, Dr. R., 38.
Sullivan, Hon. R. B., 18.
Sydenham, Lord, 11, 35.

Taché, Sir E. P., 88, 92, 93, 158.
Turgeon, Archbishop, 66, 175, 176, 181.

Viger, Hon. D. B., 18.

Whately, Archbishop, 38, 114.
Wier, Hon. B., 109.
Wilson, Hon. John, 55, 69, 77, 165, 171.
Wiseman, Cardinal, 114.
Wyse, Right Hon. Thomas, 202.

REFERENCES TO NEWSPAPERS IN THIS VOLUME.

Canadian Freeman, v., 178.
Catholic Citizen, 74, 85, 106.
Church, The, 24.
Examiner, Toronto, 106.
Forum, The, 192.
Globe, The, Toronto, 48, 132, 137, 140, 145, 150, 155, 159, 166, 169, 176, 178, 179, 180, 185.
Herald, Montreal, 108.
Leader, Toronto, 29, 130, 132, 134, 135, 136, 137, 140, 141, 159, 194.
Mercury, Quebec, 21, 159.
Minerve, Montreal, 108, 109.
Mirror, Toronto, 80, 110, 111.
Nova Scotian, 109.
Pays, Montreal, 108.
Telegraph, Prescott, 106.
True Witness, Montreal, 153.
Witness, Montreal, 193, 194.

ERRATUM.—On page 80, for "Archbishop Hughes," read "Archbishop Lynch."

16

www.ingramcontent.com/pod-product-compliance
Lightning Source LLC
Chambersburg PA
CBHW021814230426
43669CB00008B/751